FEMINIST WRITINGS

# Simone de Beauvoir

## FEMINIST WRITINGS

Edited by Margaret A. Simons
and Marybeth Timmermann

Foreword by Sylvie Le Bon de Beauvoir

UNIVERSITY OF
ILLINOIS PRESS
Urbana, Chicago, and Springfield

First Illinois paperback, 2021

1 2 3 4 5 C P 5 4 3 2 1

♾ This book is printed on acid-free paper.

The Library of Congress cataloged the cloth edition as follows:
Beauvoir, Simone de, 1908–1986.
[Works. Selections. English]
Simone de Beauvoir : Feminist Writings / edited by Margaret A. Simons and Marybeth
    Timmermann ; foreword by Sylvie Le Bon de Beauvoir.
pages    cm. — (The Beauvoir Series)
Includes bibliographical references and index.
ISBN 978-0-252-03900-3 (cloth : alk. paper)
ISBN 978-0-252-09717-1 (ebook)
I. Simons, Margaret A., editor. II. Timmermann, Marybeth, editor. III. Title.
PQ2603.E362A2      2015
848'.91409—dc23      2014027985

PAPERBACK ISBN 978-0-252-08592-5

The editors gratefully acknowledge the support of a grant from the National Endowment
for the Humanities, an independent federal agency, and a Matching Funds grant from the
Illinois Board of Higher Education. The volume also received a translation grant from the
French Ministry of Culture.

# Contents

# Foreword to the Beauvoir Series

*Sylvie Le Bon de Beauvoir*

TRANSLATED BY MARYBETH TIMMERMANN

It is my pleasure to take this opportunity to honor the monumental work of research and publication that the Beauvoir Series represents, which was undertaken and brought to fruition by Margaret A. Simons and the ensemble of her team. These volumes of Simone de Beauvoir's writings, concerning literature as well as philosophy and feminism, stretch from 1926 to 1986, that is to say throughout almost her entire life. Some of them have been published before, and are known, but remain dispersed throughout time and space, in diverse editions, diverse newspapers, or reviews. Others were read during conferences or radio programs and then lost from view. Some had been left completely unpublished. What gives them force and meaning is precisely having them gathered together, closely, as a whole. Nothing of the sort has yet been realized, except, on a much smaller scale, *Les écrits de Simone de Beauvoir* (The writings of Simone de Beauvoir), published in France in 1979. Here, the aim is an exhaustive corpus, as much as that is possible.

Because they cover more than 50 years, these volumes faithfully reflect the thoughts of their author, the early manifestation and permanence of certain of her preoccupations as a writer and philosopher, as a woman and feminist. What will be immediately striking, I think, is their extraordinary *coherence*.

Obviously, from this point of view, *Les cahiers de jeunesse* (*Diaries of a Philosophy Student*), previously unpublished, constitute the star document. The very young eighteen-, nineteen-, twenty-year-old Simone de Beauvoir who writes them is clearly already the future great Simone de Beauvoir, author of *L'invitée,* (*She Came to Stay*), *Pour une morale de l'ambiguïté* (*The Ethics of Ambiguity*), *Le deuxième sexe* (*The Second Sex*), *Les Mandarins* (*The Mandarins*), and *Mémoires* (*Memoirs*). Not only is her vocation as a writer energetically affirmed in these diaries, but one also discovers in them the roots of her later reflections. It is particularly touching to see the birth, often with hesitations, doubt, and anguish, of the fundamental choices of thought and existence that would have such an impact on so many future readers, women and men. Torments, doubt, and anguish are expressed, but also exultation and confidence in her strength and in the future—the foresight of certain passages is impressive. Take the one from June 25, 1929, for example: "Strange certitude that these riches will be welcomed, that some words will be said and heard, that this life will be a fountain-head from which many others will draw. Certitude of a vocation."

These precious *Cahiers* will cut short the unproductive and recurrent debate about the "influence" that Sartre supposedly had on Simone de Beauvoir, since they incontestably reveal to us Simone de Beauvoir *before* Sartre. Thus, their relationship will take on its true sense, and one will understand to what point Simone de Beauvoir was even more herself when she agreed with some of Sartre's themes, because all those lonely years of apprenticeship and training were leading her to a definite path and not just any path. Therefore, it is not a matter of influence, but an encounter in the strong sense of the term. They each *recognized themselves* in the other because each one already existed independently and intensely. One can all the better discern the originality of Simone de Beauvoir in her ethical preoccupations, her own conception of concrete freedom, and her dramatic consciousness of the essential role of the Other, for example, because they are prefigured in the feverish meditations, pen in hand, which occupied her youth. *Les cahiers* constitute a priceless testimony.

I conclude by thanking Margaret A. Simons and her team again for their magnificent series, which constitutes an irreplaceable contribution to the study and the true understanding of the thoughts and works of Simone de Beauvoir.

# Acknowledgments

Margaret Simons would like to thank Marybeth Timmermann whose brilliant translations, meticulous attention to detail, and warm encouragement have made our seventeen years of work together on the Beauvoir Series so wonderful. Marybeth Timmermann would like to dedicate this volume to the memory of her mother, Marylu Mathison, who gave her daughters roots and let them have wings. She would also like to express her deep gratitude and admiration for her mentor and friend Peg Simons.

We are very grateful to Shannon Mussett and Beata Stawarska for their advice on the translation of "A Review of *The Elementary Structures of Kinship* by Claude Lévi-Strauss"; to Julien Breining for his assistance with the transcription of "Women of Letters"; to David Carpenter and Sue Erickson at the Central Library of Vanderbilt University for their help in deciphering the text of "Problems for Women's Literature"; to Bill Wilkerson and Pam Decoteau for their helpful advice on this volume's introduction; to Margie Towery for her index; to Nancy Albright, for copyediting; to Anne-Solange Noble, at Editions Gallimard for her invaluable assistance with permissions and the translation grant; to Laurie Matheson, at the University of Illinois Press, for her guidance; and to the contributors to this volume for their outstanding work and their patience. We would like to extend warm thanks to Sylvie Le Bon de Beauvoir, coeditor of the Beauvoir Series, for her continuing support and encouragement; and a very special thanks to our longtime editor, Joan Catapano, who has been a constant champion of the Beauvoir Series.

This volume would not have been possible without the generous support of a Collaborative Research Grant from the National Endowment for the Humanities (NEH), an independent federal agency; a Matching Funds grant from the Illinois Board of Higher Education allocated by the Graduate School of Southern Illinois University Edwardsville (SIUE); and a translation grant from the French Ministry of Culture.

# INTRODUCTION

*Margaret A. Simons*

How many surprises could there be in a volume of feminist writings by Simone de Beauvoir, one of the best-known feminists of the twentieth century? The answer is, surprisingly many, from recently discovered feminist texts from the era of *The Second Sex* (1949) and a new translation of a famous interview announcing Beauvoir's 1972 "conversion to feminism" to texts pointing to Beauvoir's historic role linking the movements for sexual freedom and sexual equality, homosexual rights, and women's rights in France.

The recently discovered texts from 1947 that open this volume were written during Beauvoir's four-month lecture tour of the States and located from clues in her posthumously published letters to Sartre. Beauvoir's lecture tour was arranged by Philippe Soupault (the Surrealist poet and antifascist journalist who was teaching at Swarthmore College in 1947) and against the opposition of the conservative French establishment that "hated existentialism."[1] Beauvoir's friend, the anthropologist Claude Lévi-Strauss, who as an official at the French cultural embassy arranged to pay her travel expenses, told her: "A *woman* existentialist was more than they could bear."[2]

So naturally, Beauvoir's first articles written in the States were on women. Her two-part article published in the February and March 1947 issues of

1

the American francophone newspaper *France-Amérique*, is a feminist defense of contemporary French women writers.[3] Born into a world in which "women were neither theoretically nor concretely accepted as men's equals," and benefiting from their newly won legal equality, post–World War II women writers were faced with the challenge of competing for recognition in a world that remained "a world of men." As Elizabeth Fallaize explains in her introduction, Beauvoir's article provides an early formulation of a point that she will also argue in *The Second Sex*: "women's contribution to literary achievement has been constrained by their situation, and not by any inherent lack of potential." Fallaize observes that Beauvoir's criticism of women writers for "betraying difficulty in making individual experience universal," marks not only Beauvoir's goal of writing philosophy in literature but also her "desire to differentiate herself from earlier women writers, whose work had not been accorded a status approaching men's." Beauvoir's criticisms may seem harsh, but her article brought early attention to women writers later destined for fame, including Violette Leduc, "to whom," as Fallaize observes, "Beauvoir gave strong support and encouragement despite Leduc's rather encumbering passion for Beauvoir."

Beauvoir expands her analysis of women's situation in the second of our recently discovered articles: "Femininity: The Trap," published in a March 1947 issue of *Vogue*. Tracing the roots of women's situation back to World War I, which brought French women greater access to employment (and access to higher education for women of her own post–WWI generation), Beauvoir argues for the continuing relevance of feminism as women strive to overcome the greatest obstacle to their independence: the resistance of men "in the world and within their own hearts." In her introduction Nancy Bauer observes that this short text "reads like a *précis* of *The Second Sex*," raising the question of whether Beauvoir crafted these early formulations of "signature *Second Sex* passages" in response to the assignment for *Vogue*, that is, "for a fashion magazine that reveled in femininity, no less." Bauer points, for example, to a short passage "that perfectly foreshadows the philosophically momentous opening pages of the 'Myths' section of Book I of *The Second Sex*"—suggesting a project for a future researcher comparing this text with the manuscript of *Le deuxième sexe* in the archives of the Bibliothèque Nationale.[4]

A third recently discovered feminist text, "It's About Time Women Put a New Face on Love," appeared in the April 1950 issue of *Flair*, a short-lived American fashion magazine. Published a year after *The Second Sex*, Beauvoir's article calls for equality in sexual relationships, highlighting a theme of both her book and her later feminism. Sexual desire is not rooted in outdated social roles, Beauvoir argues, but in the ambiguity of human existence as incarnated consciousness. And sexual attraction thrives on difference: "the other sex has the fascination of an exotic country." Readers familiar with criticisms of Beauvoir's philosophy may be surprised by her appeal to sexual difference here. But, as Karen Vintges explains in her introduction, Beauvoir claimed in *The Second Sex* that there would always be "certain differences" in the sexual worlds of men and women. Those differences reflect a changing situation, however, and are thus not reducible to a set of fixed characteristics. "For Beauvoir," Vintges argues, "sexual difference is never a matter of pre-given identities but rather involves a continuous work of invention"—a theme evident here in Beauvoir's call to "help invent the future" of love.

Readers of our 2011 volume of Beauvoir's literary writings may be surprised by a fourth "recently discovered" text: a new translation of Beauvoir's "Foreword to *History: A Novel.*" Our 2011 volume reprinted the 1977 edition of Beauvoir's foreword to this novel by Elsa Morante, while our new translation is based on the original French text discovered in plain sight in *Les écrits de Simone de Beauvoir.* A comparison of the 1977 English version with the French original reveals deletions and mistranslations that distort Beauvoir's text and require a reappraisal of her interpretation of Morante's novel—criticized by Eleanore Holveck in her 2011 introduction for failing to appreciate Morante's achievement in "one of the finest novels to come out of World War II."[5]

English editions of Beauvoir's texts often contain mistranslations, which is especially problematic when the original French texts are missing, as they are for "Femininity: The Trap" and "It's About Time Women Put a New Face on Love." The linguistic style suggests that they were translated from French into English; and Beauvoir writes in *America Day by Day* of working with a translator in New York City in April 1947: "in the mornings I often go up to R.C.'s place to discuss the translation of the articles I'm writing."[6] But without an original French text, "correcting" these translations is difficult (what, for example, was the original French for "the go-getter" in "It's About Time Women Put a New Face on Love"?). We have, however, revised the translations for philosophical clarity wherever possible (noting all such changes in the notes). In "Femininity: The Trap," for example, we have changed the English word, *conscience* to *consciousness* (both possible translations of the French word *conscience*) to more accurately render Beauvoir's distinction between human consciousness and nature. We have also changed singular *woman* to plural *women* in the title of "It's About Time Women Put a

New Face on Love" and throughout the volume wherever Beauvoir means all women or women in general in order to avoid essentialist connotations that Beauvoir would not have intended.[7]

Even when the original French text is available, editorial corrections are sometimes necessary, as in Beauvoir's "Review of *The Elementary Structures of Kinship* by Claude Lévi-Strauss," to correct typos (e.g., *intrinsic* instead of *extrinsic*) or clarify technical terms (e.g., [*marital*] *alliance*). Lévi-Strauss's study of the universal rule against incest is an important reference in *The Second Sex*,[8] providing support for Beauvoir's claim that marriage—and heterosexuality—are not biologically determined but socially constructed. As Shannon Mussett explains in her introduction: "For Lévi-Strauss, the prohibition on incestuous marriages does not result from an instinctive repugnance or an implicit awareness of the possibilities of monstrous results, but from the necessary demand for the creation and maintenance of marital alliances." According to Lévi-Strauss, Beauvoir argues, women do not enter into the marital exchange as subjects, but as objects: "relations of reciprocity and exchange do not appear between men and women; they are established between men by means of women. A profound asymmetry between the sexes exists and always has existed." But as a cultural construct, marriage can change, thus allowing the possibility for reciprocity. As Mussett explains, Beauvoir "takes up what some might see as a rigid structuralist position and opens up its myriad existential possibilities."

Responding, perhaps, to the surprising outcry that greeted the advance publication earlier that year of the chapters from *The Second Sex* on "Sexual Initiation," "The Lesbian," and "The Mother" (which opens with an argument for birth control and abortion), Beauvoir uses her October 1949 review of Lévi-Strauss's book to defend the study of sexuality: "Those who are scandalized by the burning interest that today's men attach to [the sexual act] display a remarkable ignorance . . . for man defines his humanity by the manner in which he assumes his sexuality." The storm of protest over *The Second Sex*—and its call for sexual equality for women—may be surprising given the sexual freedom traditionally accorded heterosexual men in France. But, as historian Sylvie Chaperon explains, "the hostility triggered by *The Second Sex* was clearly focused on the chapters concerning sexuality and maternity."[9]

The outcry began in May 1949, according to historian Ingrid Galster, when the lead article in *Les temps modernes* was on women's sexual initiation: "From the second page, it was a question of 'vaginal sensitivity,' 'clitoral spasm,' and the 'male orgasm.' It was too much: 'We have literally attained the limits of the abject,' wrote François Mauriac in the May 30 issue of *Le Figaro*,"[10] launching an inquiry on the subject of decadence in literature. A conservative July 1949 article condemned Beauvoir's "disgusting apology for sexual inversion and abortion."[11] The Communists, according to Chaperon, while attacking *The Second Sex* as a product of bourgeois decadence, employed surprisingly similar terms in condemning Beauvoir for "exalting the lowest in man: bestial instincts, sexual depravity."[12]

Of course, by 1949 Beauvoir, whose relationship with Sartre was public knowledge, was already a notorious figure in France (a student from her 1937–38 philosophy class referred to a "whiff of sulfur" that surrounded their brilliant teacher).[13] In December 1941, a formal complaint against Beauvoir for "corrupting a minor" had been filed by the mother of another former student charging Beauvoir with initiating sexual relations with her 17-year-old daughter in 1938. After an extensive police investigation, the charges were dropped for lack of evidence. But in June of 1943, Beauvoir was nonetheless "relieved of her responsibilities" by the collaborationist Vichy government's Office of National Education and put on "special leave," only to be reinstated—surprisingly—after the Liberation.

Why Beauvoir was reinstated is a question addressed by Galster who explains that Beauvoir was charged by the Vichy education officials with encouraging her students to take an interest in psychiatry and "making them read Proust and Gide," who were condemned for "the spirit of jouissance [sexual pleasure] emanating from their works which, according to the dominant ideology, had led to the defeat of France." The report "highlighted her lifestyle: she was unmarried, had no home, slept in a hotel, worked in a café and lived in a relation of 'concubinage.'" A 1940 Vichy law cited in her case authorized the expulsion of public servants for failing to contribute to the "national renewal" of France. Since this meant the imposition of conservative "moral and family values" favored by the Nazis, it is logical, Galster writes, that Beauvoir was reinstated once the French Republic—and its liberal values of *Liberté-Egalité-Fraternité*—was restored.[14]

Beauvoir's dismissal by the Vichy government, which gave her a "certain cachet" in progressive circles,[15] was not the only source of her postwar notoriety. She also flaunted sexual convention in her fiction. Her best-selling novel, *She Came to Stay*, published in 1943 during the Occupation, is the story of a love triangle involving two middle-aged intellectuals and a teenage girl. The plot is driven by the older woman's attraction to the girl (although the novel contains no explicit depictions of lesbian sex). But it is hardly a feminist novel. *She Came to Stay* preaches ethical egoism and

5

concludes with the woman murdering the girl to escape the judgment she sees in the girl's look. Not surprisingly, *She Came to Stay* was denounced for its "moral anarchy" by the collaborationist press.[16] The criticisms leveled at Beauvoir during the Occupation, instead of silencing her advocacy of sexual freedom, seem to have deepened her commitment as well as her understanding of the political basis of individual freedom.[17] Her forceful argument for women's sexual freedom and sexual equality in *The Second Sex* is one result, reflecting her postwar political transformation—and new commitment to feminism.

According to Sylvie Chaperon, despite Beauvoir's feminism (declared in a November 1949 interview quoted by Chaperon below), *The Second Sex* was greeted at the time of its publication as a call for sexual freedom and not as an espousal of feminism. "At the start of the 1950s," Chaperon writes, "the minority of men and women who approved of *The Second Sex* spoke essentially of the necessary liberalization of sexuality and carefully avoided unfurling the flag of feminism."[18] "The old associations that had led the suffrage struggle still existed," Chaperon explains, "but they stayed out of the controversy," put off in part by Beauvoir's sexual politics.[19] What little support there was for *The Second Sex* came instead from "progressive Christians, . . . intellectuals of the non-Communist left, and existentialists" who, despite some reservations, "saluted 'the movement that today is pushing certain philosophies and literatures to the direct study of sexual problems.'"[20]

As historian Julian Jackson explains, the decade following the war was fraught with contradictions. On the one hand, movements for sexual freedom appeared that were "broadly inspired by the humanism of the Resistance and the human rights language that underpinned the struggle of the democracies against Nazism." But the era also demonstrated "hostility manifested toward sexual dissidence. . . . After the upheavals of war and occupation, European countries all experienced fear of social disorder and delinquency, and all aspired to reconstruct the family. . . . Throughout Europe there was increased persecution of homosexuals."[21] The attacks on *The Second Sex* reflect Beauvoir's importance as a champion of sexual freedom. In the immediate postwar period, Chaperon writes, "two targets especially were in the line of sight of the Communists and the Catholics: male homosexuality and female sexuality"—the former represented by André Gide's *Corydon* and the latter by Beauvoir's *The Second Sex*.[22] Julian Jackson refers to *The Second Sex*, as one of "two important publications that challenged sexual orthodoxies" in the post-Liberation years (the other, Alfred Kinsey's 1948 report on male sexuality, "was not so much denounced as ignored").[23]

Beauvoir's importance as a feminist advocate of sexual freedom might surprise Americans more familiar with the 1950s "playboy" philosophy of Hugh Hefner, the male homosexual culture of the Beats, or Helen Gurley Brown's *Sex and the Single Girl* that urged women to use sex to beat the system instead of overthrow it.[24] But Beauvoir's contribution to the movement for sexual freedom—and sexual equality—was substantial and it continued throughout the fifties and sixties. In her critical essay on Sade, published in 1951–52,[25] for example, Beauvoir effectively joined—and helped legitimate— a French intellectual tradition then most closely associated with André Gide, bringing a feminist voice to the cause of sexual freedom.[26]

Chaperon writes that in the mid-1950s *The Second Sex* influenced theorists of the new "militant movements" in France that drew upon existentialist ethics and "criticized the sexual morality of the era."[27] Daniel Guérin, for example, in *Kinsey and Sexuality* (1955), credits "the path opened by Beauvoir" in *The Second Sex*.[28] A "libertarian socialist" and anticolonialist who had been forced in the 1930s to hide his homosexuality from his left wing political comrades who "saw homosexuality as a bourgeois vice,"[29] Guérin utilizes Beauvoir's social constructionist analysis of femininity in his account of drag queens (rejecting Sartre's account)[30] and argues that the persecution of homosexual men is linked to women's oppression in patriarchal society.[31] Julian Jackson notes Beauvoir's influence on a critique of effeminacy in the "homophile" journal, *Arcadie*: "As one writer put it in 1958, drawing a parallel with de Beauvoir's analysis of the construction of femininity in *The Second Sex*, once 'society encloses a group in a situation of inferiority, it constructs it, making it become in some sense what it accuses it of being soon afterward.'"[32]

By August 1959 when Beauvoir's article included here, "Brigitte Bardot and the Lolita Syndrome," appeared in the American journal, *Esquire*, attitudes in France were changing. Existentialism was at the height of its popularity. Beauvoir's 1954 novel, *The Mandarins*, had won the prestigious Prix Goncourt; and her 1958 autobiography, *Memoirs of a Dutiful Daughter*, was a best seller. But the Vatican had placed *The Second Sex* and *The Mandarins* on the *Index* in 1956 and Beauvoir's sexual politics remained controversial. Beauvoir renews her attack here on conservative sexual mores, applauding the Bardot films and the novel, *Lolita*, for their challenge to sexual hypocrisy and for the new model of female sexual autonomy represented by Bardot. Although, as Elizabeth Fallaize cautions in her introduction, Beauvoir's enthusiasm for "the Bardot persona" "has to be seen in the context of the repressive sexual standards for women operating in the 1950s," Fallaize credits

Beauvoir with elaborating "a theory of situated eroticism" that continues the deconstruction of myths of femininity begun in *The Second Sex* and anticipates later feminist film criticism. But, as Fallaize observes, Beauvoir does not critique "the way in which the camera repeatedly isolates and fetishizes parts of the actress's body," as later feminist critics would. Indeed, Beauvoir's article celebrates the attractions of that body: "Femininity triumphs in her delightful bosom. . . . The line of her lips forms a childish pout, and at the same time those lips are very kissable."

Beauvoir's support of women's sexual freedom and equality in the 1950s included support for efforts to legalize contraception in France. As Karen Vintges notes in her introduction to Beauvoir's short feminist texts from that era, "family planning was still taboo and the sale of contraceptives was restricted all over the world," when Beauvoir was called upon by Dr. Lagroua Weill-Hallé, a cofounder of the Family Planning movement in France, to author prefaces to two of her books. Beauvoir's preface to *Family Planning* (1959) employs an interesting rhetorical strategy, appealing to French nationalism and addressing conservative objections to birth control that reveal her thorough study of right-wing thought. In her preface to *The Great Fear of Loving* (1960), Beauvoir challenges the popular view that "'the woman question' is settled," demands "this elementary freedom—the freedom of conception," and concludes with an activist appeal: "We must respond with more than a shrug of the shoulders" and end this "useless suffering . . . as rapidly as possible."

Beauvoir's move to the political left during the repressive era of the Cold War is evident in her 1961 article, "The Condition of Women." Written after her trip to Mao's China, Beauvoir's article calls for "an overthrow of the system of production" as a necessary (if not sufficient) condition for women's liberation. But she remains an outspoken feminist. "The Condition of Women" includes Beauvoir's classic response to a man arguing that women's role is dictated by the *"petite différence"*—referring to the menstrual cycle: "If it were imposed upon men, they would find the monthly gift of their blood superbly virile."

The era's repressive climate is also reflected in Beauvoir's preface to *The Sexually Responsive Woman* (1964). This study of female sexuality based on laboratory experiments by Phyllis and Eberhard Kronhausen, anticipates the famous study by Masters and Johnson in finding that "'the vaginal orgasm' theory is untenable."[33] But Beauvoir's preface avoids what she describes as the "forthright, courageous" language of the authors, congratulating them more abstractly on granting "women an autonomy—both physiological and psychological—equal to that of men." A similar discretion is evident in Beauvoir's 1965 article, "What Love Is—and Isn't," which provides an interesting reflection on love as an act of defiance involving an "Other." But in contrast to the focus on sex in her 1950 article that called upon women to "put a new face on love," this article makes no mention of sex at all.

Beauvoir addresses the era's antifeminism directly in "The Situation of Women Today," the first of three lectures that she presented in Japan during the autumn of 1966.[34] This key text takes up arguments from *The Second Sex* on the problems of women's traditional dependency and reaffirms Beauvoir's commitment to feminism: "in my opinion feminism is far from being out-dated [*dépassé*]. . . . [O]n the contrary, we must keep it alive." As Debra Bergoffen notes in her introduction, Beauvoir's careful attention here to the situations of women in different countries counters the "feminist critiques of her so-called essentialism." And her discussion of the barriers limiting women's success despite their legal equality confirms the "radical feminist" rejection of liberal humanism in a 1965 interview where she argues that: "The concrete fact today is that there are differences between men and women and to deny them is bad feminism—founded on a deceitful abstraction."[35]

"The Situation of Women Today" also challenges the view that Beauvoir subsumed feminism under Marxism in the mid-1960s. Rejecting a working-class model of oppression, Beauvoir quotes a homemaker contrasting her work to that of an unskilled laborer: "At least at the end of the day he has the satisfaction of knowing that he has earned his own living while I work eight or ten hours per day and at the end of the day I haven't earned a cent." Beauvoir concludes that women and men are linked in both their oppression ("the fact that women are subjugated to men leads to an enslavement of men to society") and their struggle for liberation: "Always and everywhere the struggle for the emancipation of women is linked to the struggle for progressivism in general."

In "Women and Creativity," her second lecture in Japan, Beauvoir returns to a discussion of women writers begun in her 1947 article and provides a surprising clue to a mystery that has puzzled Beauvoir scholars since the posthumous publication of her student diaries: why in later life she denied her early ambitions and achievements in philosophy. The clue comes in Beauvoir's discussion of the eleventh-century Japanese novelist, Murasaki Shikibu, whose novel, *The Tale of the Genji*, is called by Beauvoir "the greatest oeuvre in the world, I think, that has been realized by a woman." As Ursula Tidd notes in her introduction, Beauvoir shared with Murasaki the experience of early paternal encouragement. Murasaki, Beauvoir observes, "tells that when her brother studied Chinese, he had a lot of trouble learning the Chinese characters while she learned them very quickly. And the father basically said, 'What a shame that she is not the boy!'" Remembering this passage, Beauvoir later catches Murasaki in a lie, denying what we, her readers, know about her abilities in Chinese. Murasaki "takes great care to tell us," Beauvoir writes, "'I am a woman so I don't speak Chinese,' which is false, but she does not want to appear pedantic or as a bluestocking. . . . Basically she is playing, in a completely charming manner, incidentally, at being the traditional woman."

Beauvoir then makes a puzzling criticism of women writers (including Murasaki and by implication, herself): "The very great works of art are those that call the entire world into question." "And due to their condition, women are not in a position to do that!" "They do not radically contest the world, and that is why no women in the history of humanity have created a great religious or philosophical system, or even a great ideology."[36] But, as Beauvoir's readers know, *The Second Sex* calls the world radically into question. Perhaps in denying her own achievements Beauvoir, like Murasaki, is "playing . . . at being the traditional woman" in an antifeminist society, with the expectation that her readers, like Murasaki's, would find the ruse "charming." If so, then her discussion of Murasaki in this article provides a clue to solving a puzzle at the heart of Beauvoir's autobiographical writings.

During the 1960s, Beauvoir attacked the political right in her fiction, as in her critique of technocratic society in *Les Belles Images* (1966) and her depiction of women in bad faith in *The Woman Destroyed* (1968). But Beauvoir also defended courageous women writers and activists, including most famously, the Algerian freedom fighter, Djamila Boupacha, in her 1962 "Preface to *Djamila Boupacha*," and also the lesbian author, Violette Leduc, in her 1964 "Preface to *La Bâtarde* by Violette Leduc."[37] In a short article from 1969, "Love and Politics," published here, Beauvoir defends a Communist activist, Lise London, for actions during the Stalinist era, revealing both Beauvoir's support for a courageous woman under public attack, and her own very different political attitude. As Vintges notes in her introduction: "Discussing Lise London's absolute faith in communism, Beauvoir added this remark: "I myself have never had a political conviction as unconditional as hers."

Given the evidence of Beauvoir's decades-long feminist engagement, reading of her 1972 "conversion to feminism" in a famous interview from the inaugural July 1972 issue of *Ms.* can be a surprise. The *Ms.* interview, entitled "The Radicalization of Simone de Beauvoir," has the following introduction: "Here, for the first time, Simone de Beauvoir reveals a recent and very personal revolution. With Alice Schwartzer, an activist in the Frenchwoman's Liberation Movement, she discusses her conversion to feminism, her changed political philosophy, and her plans to join women at last."[38] But no mention of a "conversion to feminism" appears anywhere in the original French text of the interview or its introduction in the February 14, 1972, issue of *Le nouvel observateur*. Nor does the title of the original French text—*La femme révoltée* (*The Rebellious Woman*), an apparent allusion to Camus' *L'homme révolté* (*The Rebel*)—imply a "radicalization." In fact Schwartzer's opening question in the original French text begins with a statement—deleted in *Ms.*—that seems to rule it out: "To this day, the analysis of the situation of women that you put forth in *The Second Sex* remains the most radical. No other author has gone as far, and it can be said that you have inspired the new women's movements."

Complicating the situation further, Schwartzer's opening tribute to the radicalism of *The Second Sex* has been replaced in *Ms.* by a seemingly ridiculous claim: "When you wrote *The Second Sex* in 1949 you believed that socialism was the only true remedy for the inequality of the sexes." To add to the confusion, this statement seems to be a paraphrased quote from Beauvoir herself later in the interview: "At the end of *The Second Sex*, I said that I was not a feminist because I thought that the solution to women's problems must be found in a socialist evolution of society. By being feminist, I meant fighting for specifically women's demands independently of the class struggle."

But as Sylvie Chaperon points out in her introduction, Beauvoir declared that she was a feminist in a November 1949 interview—shortly after the publication of *The Second Sex*. Furthermore, *The Second Sex* calls for feminist solidarity, criticizing socialists, such as Louise Michel, who "spoke against feminism because it diverted the energy that should be used entirely for class struggle," and praising militant suffragettes in England and America: "the first time in history that women took on a cause as women." Since "freedom remains abstract and empty" in women, according to *The Second Sex*, "it can be authentically assumed only in revolt." For a woman "there is no other way out than to work for her liberation." The conclusion of *The Second Sex* argues that women must fight together for their rights: "one would not think of expecting gratuitous generosity from oppressors; but the revolt of the oppressed at times and changes in the privileged caste at other times create new situations; and this is how men, in their own interest, have been led to partially emancipate women: women need only pursue their rise, . . . and they will sooner or later attain perfect economic and social equality."[39]

How are we to understand Beauvoir's 1972 apparent misrepresentation of *The Second Sex*? Fortunately Chaperon has discovered another interview, from September 1968, that provides a clue. In that September 1968 interview, Beauvoir calls for women's involvement not in feminism, but in the socialist struggle—indicating her shift to the political left in the aftermath of the May 1968 political uprising of French students and workers. She worked closely (if not entirely in agreement) with young French Maoists in those years. In 1970, for example, when the editors of the Maoist newspaper, *L'Idiot international*, were jailed, Beauvoir assumed legal responsibility for the paper, defending the vital role of an alternative, muckraking press in exposing corporate and governmental abuses.[40] The September 1968 interview discovered by Chaperon suggests that Beauvoir may have also modified her interpretation of *The Second Sex* during this period, emphasizing the compatibility of her earlier work with her new Marxist politics.

Beauvoir's 1972 "conversion to feminism" may also reflect the radicalism of the Women's Liberation Movement (MLF) and its disdain for feminists of an earlier generation. As Didier Eribon explains, writing about the hostility in the radical gay movement toward Michel Foucault: "The revolutionary movements of the 1970s constructed their discourses in opposition to earlier forms of gay culture (apparently unaware that they did not themselves arise out of nothing, that they could exist only because an entire culture, a sub-cultural life, and a whole set of discourses preceded them). They had no intention of doing any historical work of rediscovery and rehabilitation." According to Eribon, Foucault was apparently "violently taken to task by the militants . . . at one public meeting," reproached for the discretion that had allowed him to survive the earlier repressive era. According to Schwarzer, Beauvoir received similar treatment by the MLF in "Women's Liberation: Year One" (as though, Chaperon remarks, history ever has a "year one"), where the militants "had been at great pains to take Simone de Beauvoir to task for being 'Sartre-fixated' and, worse still, for writing for a male publication (*Les temps modernes*)."[41] Thus for various reasons, Simone de Beauvoir, who laid the theoretical foundations of radical feminism in *The Second Sex* and defended feminism through the lonely years of the 1950s and '60s, is remembered—ironically—for a 1972 "conversion to feminism."[42]

Beauvoir responds to critics of the February 1972 interview in a March 1972 article included here, where she attacks essentialist views of woman's "nature," while affirming the possibility of liberation for women with children, defending homosexuality, and recalling that *The Second Sex* was criticized at the time of its publication for a "lack of confidence" in socialism.

Beauvoir's activities in the 1970s reflect her continuing support for sexual freedom and sexual equality, as in the April 1971 Manifesto of the 343 for abortion rights and the Choisir (To Choose) association that took on the legal defense in the famous Bobigny abortion trial of 1972. As Chaperon explains in her introduction, the three texts on the Bobigny trial included here provide insights into French feminist politics of the era, while recording Beauvoir's involvement in a trial that transformed French attitudes on abortion.

As the political opposition hardened and the MLF matured in the 1970s, Beauvoir put "her notoriety and her connections at the service of this movement of young rabble-rousers without ever claiming to lead it in any certain direction," according to Françoise Picq in her introduction. Beauvoir supported those feminists interested in legal reform through the creation of a League of Women's Rights and those "who preferred to fight sexism by denouncing it with perspicacity and humor," through the "Everyday Sexism" column in *Les temps modernes*. She lent her support to a successful campaign for divorce law reform and an unsuccessful one for a law banning sexism, which, as Picq explains, won the support of the Secretary for Women's Rights in the new Socialist government in 1981, but failed after vehement opposition from advertisers and the press.

In 1979, Beauvoir joined an international campaign—also unsuccessful—to defend the rights of women in the Iranian Revolution. In 1980, when as Picq remarks "the 'feminism of the 1970s' symbolically came to a close," Beauvoir took sides in a public dispute among French feminists, condemning a group whose actions divided the MLF as never before. Finally, in her preface to *Mihloud*, the last text in this volume and the final publication before her death in 1986, Beauvoir endorses "a homosexual love story touched by AIDS," bringing her support to issues that were "still considered virtually unmentionable in 1980s France," as Lillian S. Robinson and Julien Murphy write in their introduction. Beauvoir's last publication thus reaffirms her decades-long commitment to sexual freedom and sexual equality, homosexual rights, and women's rights in France.

## NOTES

1. "Philippe Soupault . . . avait fait inviter Simone de Beauvoir par diverses universités américaines, permettant ainsi son voyage, ce dont elle lui sut toujours gré" (She was always grateful to Philippe Soupault for having arranged the invitations from various American universities that made her trip possible). Simone de Beauvoir, *Lettres à Sartre* (*Letters to Sartre*)

(LAS), ed. Sylvie Le Bon de Beauvoir, 2 vols. (Paris: Gallimard, 1990), II: 281, n. 1; "un vieux professeur français de Harvard . . . était un de ceux qui voulaient m'empêcher de venir, par haine de l'existentialisme." (An old French professor at Harvard . . . was one of those who wanted to prevent me from coming, out of hatred of existentialism.) LAS II: 282.

2. "Il m'a dit qu'une *femme* existentialiste c'était plus qu'ils n'en pouvaient supporter." LAS II: 284.

3. The first reference to the two-part article is in a letter from New York dated February 3, 1947: "A midi ½ j'ai été voir Prolers, directeur de *France-Amérique* . . . qui m'a proposé des articles" (At 12:30 I went to see Prolers, the director of *France-Amérique* . . . who suggested some articles) (LAS II: 290). She describes her work on the article in a letter dated February 17, 1947: "J'ai travaillé tout le matin à un article pour *France-Amérique* que je n'avais pas commencé et qui était promis pour aujourd'hui. . . . Puis de 7h. à 9 h. j'ai fini mon article. . . . [The next morning] je vais dicter mon article à *France-Amérique*" (I worked all morning on an article for *France-Amérique* that I hadn't started and that was due today. . . . Then from 7 to 9 I finished my article. . . . [The next morning] I am going to dictate my article *to France-Amérique*) (LAS II: 306). And in a letter from Chicago dated February 28, 1947, she writes of completing the article: "J'ai . . . hâtivement travaillé à un article pour *France-Amérique* qu'il me fallait envoyer en toute hâte" (I . . . hurriedly worked on an article for *France-Amérique* that I had to send right away) (LAS II: 313).

4. See Catherine Viollet, "Le manuscrit du *Deuxième sexe*" (The manuscript of *The Second Sex*), in *Cinquantenaire du Deuxième sexe* (Fifty Years after *The Second Sex*), ed. Christine Delphy and Sylvie Chaperon (Paris: Syllepse, 2002), 143–51.

5. Eleanore Holveck, Introduction, in Simone de Beauvoir, *"The Useless Mouths" and Other Literary Writings*, ed. Margaret A. Simons and Marybeth Timmermann (Urbana: University of Illinois Press, 2011), 309.

6. *America Day by Day*, trans. Carol Cosman (Berkeley: University of California, 1999), 314. The translator mentioned in this diary entry may have been Robert Cornman (1924–2008). Often referred to by his initials, Cornman was a pianist/conductor from Brooklyn. He served in the military in Europe during WWII, returning after the war to New York where he presented a recital in 1947. According to his website, he was "bilingual in French and English; often translated articles and books"; http://www.archeophone.org/cornman/cveng.php (accessed April 10, 2014).

7. On Beauvoir's rejection of essentialism, see her 1965 interview with Francis Jeanson: "j'admets absolument que *les* femmes sont profondement differentes *des* hommes. Ce que je n'admets pas, c'est que *la* femme soit differente de *l'*homme." (I admit absolutely that women are profoundly different from men. What I do not admit is that woman is different from man), in Jeanson, *Simone de Beauvoir ou l'entreprise de vivre* (Simone de Beauvoir or the enterprise of living) (Paris: Seuil, 1966), 263.

8. *The Second Sex*, trans. Constance Borde and Sheila Malovany-Chevallier (New York: Knopf, 2010), 7, n. 4.

9. Sylvie Chaperon, *Les années Beauvoir: 1945–1970* (*The Beauvoir Years: 1945–1970*) (Paris: Fayard, 2000), 180–81.

10. Ingrid Galster, "Les limites de l'abject" (The limits of the abject), in *Beauvoir dans tous ses états* (Beauvoir in all her states) (Paris: Tallandier, 2007), 183–97; 184.

11. Cited by Chaperon, *Les années Beauvoir*, 182; and by Galster, "Les limites de l'abject," 188.

12. Chaperon, *Les années Beauvoir*, 175–77.

13. Ingrid Galster, "'Nous sentions un petit parfum de soufre.' Entretien avec Jacqueline Gheerbrant" (Interview with Jacqueline Gheerbrant), in Galster, *Beauvoir dans tous ses états*, 54.

14. Galster, "Juin 1943: Beauvoir est exclue de l'université," in Galster, *Beauvoir dans tous ses états*, 98–99.

15. Hazel Rowley, *Tête-à-Tête* (New York: HarperCollins, 2005), 133.

16. Galster, *Beauvoir dans tous ses états*, 149.

17. On Beauvoir's political transformation during the Occupation, see her *Wartime Diary*, trans. Anne Deing Cordero, ed. Margaret A. Simons and Sylvie Le Bon de Beauvoir (Urbana: The University of Illinois Press, 2009), 8–33.

18. "Au début des années 1950, celles et ceux, minoritaires, qui approuvent l'ouvrage [*The Second Sex*] parlent essentiellement de la nécessaire libéralisation de la sexualité et se gardent bien de déployer l'étendard féministe." "Ce n'est plus le droit qui est pris comme révélateur des écarts, mais les comportements des individus eux-mêmes, notamment sur le terrain de la sexualité. C'est précisément ce dernier point qui éloigne les anciennes générations du DS" (It was no longer the law that was seen as revealing inequities, but the behavior of the individuals themselves, especially in the field of sexuality. This last point is precisely what distanced the older generations from the SS) (Chaperon, *Les années Beauvoir*, 188, 201).

19. Sylvie Chaperon, "Beauvoir et le féminisme français" (Beauvoir and French feminism), in *Beauvoir*, ed. Eliane Lecarme-Tabone et Jean-Louis Jeannelle (Paris: L'Herne, 2012): 277–83; 277.

20. Sylvie Chaperon is quoting Jean-Marie Domenach's remark in *Le Figaro littéraire*, June 25, 1949, in her article, "Kinsey en France: les sexualités féminine et masculine en débat" (Kinsey in France: A debate about feminine and masculine sexualities), in *Le mouvement social* (The social movement) 2002/1 (no 198), 91–110; paragraph 13; http://www.cairn.info/revue-le-mouvement-social-2002-1-page-91.htm#retournoteno36 (accessed April 10, 2014).

21. Julian Jackson, *Living in Arcadia: Homosexuality, Politics, and Morality in France from the Liberation to AIDS* (Chicago: University of Chicago Press, 2009), 113–14.

22. Chaperon, "Kinsey en France," paragraph 12.

23. Jackson, *Living in Arcadia*, 44–45.

24. See Lina Salete Chaves, "Sexually Explicit, Socially Empowered: Sexual Liberation and Feminist Discourse in 1960s Playboy and Cosmopolitan," (MA thesis, University of South Florida, 2011); http://scholarcommons.usf.edu/etd/3041/ (accessed April 10, 2014).

25. Simone de Beauvoir, "Must We Burn Sade?" in *Political Writings*, ed. Margaret A. Simons and Marybeth Timmermann (Urbana: University of Illinois Press, 2012), 37–101.

26. On a Communist newspaper condemning Gide as "a theoretician of, obsessed by homosexuality," see Chaperon, "Kinsey en France," paragraph 12.

27. Chaperon, "Beauvoir et le féminisme français," 278.

28. Daniel Guérin, *Kinsey et la sexualité* (Kinsey and sexuality) (Paris: Julliard, 1955), reprinted in his *Essai sur la révolution sexuelle; après Reich et Kinsey* (Essay on the sexual revolution: After Reich and Kinsey) (Paris: Éditions Pierre Belfond, 1969), 31–125; 1955, 12, n.3; 1969, 32, n.2.

29. Jackson, *Living in Arcadia*, 95.

30. Guérin, *Kinsey et la sexualité*, 1955, 66; 1969, 62; on Sartre: "'Elles' ne se font pas 'femmes,' comme dit Sartre, elles se font, plus exactement, telles qu'elles se représentent la femme, c'est-à-dire poupées et putains" (They do not make themselves "women," as Sartre says; they make themselves, more exactly, into their image of woman, that is dolls and whores) (1955, 72, n.1 cont.; 65, 1969).

31. Guérin, *Kinsey et la sexualité*, 1955, 139–40; 1969, 101.

32. Jackson, *Living in Arcadia*, 115 and 127, n. 97, citing Robert Amar, "Pages de carnet," *Arcadie* 52 (April 1958): 49.

33. Phyllis and Eberhard Kronhausen, *The Sexually Responsive Woman* (New York: Grove Press, 1964), 118.

34. "Women and Creativity," the second lecture from Japan, is included here, while the third, "My Experience as a Writer," is in *Literary Writings*, 275–301.

35. Jeanson, *Simone de Beauvoir ou l'entreprise de vivre*, 262–63.

36. Beauvoir's explanation here for women's failure to radically contest the world compounds the confusion: "[I]n order to call the world completely into question, one must feel profoundly responsible for that world. Yet women are not responsible for the world, insofar as it is a man's world." But readers of her 1963 autobiographical volume, *Force of Circumstance*, will remember Beauvoir writing that in the immediate postwar period (when she conceived *The Second Sex*), she, with her fellow writers on the Left, did sense that they were assuming a responsibility for the world: "'Politics is no longer dissociated from individuals,' Camus wrote in *Combat* at the beginning of September 1944. 'Politics is man speaking directly to other men.' Speaking to men was our role as writers. Before the war, few intellectuals had tried to understand their era; all—or almost all—had failed. . . . We had to take over [*assurer la relève*]." Then, in a passage that echoes Murasaki "playing at being a conventional woman," Beauvoir turns the discussion to Sartre: "But as I said I had no philosophical ambition." *La force des choses*, I (Paris: Gallimard/Folio, 1988), 14–15; my translation.

37. "Preface to *Djamila Boupacha*," in Beauvoir, *Political Writings*, 260–82; "Preface to *La Bâtarde* by Violette Leduc," in *Literary Writings*, 165–87.

38. Alice Schwartzer and Simone de Beauvoir, "The Radicalization of Simone de Beauvoir," trans. Helen Eustis, *Ms.* 1:1 (July 1972): 60.

39. *The Second Sex*, 141, 143, 664, and 764.

40. See Simone de Beauvoir, *Tout compte fait* (*All Said and Done*) (Paris: Gallimard, 1972), 491–92.

41. Alice Schwarzer, *Simone de Beauvoir aujourd'hui: Entretiens* (Paris: Mercure de France, 1984) (*After "The Second Sex": Conversations with Simone de Beauvoir*), 13; Chaperon, *Les années Beauvoir*, 377; Didier Eribon, "Michel Foucault's Histories of Sexuality," *GLQ: A Journal of Lesbian and Gay Studies* (2001) 7(1): 31–86; 65–66. Note the spelling variants: "Schwartzer" in *Le nouvel observateur* and *Ms.* and "Schwarzer" in *Simone de Beauvoir aujourd'hui*.

42. See my "*The Second Sex* and the Roots of Radical Feminism (1995)," in *Beauvoir and The Second Sex: Feminism, Race, and the Origins of Existentialism* (Lanham, Md.: Rowman & Littlefield, 1999), 145–65.

# French Women Writers

# INTRODUCTION

*by Elizabeth Fallaize*

"Problèmes de la littérature féminine" (Problems for women's literature) and "Femmes de lettres" (Women of letters) constitute the two halves of a substantial article on French women writers that Beauvoir wrote and published during her lecture tour of America, in the spring of 1947. The article, which has come to light only in the course of the preparation of this volume, throws light on Beauvoir's thinking on the subject of women writers at an early stage of her work on *Le deuxième sexe*. Like the analyses of *Le deuxième sexe*, and those of the lecture on women and creativity, which she gave in Japan nearly two decades later, in 1966, this article also indirectly suggests some of the constraints under which Beauvoir may have considered herself to be working as a woman writer.

The title of the first half of the article, "Problèmes de la littérature féminine," sets the tone for Beauvoir's report to an American audience on contemporary French women writers—in fact, not only the first piece but both halves of the article focus on the constraints that Beauvoir considers to have handicapped women in the pursuit of great literary achievement and on the consequent weaknesses of women's writing. Her aim is to demonstrate the point that she will also argue in *Le deuxième sexe*: women's contribution to

19

literary achievement has been constrained by their situation, and not by any inherent lack of potential. There may have been no great women writers of the past, but the future remains open to change, as women's situation changes. Although this message is clear, at this stage in her thinking she has not yet elaborated all of the arguments underpinning women's situation; the reasons for women's lack of achievement are less compellingly set out and her conclusions are less combative than in *Le deuxième sexe*. Nonetheless, it is clear that the subject is of considerable interest to her and that she has made progress in developing her ideas.

She begins her assessment of the situation of women writers with the central argument that women have been marginalized in a man's world and refused recognition as equal participants in human society. The only routes previously open to women writers have therefore been either the pursuit of the struggle for recognition, a route Beauvoir considers inimical to literary achievement, or a focus on the domains traditionally reserved for women. She cites Colette as a supreme example of a woman writer who has achieved great success in the literary expression of a universe centered on childhood, on nature and domestic animals, on love and sensuality, and on the joys of a harmonious domestic interior. However, Beauvoir considers the focus on the search for happiness and on the self to be a major stumbling block for women writers, preventing them from giving their work the universal dimension that she considers the hallmark of great writing. Women writers of the current generation have been emboldened by their new status and rights (Beauvoir is presumably thinking of the right to vote, conceded to French women in 1945), and are now tackling subjects of universal interest, such as war and major social problems. Despite this progress, according to Beauvoir they nevertheless still tend to use these subjects as a mere backdrop to a continuing preoccupation with happiness and with the individual destiny of the heroine. Worse still, the self-portrayal, which she identifies as at the heart of all women's writing, is unable to match the best of male writing on the subject of the self, though contemporary writers are achieving a lucidity in self-portrayal previously absent.

Why do women continue to be preoccupied with the self, and why do they not excel at self-portrayal? In *Le deuxième sexe*, Beauvoir explores in considerable detail the way in which girls' early psychological conditioning and education predisposes them to a narcissism that is almost impossible to shake off. She also shows how that narcissism encourages a false consciousness of the self, which impedes the radically honest portrayal of the self that marks the writing of a Proust or a Joyce. At the time of writing this article,

Beauvoir appears not to have formulated those arguments yet. Instead, she explains women writers' continuing preoccupation with the self as resulting from their acute consciousness that the equality battle is in fact still far from over. This creates an inferiority complex, which combines with a lack of audacity to inhibit women from the bold overthrowing of received ideas or the frank disclosure of the self that men are more often in a position to achieve. Beauvoir points out that centuries of identification of the feminine with the modest does not encourage women to be audacious, and that public reaction to frankness on the part of a woman is unlikely to be as sympathetic as it would be to a man. This is a prescient remark in view of the public reaction to sections of *Le deuxième sexe*, which Beauvoir was soon to endure.

The second half of the article, "Femmes de lettres," examines in more detail women writers' treatment of two traditional themes, childhood memories and nature, and one new theme, that of violence. Beauvoir produces a strong analysis of why women's nostalgia for their childhood is so common—childhood represents for women the lost paradise of an existence in which they existed as autonomous beings. Although the argument is not developed here, it recalls the argument made in *Le deuxième sexe* that it is at puberty that the young girl comes face to face with the realization of her future secondary existence. A parallel argument is made in relation to the depiction of nature: a woman's attraction to nature can be explained in terms of the direct relation that she is able to have with the natural world, as opposed to her indirect relation to the social world, which she can only act on through the intermediary of the male. In the case of both these subjects traditionally treated by women writers, Beauvoir sees her contemporaries as having made progress over their predecessors— nature and childhood are not presented by them simply as a source of escapism. However, Beauvoir is inclined to see the newer theme of violence as falling into the escapism trap.

The compilation of problems with which women writers wrestle has become, by the closing stages of the article, a rather overwhelming list—and Beauvoir feels obliged to concede that her review appears severe. Although contemporary women's writing strikes her overall as lacking authenticity and betraying difficulty in making individual experience universal, she underlines the fact that the current generation is nevertheless opening up new ground from which future generations will benefit. Her main examples of prewar writing are Colette, a writer who features more than any other in *Le deuxième sexe*, and whose work Beauvoir clearly knows extremely well, and Anna de Noailles, again a writer whose work is frequently cited in *Le deuxième sexe*,

21

most usually as an example of women's problems and self-absorption. Interestingly, there is no mention yet of Virginia Woolf, whose 1929 essay *A Room of One's Own* Beauvoir drew on enthusiastically in *Le deuxième sexe*, as well as in her novels. Going back to the nineteenth century, she also cites Emily Brontë—a woman writer for whom Beauvoir expresses the greatest admiration both in *Le deuxième sexe* and in her memoirs, and who is one of the few women writers Beauvoir credits with the ability to create convincing male characters. Among the contemporary writers whose work she presents, the most interesting names are those of Elsa Triolet, Colette Audry, Clara Malraux, Violette Leduc, and Marguerite Duras. Elsa Triolet had won the prestigious Goncourt prize in 1944 for a novel inspired by her participation in the Resistance; she and her partner, poet and novelist Louis Aragon, were both known to Beauvoir. Colette Audry was a close friend and former colleague, whose work Beauvoir draws on frequently in *Le deuxième sexe*; Clara Malraux, the former wife of André Malraux, was also known to Beauvoir and wrote a number of interesting memoirs and fictions raising feminist issues. The literary reputation of Violette Leduc, to whom Beauvoir gave strong support and encouragement despite Leduc's rather encumbering passion for Beauvoir, has grown considerably since the 1940s, and Beauvoir has the merit of having encouraged a rising star. The most surprising name, however, is that of Marguerite Duras, whose first novel is mentioned here by Beauvoir. Duras could now plausibly be described as the best known French woman writer of the twentieth century, but there was no indication in 1947 of the radical turn her work was later to take, or of the international recognition her work would achieve from the 1980s onward. Beauvoir therefore shows considerable foresight in mentioning at least two contemporary women writers who were destined for literary fame.

What does this article tell us about Beauvoir's own fictional project? The author of three novels and a play in 1947, and a collection of short stories that had been rejected for publication, Beauvoir had certainly tackled the major topics of war and resistance, which she urges in this article as crucial subjects for women to take on. Her published novels and play included male narrative viewpoints, reflecting a concern expressed here that women writers might balk or fail at the convincing portrayal of men. Her concern throughout her writing career to give her work a universal and metaphysical dimension, a concern which she was still stressing in her Japanese tour of 1966, can be seen in the light of this article not only as a personal vision of literary creation, but also as a marker of her desire to differentiate herself from earlier women writers, whose work had not been accorded a status approaching men's. The refusal of her volume of short stories, which focused on the portrayal of women's lives, no doubt played a part in determining her view that this was not the way ahead for women writers. Ironically, the women writers today considered the great writers of the twentieth century—such as Virginia Woolf and Marguerite Duras—did not pursue the universalist and metaphysical agenda that Beauvoir set out for women writers of the future, though they did display the radical vision she also identifies as crucial. From the vantage point of the twenty-first century, Beauvoir's strong conviction that writing must have a universal dimension can itself be understood as a product of her positioning as one of the first generation of women to be theoretically admitted on equal terms to traditionally male domains. Her analysis of the constraints on women writers remains compelling and becomes even more so in *Le deuxième sexe*, in which she ends her chapter on the independent woman by calling for women writers to be given their chance in the interests of the whole of humanity.

# PROBLEMS FOR WOMEN'S LITERATURE

TRANSLATION AND NOTES BY VÉRONIQUE ZAYTZEFF

AND FREDERICK MORRISON

Critiquing a novel written by a woman, Thierry Maulnier[1] one day remarked that literature by women has put the problem of happiness in the foreground of its concerns. As a matter of fact, in their works as well as in their lives, women have long been particularly interested in the construction of their own existence and have usually sought to tell the story of individual successes or failures. It is easy to understand the reason for this.

For centuries it has been men and men alone who have fashioned the world in which we live. That is to say that this world belongs to them. Women have their place in it, but are not at home there. It is natural that a man seeks to explore the domain of which he feels himself the master; that he searches with curiosity to know it, strives to dominate it with his thought, and even claims, through the medium of art, to create it anew. Nothing stops him, nothing limits him. But, up until these last few years, women's situation was completely different.

Women were neither theoretically nor concretely accepted as men's equals. A woman could not attempt to surpass the given world; she did not yet have a true hold on it, and this hold was what she had to conquer first. Two paths were open to her: either she could fight to have her rights acknowledged or she could put to their best use the means she already had available to her in order to gain access to the richest possible existence. In both cases, her drama was entirely personal. She had to reach a man's level or accept living in his shadow. The second solution was the most conducive to the blossoming of a literary oeuvre, since a propagandist agenda and the stubborn defense of a thesis pose obvious dangers in the domain of art. The strictly feminist novels of the preceding generation have hardly left any trace at all. If, on the contrary, a woman were to endeavor to describe the domains that were reserved for her, she could, within her limits, demonstrate the gifts of invention and expression that make the true writer. Colette's success proves this in a resounding way.[2] However, Colette's oeuvre is precisely centered in its entirety on the search for happiness. Thrown into a world that goes beyond her and upon which she does not claim to act, a woman must create for herself the coziest possible nest. She explores her riches, gathers her treasures: her childhood memories; the earth with its flowers, pets, springs, and seasons; love and affection; and home, which embodies the harmonious unity of a life.

However, over the course of the last few years, women's situation has been profoundly changed. Their demands have been heard. They have been granted a direct hold on the world. It is interesting to consider the consequences of this evolution in women's literature today.

There are two different but not irreconcilable tendencies dominating contemporary French literature. Young writers try to increase their external knowledge of the world; they want to integrate the vastest possible experience into literature. This leads to the current importance and success of all forms of news reporting, and the development of this complex genre that could be called the journalistic novel. On the other hand, they also seek a deepening of their internal knowledge of themselves. They turn toward philosophy; they want to integrate into literature the most mysterious regions of their being.

Women too are carried along by these two currents. Some women have been war correspondents; some passionately devote themselves to journalism; they travel, they tell what they have seen, and they succeed as well as men in observing and communicating the fruits of their observation. Others take up theoretical studies; they write critical, philosophical, and psychological essays, and in this field of pure abstraction they show themselves no different from men. However, when they try to express their concrete vision of existence in the strictly literary field, then their condition as women reveals itself. This condition is very ambiguous.

25

In fact, theoretically, the quarrel over feminism has just been concluded in women's favor. Women are invited to participate in the edification of the world; they no longer have to fight to conquer their rights. They have conquered them. Their work no longer needs to be negative, but positive. They know that, and they also know that the curious are waiting to see what profit they will be able to derive from their victory. They are thus doubly incited to turn away from their own problems and apply themselves, as men do, to subjects of universal interest. Now that they have a role to play in political and social life, this life has truly become their life; they feel an authentic need to talk about it in their books. Still, an external obligation weighs them down. They must show men that they are capable of exploiting the fields that have just been opened to them. Thus, women today write like men: about resistance, war, and social conflicts.

Yet, it is not true that their present condition is already that of a man. Precisely because their conquests are recent, this world into which they have been admitted remains a world of men, and it is abstract and theoretical to claim that the singularity of their situation has been abolished. Women know it; they are still conscious of their personal difficulties and wish to remedy them. This is why Thierry Maulnier's remark remains true, even today. They are still preoccupied with what they call happiness, and one of the original aspects of their literature is their effort to reconcile this concern with the interest that they bring to the universe and history. What is striking about Edith Thomas and Elsa Triolet is that their novels borrow their materials from great events, such as the Spanish civil war, the Phony war, the exodus, and the Resistance, yet these topics are addressed through the singular story of a female heroine.[3] What appears to be essential is not so much the great human drama in its general terms but the connections this heroine has with the circumstances into which she has been thrown. The true subject of these works is how, in today's world, a woman's singular destiny is accomplished or broken down. The common thesis of all the short stories in the recently published collection by Colette Audry, *On joue perdant* [Playing a losing game] [1946], is the failure of every attempt at individual happiness in today's world: the failure of love, of domestic life, of motherhood, of dreams, and even of renunciation.[4] In the majority of these books by women, the social and historical world, i.e., the real world, is present, but only on the horizon: it is not the very subject matter that the writer intends to handle and control.

This timidity should not surprise us and in no way does it foretell the future. I must reiterate that women will have the same opportunities as men only when they are settled on this earth as solidly as men are. They are still novices and they hesitate. This hesitation is found again when they speak not of external events but of themselves. One would think that their individualism and their subjective sense of existence would bring them to profound inner discoveries. One must admit that they lack the audacity of a Proust, a James Joyce, or a Sartre. Colette was famous for having pushed back the limits that had been assigned to women until that time. She approached sexual themes with frankness. However, she treated them with such elegance and reserve that, to tell the truth, she barely touched the surface. Moreover, the sensuality she describes is close to greediness. The savor of a kiss seems to have for her the simplicity of savoring a piece of fruit. On this question other women could most certainly provide very different testimonies. After Colette's books, almost everything still remains to be said. Yet, women scarcely do so. The short book *L'asphyxie* [*In the Prison of Her Skin*] [1945], by the newly published writer Violette Leduc, gave rise to a movement of keen interest because, perhaps for the first time in France, a woman strove, with a man's audacity, to deliver an authentic sensuality.[5] They were still no more than suggestions, but they were so cruel, so disturbing that they seemed rich with promise. And yet, this case is more or less unique. Clumsy at speaking about men, whom they know only from the outside, women hardly dare to talk aloud about themselves.

Here again their timidity is quite natural. Each time a man attempted to shed a new light on the darkness of his body or his heart, he provoked a scandal. One needs a great deal of proud certitude to dare focusing on oneself the malicious attention that any truly sincere disclosure arouses. The scandal and the malice are multiplied if it is a woman who incites them. And she is not as fully armed as a man to face them. Moreover, on this daring path men have behind them the help of a tradition stemming from Greece and Rome. Women have been lauded above all for their discretion and their decency. If one of them wishes to renounce this measure, she must invent everything, her technique and her very language. It is not an easy enterprise.

There is another reason that explains why women do not willingly take this risk. It is due to the fact, as I have already mentioned, that their victory is still only an appearance. Men only appear to consider women as equals, while to tell the truth, they think of themselves as superior to women. In regards to men, women still suffer an inferiority complex whose irritating reflection is sent back and forth among them. They are conscious that the struggle is not over, and while they no longer write feminist books, feminist concerns are nonetheless not absent from their work. They still need to

27

defend themselves in men's eyes and exhort each other to have confidence in themselves. This leads to a moralistic aspect in their writings. And we know that ethics and psychology do not always get along. Psychology is all the more audacious and valid when it tries to be more sincere. The concern for what one ought to be prevents one from describing exactly what one is. When women portray some heroine, they are pursuing a moral goal rather than attempting to give a disinterested testimony. And this moral that emerges from their books is significant. For them, it is above all a question of exalting a type of woman who possesses the same qualities as a man, yet without losing her femininity. Contemporary heroines are neither enchantresses nor resigned women. They are women who accomplish their destiny with a man's toughness, courage, and honesty, and especially with lucidity. This is a word that one encounters in women's novels at each turn of the page. Since they cannot modify their condition overnight, women are determined to at least face it. Lucidity is the opposite of flight; it is a thoughtful acceptance of the situation and the first condition of a veritable independence.

One could not but approve this will manifested by today's women: to see clearly, to not lie, and to not accept being told lies. But they must be alert to the fact that lucidity is not sufficient to win the game, and that understanding the ambiguity of a situation neither dispels it nor controls it. A woman who questions herself lucidly before yielding to her senses, like Clara Malraux's Grisélidis, has not by that behavior eliminated the true problems of women's sensuality.[6] In this will to lucidity there is a rationalism that is, above all else, a combat weapon. One understands quite well that only people who feel secure in themselves would indulge in the luxury of anxiously questioning themselves. Women still feel themselves too lost in this world to attempt losing their way even more. They first need to try to put things together, to take stock. However, this is only a first stage. When it seems to them utterly natural to possess what they call, with still too much humility, men's virtues, then they will be able to begin bringing truly new contributions to the knowledge of human reality, such as they find it in themselves.

## NOTES

The article entitled "Problèmes de la littérature féminine" in *France-Amérique* 14, February 23, 1947, 1, 5 (© Sylvie Le Bon de Beauvoir) was preceded by the following introduction:

"Philosopher, reporter, and novelist, Simone de Beauvoir is in the foreground of French literary life. Her novels and plays, *Le sang des autres* [*The Blood of Others*] [1944], *Les bouches inutiles* [*The Useless Mouths*] [1945], and *L'invitée* [*She Came to Stay*] [1943] are read, commented upon, and discussed by a vast public.

Having arrived in the United States for a lecture tour, Simone de Beauvoir will give *France-Amérique* a series of articles. The following article is the first of the series."

1. Thierry Maulnier (1909–88) was a French writer, essayist, and journalist. He was a member of the Académie Française.

2. Sidonie-Gabrielle Colette (1873–1954) is considered not only a major twentieth-century woman writer but also a major literary figure of the first half of the century.

3. Edith Thomas (1909–70) was a French reporter and a writer. She wrote extensive articles on the Spanish Civil War and was a member of the Communist Party for seven years. From 1947 until her death, she was the curator of the National Archives in France. Elsa Triolet (née Kagan) (1896–1970) was a French novelist born in Moscow. She was a member of the Communist Party and companion of Louis Aragon (1897–1982), who was a Surrealist poet and leading figure in the French Resistance to the German Occupation of France; the Spanish Civil War lasted from 1936 to 1939. The leftist government of the Spanish Republic was besieged by the Nationalist forces led by General Francisco Franco, who was backed by Nazi Germany and Fascist Italy. Many Spanish intellectuals either were killed or forced into exile; the Phony War (September 1939–Spring 1940) was the period marked by no Allied military operations in Continental Europe despite the attack by Germany on Poland; and the exodus refers to the flight of French civilians from the invading German army in 1940.

4. Colette Audry (1906–82) was a prolific French writer, a Resistance member, and a life-long left-wing activist. She was a close friend of Simone de Beauvoir and Jean-Paul Sartre.

5. Violette Leduc (1907–72) was a French writer sometimes referred to as France's greatest unknown writer. She was a contemporary of Beauvoir, Sartre, Camus, and Cocteau.

6. Clara Malraux (1897–1982) was a French writer whose novel, *Portrait de Grisélidis* (Portrait of Grisélidis), was published in Paris in 1945 (Éditions Colbert). She was married to the French novelist and politician André Malraux.

# WOMEN OF LETTERS

TRANSLATION BY VÉRONIQUE ZAYTZEFF

AND FREDERICK MORRISON

NOTES BY VÉRONIQUE ZAYTZEFF

Perhaps because women neither yet dare to tackle head on the great problems facing the world, nor to look very deeply inside themselves, their literature partly remains an escapist literature. One knows that, much more than men, they have always sought to create in imagination or to re-create by recollection a domain that is true to their yearnings. They have, in particular, readily looked for refuge in their childhood memories, in nature, or in dreams of love. Today we still find these themes in most of the novels written by women. Nevertheless, they are now handled in a totally different way than they were in the preceding generation.

What is striking is that women have always turned nostalgically toward their childhood. This trait does not belong solely to women writers: almost all women retain a heartfelt regret for a lost paradise. When they love a man, their first concern is to open to him the doors of this past; unhappy and disappointed, they return there on long, solitary pilgrimages. A man is far less likely to attach so much joy to his early years and men rarely devote to it a very large place in their books. It is perhaps because a woman is aware of having been in her childhood, and solely in her childhood, a perfectly autonomous being. At the time, she felt, as all little boys did, that she too was the center of the universe. Later on, in submission or in revolt, she learned dependence, and whether or not she found any happiness therein, she now has the feeling of a sort of abdication. This is why she tries to re-create that time when she was a sovereign, indomitable consciousness, and why she tries to resurrect the sweet promises offered her in that world.

This idea is expressed very forcefully, for example, in *Souvenirs* [Memories] by Colette Audry,[1] whose short stories I have already mentioned.[2] She thinks she has been demeaned in becoming a grownup. Nevertheless this book, as well as *Asphyxie* [*In the Prison of Her Skin*] [1946] by Violette Leduc, also devoted to childhood memories, is far from depicting those long-gone years as a marvelous paradise.[3] By choosing to have their share in the real world, today's women have deliberately turned their backs on the marvelous. They do not use the tenderness they still feel for their childhood as an excuse for inventing mirages; there again, they want to see clearly. They put their past back within the framework of the real. Violette Leduc's memories are utterly cruel; she evokes with pitiless precision the world in which she grew up, as well as an entire social and sensual background that alone makes the tragic figure of her mother intelligible. Her childhood is an apprenticeship for life in all its harshness and terrible mysteries; it is already heavy with all the difficulties of a woman's destiny. Colette Audry's tone is more objective. However, through a childlike vision, a whole bourgeois and provincial universe is depicted for us, with its pettiness, its routines, and the intolerable ennui that this universe emits. In both cases we are far from the young carefree attitude of a Claudine.[4] Here again, the authors have tried, above all, to place themselves in the world as a whole, without complacently surrendering to subjective images and emotions.

A similar tenderness characterizes the manner in which the theme of nature is broached, a theme which comes into play much more directly than in the past and under a different light. Formerly, nature played quite a privileged role in women's lives: it was the sole figure of the absolute that was directly accessible to them. A woman had contact with human realities only through the intermediary of men, but nothing stood between her and trees, springs, sky, animals, and flowers. In the face of these beauties, of these pleasures which have nothing to do with people, she could rediscover the lost independence of her childhood. The link between the two themes is noticeable in Anna De Noailles or Colette, for example, as well as the British women novelists.[5] Even nowadays, landscapes and silent plants are a woman's most easily captured prey, and she still likes to talk about them. However, since she is no longer resigned to possess nothing by rights but

31

this single possession, neither does she grant it the first place in her books. Nature is very often present in modern novels by women, but it is a setting, or even a furtive refreshment, and no longer a haven where one rests nor a mystical, uplifting passion. In Violette Leduc or in *La vie tranquille* [The quiet life] [1945] by Marguerite Duras, nature is perceived and evoked with sensitivity and force, but this is in its relationship with the human world.[6] For in this domain as well, women no longer choose to yield to the escapist temptations offered to them.

The domain of the pure imagination is where women abandon themselves more; and it is perhaps here that their intuition is most characteristic. Certainly, it is no longer a question of love affairs in flowery dresses. However, the stories invented by our young women novelists often have no more truth in them than the vapid romantic idylls that they deliberately oppose.

From this point of view, what seems to me the most striking element is the important role given to violence in these works. The book by Marguerite Duras, referred to above, that has in other respects such an authentic tone, begins with violence and unfolds in a climate of violence. *Pascal Vituret* [Pascal Vituret] [1945] by Claude Le Coguiec has a violent end. There is violence again in *La voile noire* [The black sail] [1943] by Marie Le Hardouin and *Les marais* [The swamps] [1942] by Dominique Rolin.[7] Certainly, influences of earlier writers are evident here: that of Emily Brontë and closer to us that of Faulkner. However, these influences are not sufficient to explain the phenomenon. Perhaps women do wish to reject the qualities of discretion and charm to which they have so long been limited; they wish to display vigor, cruelty, and audacity. This may also be a form of escapism they allow themselves because they do not recognize it as such; they can express in these inventions the interior dramas that they dare not expose directly.

I wrote that their situation was ambiguous. In this period of crisis, dramas are unfolding within them, and the bloody and passionate images they invent are surely a way of externalizing these dramas.

In rereading this brief outline, I notice that it may appear harsh. Women's literature today seems to lack a certain authenticity. This is quite a serious criticism, and some men will perhaps take it to mean that women should once again return to their hearth, garden, and children in literature as in life. Indeed, many men commonly declare that a woman is only able to bring anything of value if she confines herself to a specifically feminine domain: let her renounce her intrusions into the world of men. It is easy to burden her with the weight of great names and demonstrate that she is not up to their stature. "Women," a male writer once told me, "do not know how to escape from the particular in order to soar to true greatness." There is a great deal of truth in this statement. Women are adept at grasping the concrete; their style often has a carnal quality that is lacking in men's writing, but women are often clumsy in bringing out the universal truth of their experience.

Nevertheless, I do not think that this will always be true. The present generation is hesitant and lacks self-confidence because it is trying its hand at new conquests; it no longer has the inner harmony that allowed Madame de La Fayette, or Colette to write their masterpieces.[8] And it may not offer any one name capable of matching these great names, but it is paving the way for something new. I am convinced that the women of tomorrow will reap the fruit of the efforts put forth by the women of today. The latter still move forward by trial and error in this world to which men reluctantly invite them. And if one chooses to be spiteful, one will say that they are chasing rainbows, that they refuse to express their singular truth, and that they do not have enough strength to express universal truths. The mixture of self control and audacity that is found in their works and reflected in their very style already gives their books an ambiguous charm, slightly caustic and from time to time containing a touch of pathos that takes hold of one's heart. Perhaps none of the books I have quoted deserves to be called a great book, but they are rich in promises and such an abundant richness is already an accomplishment.

## NOTES

The article "Femmes de Lettres" (*France-Amérique*, March 9, 1947, vol. 14, no. 43: 1, 5; © Sylvie Le Bon de Beauvoir) was preceded by the following introduction: "Two weeks ago, we published Simone de Beauvoir's masterful study of the problems for women's literature today. In the article that follows, the author of *L'invitée* [*She Came to Stay*] [1943] and *Le sang des autres* [*The Blood of Others*] [1945] presents the conclusions derived from her research and indicates the paths now being taken by women writers in France."

1. Colette Audry (1906–90), a close friend of Beauvoir, was an author, screenwriter, and dialog writer who was awarded in 1962 the "Prix Renaudot" for her novel *Derrière la baignoire* (*Behind the Bathtub*). Here, Beauvoir is probably referring to Audry's 1947 novel *Aux yeux du souvenir* (In the eyes of memory).

2. Beauvoir discusses Audry's 1946 short story collection *On joue perdant* [Playing a losing game], in "Problems for Women's Literature," which was published in a previous issue of *France-Amérique*, and appears in English in this volume.

3. Violette Leduc (1907–72) was a French writer sometimes referred to as France's greatest unknown writer. She was a contemporary of Beauvoir, Sartre, Camus, and Cocteau.

4. Simone de Beauvoir is alluding to Colette's *La maison de Claudine* (*My Mother's House*) (1922), which depicts the peaceful world, idyllic nature, and the mother-daughter bond.

5. Anna de Noailles (1876–1933) was a poet and leading literary figure in France in the pre–World War 1 period; Sidonie-Gabrielle Colette (1873–1954) was an outstanding French writer of the first half of the twentieth century. She wrote over fifty novels, numerous short stories, and was elected to the Académie Goncourt in 1944. Her main themes were the pleasure and pains of love, female sexuality, and the disappointing world of men.

6. Marguerite Duras (1914–96) was a prolific author and screenwriter (*Hiroshima mon amour*) (1967) who was born in Indochina.

7. Marie Le Hardouin (pen name of Sabine Vialla) (1912–67) was a French author who was awarded the "Prix Femina" in 1949 for her novel *La dame de coeur* (Queen of hearts); Dominique Rolin (1913–2012) was a Belgian-born author of several novels such as, among others, *Les quatre coins* (The four corners) (1953) and *La maison de la forêt* (The house in the forest) (1965).

8. Marie Madeleine, countess of La Fayette (1634–93), known as Madame de La Fayette, was a French writer who is best known for the early novel *La Princesse de Clèves* (*The Princess of Cleves*) (1678).

**2**

Femininity: The Trap

# INTRODUCTION

*by Nancy Bauer*

In January of 1947, Simone de Beauvoir flew from Paris to New York to begin her first tour of the United States. It was to be a momentous four months. Under the auspices of the French government, Beauvoir gave two dozen lectures at colleges and universities across the country on the topic "the ethical problems of the post-war writer." Her friendship with the novelist Richard Wright and his wife, Ellen, who took her under their wing during her whirlwind first weeks in New York, sensitized her to the pervasiveness of racism that she would witness in America, which she chronicled with startling (and, still, underappreciated) insight in *America Day by Day*. In late February, on her initial visit to Chicago, Beauvoir met the writer Nelson Algren, with whom she fell more passionately in love than she had or would with any other man. And then there was the effect her trip surely had on the little book Beauvoir had begun writing half a year earlier, in June of 1946, a book on what the author blurb for "Femininity: The Trap" describes as "the new role of women in France."

Unlike much of the rest of the blurb, which announces that Beauvoir, "the leading disciple of Jean-Paul Sartre's *Existentialist* philosophy," is "a woman who thinks like a man," *Vogue*'s characterization of the scope of the incipient

*Second Sex* was not decidedly skewed. The book was in fact born of Beauvoir's desire to tell her story as a woman who had resisted the usual life course for a bourgeois French woman, and the opening paragraph of "Femininity: The Trap" sets things up as though Beauvoir is reporting on the state of affairs for women in her home country. As Beauvoir notes, that state of affairs had changed dramatically during the Second World War, when the "Rosie the Riveter" phenomenon rendered the ancient Napoleonic civil code, which denied women the status of full citizenship, intolerable. In 1944, just three years before Beauvoir's trip to America, French women were finally granted a reasonably wide range of rights, most critically the right to vote and the right to hold office. This sea change appeared to guarantee women's equality with men and thereby to make feminism, understood as equality before the law, as a thing of the past.

The problem, of course, is that on-paper equality is not a guarantee of real-life equality. To declare that all people "possess the same value, the same dignity" is not to say anything about whether women will be able to take advantage of their new legal status. Women's actual well-being depends on what Beauvoir calls "position and opportunities," and these things are in turn a function not only of socioeconomic factors but also of how men and women conceive of what it is to be a sexed human being. Beauvoir immediately makes clear that these conceptions are far from straightforward. Men, even well-intentioned ones, laud women for being "intuitive, charming, sensitive"; flattered, women respond by *being* intuitive, charming, and sensitive. But each of these terms is a cover for something ugly. "What men actually mean when they speak of the sensitivity of woman is lack of intelligence, foolishness when they say charm, treachery when they say caprice." The implication is that women who have been brought up to understand themselves as beholden to men's insidiously two-faced expectations—perhaps especially women who are legally equal to men and to that extent do not suffer overt political injustice—risk compromising themselves in myriad ways, including morally. *Et voilà*: only three paragraphs into this essay, we find ourselves well beyond the situation of French or even American women and in deep philosophical waters.

Indeed, the importance of this little article lies precisely in that fact: "Femininity: The Trap" reads like a *précis* of *The Second Sex*. That the *querelle de féminisme* might not be a thing of the past, that reopening it might "irritate" women, that the myth of the eternal feminine is false, that "man" is a word that means "universally human," that men see women's ideas as a function of their sex and forget that they themselves have glands and hormones, that women's relative physical weakness does not disadvantage them in a mechanized world, that housework is repetitive, that all of our mythologies weigh against the liberation of women from their stereotypical roles, that women "have rarely up to now achieved what is called genius," and that women often must choose between success in being feminine and other sorts of success, including professional advancement—all of these claims play pivotal roles in *The Second Sex*. In fact, in several cases the views Beauvoir expresses in "Femininity: The Trap" appear verbatim, or just about, in the book. Is it possible that these signature *Second Sex* passages of Beauvoir's, appearing in this article for the first time in print, were a product of her efforts to fulfill this assignment for *Vogue*?

We may never know for sure, since "Femininity: The Trap" is about as neglected as anything Beauvoir ever published. There's no mention of it in the reference bible for Beauvoir's *Nachlass*, Claude Francis and Fernande Gontier's *Les écrits de Simone de Beauvoir*. From *America Day by Day*, we know that on her inaugural trip to the United States Beauvoir often spent her evenings in New York at cocktail parties populated by literary types, including employees of Condé Nast, the publisher of *Vogue*. It appears from her letters to Sartre that on January 31st Beauvoir discussed the idea of an article in the magazine with *Vogue*'s Jean Condit, who apparently threw a party in Beauvoir's honor a few days later. Beauvoir reports that on February 6th she agreed to do the *Vogue* piece. She tells Sartre that she spent part of the morning of February 10th working on her essay and dictated it to a typist at *Vogue* on February 12th, the last day of her opening stint in New York.[1] So it's at least conceivable that in the couple of days she spent working on "Femininity: The Trap," Beauvoir penned preliminary versions of some of the most memorable passages that would appear in the magnum opus of feminism—and for a fashion magazine that reveled in femininity, no less.

The irony here, however, may be less potent than it seems. The title of Beauvoir's essay, which was almost surely imposed by the editorial staff, doesn't fit the content. Beauvoir never suggests in the piece that femininity, per se, is a "trap." In fact, she mentions femininity only twice, once in the context of vigorously denying the "myth" of the "eternal feminine" and again in describing the quandary facing women who attempt to find success in the world. Women rarely approach genius, Beauvoir argues, because they are socialized to allow others to judge them, rather than to judge the world for themselves. As a girl accommodates herself over time to the demand that she regard herself essentially as an object of others' evaluations—and, as in *The Second Sex*, Beauvoir argues here that the female child in this way *becomes* the woman she is not born as—she begins to police herself. She loses the desire to do anything but color within the lines and comes to find natural the habit of being timid and agreeable with respect to men's desires. Insofar as real-world success requires boldness and innovation, women are in a bind. A woman who seeks this success is likely to feel that it will come at the cost not just of her agreeableness, but also of her femininity.

By "femininity," I submit, Beauvoir has something in mind along the lines of what *Vogue* in its signature way has always promoted: comporting oneself so as to enhance one's "powers of seduction" over heterosexual men. Beauvoir is thus arguing that women are raised to imagine that acting on ambitions reaching beyond this enhancement enterprise will make them less attractive to men. We might note in this context that Beauvoir is described by *Vogue* in an editor's note as "a slender, handsome, thirty-eight-year-old Frenchwoman, with a strong-boned face" who "looks and speaks like the schoolteacher she once was," while André Malraux, profiled in the same issue, is identified as a "literary strong man" and a "still faithful DeGaullist and enemy of the communists." And lest we imagine that we now live in a radically different era, in which femininity is not at odds with worldly strength, it's worth reflecting on the extent to which we still tend to view femininity as incompatible with the power to get things done in the world. Consider, for instance, the sartorial challenges faced by women in politics and business, who, unlike their male counterparts, do not have the option of comporting themselves in a sex-neutral way. What she wears, how she styles her hair, how much makeup she wears: these things invariably draw our attention to a professional woman's femininity, or lack thereof, and can even seem to mock her ambitions. No wonder so many women, even those who are well-placed enough socioeconomically to dare to challenge the status quo, continue to lack what Beauvoir calls "the seed of folly" that allows an otherwise sane person not to care about how he or she appears in others' eyes.

In the last two paragraphs of "Femininity: The Trap," Beauvoir argues that the transformation of the status quo is ultimately dependent not on women's abandoning—or celebrating—their femininity but on men's letting go of their investment in women's inferiority. This investment, she claims, runs very deep—so deep that men will have to be "indoctrinated" (though the would-be author of *The Second Sex* does not specify how) to give it up. For men, Beauvoir claims, are threatened by the prospect of what she calls the "evolution" of women not just—perhaps not even mainly—because they fear economic or social competition. Rather, Beauvoir claims in a short passage that perfectly foreshadows the philosophically momentous opening pages of the "Myths" section of Book I of *The Second Sex*, men's reasons for resisting change are *ontological*.[2] Following Hegel's master-slave dialectic, Beauvoir suggests that man needs an inferior being to confirm his "superiority and power." But, as Hegel stressed, a mere thing—an inert piece of nature—though inferior, lacks the capacity to confirm a man's right to domination. Thus, for man, woman *is*, as Beauvoir meant to put it, "both nature and consciousness."[3] She is an object with the human capacity to recognize a man's humanity without demanding in return that he recognize hers. In *The Second Sex*, Beauvoir makes clear that this understanding of what it is to be a woman, to which she thinks women readily acquiesce, explains the relentless intractability of the man-woman hierarchy. For unlike the Hegelian slave, we women are so heavily rewarded for turning ourselves into man-recognizing machines that we do not over the course of time lose the will to pretend to ourselves that we are essentially objects.

Of course, even the most philosophically minded reader of "Femininity: The Trap" could hardly have caught the Hegelian inflection in the article's final paragraphs. But for the contemporary reader, this little essay, long ago forgotten, provides another bit of proof that *The Second Sex* is, in the first place, a philosophical reflection on what it is to be a woman.

## NOTES

1. See Simone de Beauvoir, *America Day by Day*, trans. by Carol Cosman, foreword by Douglas Brinkley (Berkeley: University of California Press, 1999), 40; and Beauvoir, *Letters to Sartre*, trans. by Quentin Hoare (New York: Little Brown, 1992), 419, 423, 427, and 430.

2. The "Myths" section of *The Second Sex* is one that we know that Beauvoir drafted *before* her American trip, though we don't know whether this critical philosophical opening was already a part of it.

3. See note 1 in "Femininity: The Trap," for the reason I use the word "consciousness" here, rather than "conscience."

# FEMININITY: THE TRAP

*by Simone de Beauvoir*

NOTES BY MARYBETH TIMMERMANN

The French have never been feminists. Of course, they've always loved women, but in the manner of Mediterranean peoples, which is the way ogres love little children—for their personal consumption. In the middle ages, the law denied French women the possession of land and separated them from the political scene. Later, the civil code denied them the same rights as men. It is also known with what stubbornness aging senators have consistently turned a deaf ear when the feminists claimed the vote and full rights of citizenship. Since the war of 1914–18, the situation has changed somewhat. Lack of manpower brought women into many fields to replace men, and they began to acquire economic independence. This war completed the evolution. In the Resistance, in concentration camps, women proved their right to participate in the reconstruction of their country on an equal basis as men. The civil code was modified in their favor and they were given the right to vote, to be elected; there are few jobs which are today forbidden them. It appears, therefore, that in France the old quarrel between feminists and antifeminists is settled, and there is no reason to return to it. But I ask myself if on the contrary it is not today that the question rises most acutely. The world of men is open to women; it is now that they must prove themselves. Men have recognized them as equals, but what exactly is going to be women's place, and will they get the same opportunities as men?

I know that the simple statement of these questions will irritate more than one woman. Men in France, as in America, think that once and for all women are equal to men and that we must talk of something else. But if it is true that all human beings who are conscious and free possess the same value, the same dignity, it is also true that the position and opportunities determine the questions which belong to each.

I myself think that there is no myth more irritating and more false than that of the eternal feminine which was invented, with the help of women, by men, who describe her as intuitive, charming, sensitive. Men have the ability to give these words a flattering resonance, so much so that many a woman is taken in by the image. She unfolds the mysteries of her heart, the secret of her intimate flutterings; meekly she offers men the reflection of their own desires and backs them up in the sense of their superiority. But what men actually mean when they speak of the sensitivity of woman is lack of intelligence, foolishness when they say charm, treachery when they say caprice. Let us not be dupes. It is evident that it is only on legal papers and in civil registries that the two sexes appear as equal. Even the word *Man*, in many countries, means at the same time male and the human race.

I have often been annoyed when a man said to me, "You think that because you are a woman." I think that I could only answer: "I think that because it is true." It is taken for granted that he is in his right in being a man, and that it is I who must be in the wrong. It is he who represents the ideal human type. And everything that differentiates women is blamed on them and considered a fault. Women are supposed to think with their glands; men superbly forget that they too have glands and hormones. They think of themselves as purely mental and objective.

Men try to justify rationally this thought by leaning heavily on observations of what they call "nature." It is true that women are physically weaker than men. That they are slaves to the hard functions of child-bearing. Women handle themselves with difficulty or clumsiness in a man's world because it is only as guests that they are admitted into this world. They are not as yet at home there; it is a world not created by them, and not as yet conquered by them.

Originally the world was built on physical force. Today it often takes no more than the pressure of a finger to be able with the help of machines to command immense forces; it is by thought and not muscular exercise that the world is now conquered. That is why the physical inequality has almost entirely lost its importance. The thrust of the present toward the future, which in truth defines humanity, was first realized by men alone. Women were housewives and mothers, and as such no principles of progress could come from them. As guardian of the home they were turned toward tradition, toward the dead past. Men alone invented the future. The role of the housewife does not consist of positive construction but of struggling against destruction.

It is one of the most exhausting tasks, because it is not directly productive. Everyone knows the story of the valet who, when reproached for not having polished his master's boots, answered wearily, "What's the use? They will only be dirty again tonight." In this sense every housewife is Penelope. Each night undoes the work of her day. That in this radically dependent position women were or were not able to find happiness is a vain question; rather like asking whether men were happier and better off in the days when there were no machines. The fact remains that today there are machines. The fact remains that for many reasons women today must work and want to work, which is another way of saying that they want independence from men.

What we are trying to define here is how the newness of this effort is experienced by women. In mythologies, in the fairy tales read to children, women are always assigned the same roles. They are Ariadne abandoned, Penelope at her needlework, Andromeda in chains. They are Cinderella, or the Sleeping Beauty waiting to be saved by Prince Charming. They are the ones who wait, who cannot find their place in the world except through the love of a man. Consider what would have happened if Shakespeare had had a sister as gifted as he. Without culture, without independence, she could only have expressed herself by foolish adventures which undoubtedly would have ended tragically.

## A Future Question Mark

The past proves nothing against the future of women, mainly because they never had a chance: but it does throw light on the present. A little girl learns early to devote her admiration to men: the traditional heroes. Very often, she feels nothing but pity and scorn for her mother's petty housewife's life, her illnesses, her tears, her frivolities, her worries. In contrast, the personality of her father is exalted; it is he who represents strength, power, and the window to the world, life, and the future. In her desire to identify herself with him the little girl recognizes and admits the superiority of [the] man over that of the woman she is destined to be. The taste for pleasing is profound in all children. Children love to feel alive. In games they gain a sense of the independence of life but it is equally important for them to feel that above their head is the reassuring ceiling of adult approval. The little boy learns early that to obtain this adult esteem, he need not too directly try to please them. He must be strong, independent, adventurous, to force himself to conquer the world and dominate his comrades. But the little girl is encouraged by parents, teachers, friends; the whole world, in fact, encourages her to develop her powers of seduction, to be gracious, well dressed, amiable. These requirements prevent her from tasting as spontaneously as the boy the pleasures of play, of sport, of comradeship.

A vicious circle begins to tighten. The more docilely she conforms to this ideal which is imposed on her, the less she develops her personal possibilities, the less she finds resources within herself. All the time she is urged to turn toward men, to seek help from outside. Her sense of dependence and weakness grows. When I was a student at the Sorbonne I was struck by hearing young women say to me with humility: "It's a book for men. We just aren't able to get through it." The fact that they believed in it made their inferiority become real.

## Acceptance, a Fault

In this way one can explain why women have rarely up to now achieved what is called genius. Geniuses are exceptional people who have dared, in specific instances, what no one dared before them. This in itself presupposes solitude and pride. Presupposes that they did not anxiously search the faces of others in order to discover approbation or blame but looked courageously toward still unsuspected horizons. Education—the whole world, in fact—teaches women timidity. That is the reason they ordinarily lack the seed of folly, the mixture of humor and pathos found among certain men who have been known to lift themselves above the ordinary run of humans in order to judge and dominate humanity.

Frivolous or grave women remain always serious. In other words they accept the world: their effort is only to find their proper places in it. Women are afraid that if they lose that feeling of inferiority they will also lose what gives them value in the eyes of men—femininity. The woman who feels feminine does not dare become involved in his political and intellectual activities or to consider herself the equal of man. Yet inversely, if a woman is stripped of her inferiority complex toward men, if she succeeds with brilliance in business, in social life, in her profession, she often suffers an inferiority complex in comparison to other women. She feels herself less charming, less amiable, less agreeable because she is deprived of this femininity.

She knows that in the eyes of men her success does not constitute an asset, but on the contrary she may be running the risk of alienating them from her. A man, on the other hand, has to fight on only one level. He has perfect unity in the manner in which he tries to integrate his personality. If he acquires power in the world, prestige in the eyes of other men, and a proud assurance within himself, he acquires at the same time greater masculinity in the sentimental and sensual fields because it is precisely independence and force that women look for in a man. It is this contradiction which afflicts many women today. Either they renounce in part the integration of their personalities, or they abandon in part their power of seduction over men. It is a masculine world; men, by their wishes, hopes, and fears, create the conditions which women are trying to battle on their way to the surface.

If one questions oneself on the future of women, one realizes that men are the first who must be indoctrinated; aside from all economic and social reasons, they are the ones who feel regret at sight of the evolution of women. Every man hopes for proof of his superiority and power, and can only find it through someone who is inferior. He has no power except if there exist objects to obey him. There are plants and beasts which he is allowed to dominate, but which remain silent and inert and do not drag him from his loneliness. A woman is both nature and consciousness;[1] she is flower, fruit, bird, and precious stone; she is human, capable of loving and wanting. So well does she appear "naturally inferior" that it is possible to dominate her without sense of injustice.

Men like to think of themselves as coming to her in the role of generous cavaliers ready to fight in her defense. But to need this generosity she must be fragile or enchained. It is possible only to deliver Andromeda if she is not free; to waken Sleeping Beauty if she is asleep. Men look to women for a projection of their own desires, the accomplishment of their own will to power. If women had totally won their independence so that their association with men was perfectly equal, a certain docility[2] would be lost to men. They are conscious of this, and it is their resistance—admitted or denied—which creates the greatest obstacle that women have to overcome in the world and within their own hearts.

## NOTES

Originally published in English as "'Femininity, the trap' . . . A French View," in *Vogue*, March 15, 1947, 171, 232, 234; translator unknown; reprinted in French translation by Sylvie Le Bon de Beauvoir, in *Simone de Beauvoir*, Gérard Bonal, Malka Ribowska, and Christophe Loviny (Paris: Seuil, 2001); © Sylvie Le Bon de Beauvoir. This article was originally published in English, and the original French text has not been found, but given Beauvoir's rejection of essentialism, we have made slight changes to the text in order to avoid essentialist connotations that Beauvoir would not have intended and to maintain consistency throughout the volume. Singular "woman" and singular "man" have been changed to plural "women" and "men" in cases where Beauvoir means all women or men, or where she is referring to women or men in general. Also, "woman" and "man" have been changed to "a woman" and "a man" in cases where Beauvoir is referring to any one woman or man (i.e., a generic woman or man).

Following the title in *Vogue* is the following: "Equal in law, unequal in the minds of both sexes, the status of women in a world that still believes in the fable of the 'eternal feminine,' examined by a French writer-philosopher." At the end of the article appears the following "Editor's Note": "Simone de Beauvoir, the leading disciple of Jean-Paul Sartre's *Existentialist* philosophy, is now lecturing in America. A slender, handsome, thirty-eight-year-old Frenchwoman, with a strong-boned face, she looks and speaks like the schoolteacher she once was. For ten years she taught philosophy in the provinces and in Paris and later wrote for the clandestine press during the Occupation. In three novels, *L'invitée* [*She Came to Stay*], *Le sang des autres* [*The Blood of Others*], *Tous les hommes sont mortels* [*All Men Are Mortal*], she demonstrated an intensely trained philosophical mind. Her play *Les bouches inutiles* [*The Useless Mouths*] was produced in Paris in 1945. A woman who thinks like a man, she plans a book on the new role of women in France, which will contain some of the ideas expressed in this article."

1. The *Vogue* article has "conscience" here, which would be one possible translation of the French word *conscience*. In this context, however, the correct term is "consciousness," since Beauvoir is contrasting women's human capacity to love and desire with the lack of these modes of consciousness in what she calls "nature."

2. The *Vogue* article has "gentleness" here. Since we don't have Beauvoir's original French essay, we can't know which French word Beauvoir originally used. However, as Nancy Bauer has pointed out to us, "gentleness" does not make sense in this context. We find a very similar context in the opening pages of the "Myths" chapter of *The Second Sex*, where the French word *docile* is correctly translated as "docile." This word, which connotes submissiveness, is more appropriate in the present context, where, as in the "Myths" chapter, Beauvoir is gesturing at Hegel's master-slave dialectic and to men's need for women to recognize them; see *Le deuxième sexe*, I (Paris: Gallimard, 1949 [rev. edition Blanche with new pagination, 2003]), 189; *The Second Sex*, trans. Constance Borde and Sheila Malovany-Chevallier (New York: Knopf, 2010), 161.

## 3

A Review of *The Elementary
Structures of Kinship*
by Claude Lévi-Strauss

# INTRODUCTION

*by Shannon M. Mussett*

In January 1929, Simone de Beauvoir did her practice teaching in philosophy at the Lycée Janson de Sailly with Maurice Merleau-Ponty and Claude Lévi-Strauss. In *Memoirs of a Dutiful Daughter* she writes of the latter that his "impassivity rather intimidated me, but he used to turn it to good advantage. I thought it very funny when, in his detached voice, and with a dead-pan face, he expounded to our audience the folly of the passions."[1] Despite his dispassionate affect, Beauvoir clearly maintained a high level of respect for her intellectual colleague throughout her life. In fact, almost twenty years after her training with the young Lévi-Strauss, she would utilize his discoveries from *The Elementary Structures of Kinship* in her groundbreaking study of woman as Other in *The Second Sex*.[2] Twenty years after this, Beauvoir would again return to the insights of the then leading French anthropologist in her ambitious study of old age, *The Coming of Age*.[3] Beauvoir's association with Lévi-Strauss thus spanned the course of her philosophical maturation, and the impact of his discoveries on her own work is oftentimes profound.

The review of *The Elementary Structures of Kinship* appeared in the July 1949 edition of *Les temps modernes*—the same year that *The Second Sex* was published as a complete monograph.[4] This book in particular illustrates most clearly the concordance between Lévi-Strauss and Beauvoir's philosophy. In her autobiography, *The Force of Circumstance,* she tells us,

> Since the beginning of May [1948], my study on *La femme et les mythes* had begun appearing in *Les temps modernes.* [Michel] Leiris told me that Lévi-Strauss was criticizing me for certain inaccuracies in the sections on primitive societies. He was just finishing his thesis on *Les structures de la parenté,* and I asked him to let me read it. I went over to his place several mornings in succession; I sat down at a table and read a typescript of his book; it confirmed my notion of woman as *other;* it showed how the male remains the essential being, even within the matrilineal societies generally termed matriarchal.[5]

Beauvoir admits that her reading of Lévi-Strauss directly confirmed her theories on woman as the Other sex, and this decisive agreement led to her utilization of his insights to support many claims throughout *The Second Sex.* In one of the few footnotes that she gives in this work she writes, "I thank Claude Lévi-Strauss for sharing the proofs of his thesis, which I drew on heavily, particularly in the second part, pp. 76–89."[6] The influence of Lévi-Strauss is clear in Beauvoir's focus on the construction of primitive societies (with specific mention of various tribes studied by Lévi-Strauss), her extension of his discussion of various cultural oppositions and norms, and her numerous direct quotations from his manuscript. Although Beauvoir is a dedicated existentialist, she finds many points of concurrence with Lévi-Strauss's anthropological hypotheses.

As a structural anthropologist, Lévi-Strauss believes in certain rudimentary and largely unconscious social structures that transcend time, location, and situation. These mental structures manifest themselves in concrete cultural institutions and practices that the anthropologist studies. Rather than focusing on social phenomena in isolation, Lévi-Strauss emphasizes the relationships between phenomena in order to discover the fundamental nature of the systems under investigation. In *The Elementary Structures of Kinship,* the primary focus of his study is the rule of the incest prohibition that appears in every culture in some form. For Lévi-Strauss, the prohibition on incestuous marriages does not result from an instinctive repugnance or an implicit awareness of the possibilities of monstrous results, but from the necessary demand for the creation and maintenance of marital alliances. Nature controls the genetic transmission of traits, but culture intercedes by dictating whose traits will be united and proliferated by employing rules of consanguinity. The rule of incest prohibition is set up so as to ensure that individual desire does not in any way destroy the cohesion of the group. Dominated by the principle of collective intervention, which intervenes in situations of scarcity (desirable women being the scarcest and most valuable commodity in any given group), the incest prohibition operates as the driving principle of exchange by determining who is able to marry whom.

The prohibition of incest is not merely a prohibition but also a command. As a man is denied access to a particular woman, she is made available to a second man. And as a woman is denied to the second man, so is she made available for the first. As such, "The prohibition of incest is less a rule prohibiting marriage with the mother, sister or daughter, than a rule obliging the mother, sister or daughter to be given to others. It is the supreme rule of the gift."[7] In a subtle manner, Lévi-Strauss shows us that *women* are the existents for whom the rules are enacted. It is not men who are prohibited or encouraged to marry, but women who are thus ordered *for* the men. This insight plays a role of great importance in Beauvoir's analysis in *The Second Sex* where she finds that women are consistently utilized as mediating objects for the benefit of male identity and power.

All of the aforementioned themes appear in Beauvoir's review of Lévi-Strauss's *The Elementary Structures of Kinship* for *Les temps modernes*, thus illustrating her thoroughness in reading the book and the depth of her meditations on its arguments. Beauvoir admits that her job in reviewing this book is not to criticize but to appreciate the tremendous accomplishment of her peer. She begins the review by hailing the brilliant awakening of French sociology with the arrival of Lévi-Strauss's work. Utilizing the best aspects of the Durkheimian and American schools, Lévi-Strauss also avoids the pitfalls of metaphysical speculation in the former and the mere fact-collecting of the latter. Rejecting abstract metaphysical interpretations of human phenomena, while simultaneously refusing to cast the world into a desert of disorder and absurdity, he discovers the human spirit in the heart of reality.

What Beauvoir aptly finds to be the most fascinating problem dealt with (and one which has a significant impact on her own analysis of women in *The Second Sex*) is the universal phenomenon of the incest prohibition. The magnitude of this phenomenon is tied to its singular position among human practices. For, as Beauvoir points out, it escapes classification as a purely natural *or* cultural occurrence. In fact, rather than masking this ambiguity peculiar to the incest prohibition, Lévi-Strauss highlights the pivotal role it plays in universally marking the transition from nature to culture. Forming the basis for exchanges of women in particular, the incest prohibition is the driving force behind exchange in general. Beauvoir astutely references Lévi-Strauss's argument that it is not on the basis of individual (natural) desire that women are distributed, but on the basis of their collective (social) utility. The negative prohibition against incestuous unions also has a positive implication in that it inaugurates a social organization through exogamous exchanges. This rule is consequently the affirmation of human *reciprocity*, which mediates and alleviates the oppositional relationship between self and other. In fact, without the abstract demand for reciprocity, the concrete socioeconomic structure of exchange would not exist. The transfer of values between individuals through the formation of alliances is so vital because, as Beauvoir points out, "a human 'mitsein' can only be established under this condition."

Highlighting the connections between the exchange of gifts and the practice of exogamy, Beauvoir's review moves into the intricacies of the simultaneous prohibition and obligation that the exchange of women institutes. Here, she lingers on what she finds to be an extremely important point: "relations of reciprocity and exchange do not appear between men and women; they are established between men *by means of women*. A profound asymmetry between the sexes exists and always has existed." The critical asymmetry to which Beauvoir alludes is that reciprocity and exchange—fundamental features in the definition of our very humanity—are not practiced between all human beings in equal measure, but only between men through the vehicles of women. In *The Second Sex*, Beauvoir goes to great lengths to describe the ways in which women are constituted as intermediate objects between natural determinacy and human freedom, thus allowing them to function as mediating objects in masculine identity formation and exchange.[8] Therefore, Lévi-Strauss's claim that women are not the controllers of exchange but the objects being exchanged between men plays a role of enormous significance in Beauvoir's analysis of women's situation. Wholly in line with these same presuppositions, Beauvoir writes in *The Second Sex*,

> For men, the counterpart—or the other—who is also the same, with whom reciprocal relationships are established, is always another male individual. The duality that can be seen in one form or another at the heart of society pits one group of men against another; and women are part of the goods men possess and a means of exchange among themselves.[9]

In short, women have no control over their use as it is up to the men of the different groups who view each other as equals to make such decisions.[10]

This determination of women as intermediate objects in masculine economies of exchange plays no small role in their positioning as the Other sex.

Following her brief, albeit highly consequential observation about the sexual asymmetry at the heart of exchange, Beauvoir's review moves into Lévi-Strauss's intricate analysis of dual systems—specifically the phenomenon of cross-cousin marriage—in order to elucidate the bond between marriage and exchange. Through this analysis, we are provided with insight into how women are branded as gifts to be yielded up or received, and how the entire system of exchange is in fact predicated on the absolute circulation of women. Beauvoir also emphasizes the fact that the "sign of alterity" is a necessary component in human interrelations. Alterity impacts sexuality, which in turn profoundly shapes human existence; in fact, "man defines his humanity by the manner in which he assumes his sexuality." This elaborate discussion grants insight into Beauvoir's incisive grasp of the system operating in Lévi-Strauss's monumental text. Anyone familiar with the methods and writings of Lévi-Strauss is aware of the incredibly complicated tables and detailed discussions that he employs in his investigations. In her presentation of the material, Beauvoir handles the complex formulas and dense terminology with accuracy and ease.

She concludes the review by drawing us into the philosophical wealth inherent in Lévi-Strauss's book. She finds its premier merit to be in its refusal to accept that all human acts are either completely intentional or else utterly meaningless. In focusing on the ambiguous crossroads between nature and culture, Lévi-Strauss upholds the fundamentally ambiguous nature of human existence. Although she observes that the author refuses to venture onto philosophical terrain, she finds that his thought is directly tied to the great humanist tradition that emphasizes the idea that human existence gives itself its *own* meaning. As such, Beauvoir finds links to Marx, Engels, and Hegel in Lévi-Strauss's work. For all of these thinkers, humanity is *antiphysis*; it realizes itself through its struggle against nature and in the oppositional tensions of self-definition between individuals and groups. In fact, Beauvoir even finds particular points of concord between the theses of Lévi-Strauss and existentialism: first, that existence posits itself and its laws in a single movement of transcendence and second, that the other is necessary in the assertion of the self. She closes by claiming that no review can do this work justice because it must be read on its own.

It may be surprising that Beauvoir would find existential resonances in Lévi-Strauss's structural anthropology and the admittedly universal and normative character of the incest prohibition. For it is precisely humanity's

*freedom* from determination—whether in the form of unconscious structures or conscious institutions—that interests Beauvoir throughout her
life. However, by the time she writes *The Second Sex*, Beauvoir is sharply
attuned to the forces of situation on one's freedom. The incest prohibition,
and the practices of exogamy that it engenders, illuminate a critical moment
of transition between the rigid confines of the situation and the assertion
of freedom. The situation demands that human beings exist in relationship
with one another; in fact, there is no concrete freedom without community
according to Beauvoir.[11] Thus, various forms of exchange must be enacted.
Those forms include the exchange of goods through trade, the exchange of
words through language, and in the case of *The Elementary Structures of
Kinship*, the exchange of women through marriage. But Beauvoir sees these
demands for exchange as more fluid and widely varying in their application
through time and space. How we respond to the limitations of the situation
through the assertion of individual and social freedom characterizes human
existence more than the abstract rules that set up the parameters of the situation in advance. In this way, Beauvoir takes up what some might see as a
rigid structuralist position and opens up its myriad existential possibilities.

## NOTES

1. Simone de Beauvoir, *Mémoires d'une jeune fille rangée* (Paris: Gallimard, 1958), translated as *Memoirs of a Dutiful Daughter* by James Kirkup (1963; reprint, Middlesex: Penguin
Books, 1986), 294.

2. Claude Lévi-Strauss, *Les structures élémentaires de la parenté* (Paris: Presses Univer-
sitaires de France, 1949), translated as *The Elementary Structures of Kinship* by James Harle
Bell and John Richard von Sturmer, ed. Rodney Needham (Boston: Beacon Press, 1969);
Simone de Beauvoir, *Le deuxième sexe* (Paris: Gallimard, 1949), translated as *The Second
Sex* by Constance Borde and Sheila Malovany-Chevallier (New York: Alfred A. Knopf, 2010).

3. In her biography of Beauvoir, Deirdre Bair tells us that Beauvoir "revived a long-dor-
mant friendship with Lévi-Strauss so that she could use the materials he and his colleagues
had assembled" in her study of old age. *Simone de Beauvoir: A Biography* (New York: Sum-
mit Books, 1990), 531.

4. Although excerpts of *Le deuxième sexe* appeared in *Les temps modernes* in 1948, it was
not published in its entirety until 1949.

5. Simone de Beauvoir, *After the War: The Force of Circumstance*, vol.1, trans. Richard
Howard (New York: Paragon House, 1992), 167–68.

6. *The Second Sex*, 7. In the second chapter of "History" in *The Second Sex*, Beauvoir's references to Lévi-Strauss are numerous and philosophically rich, thus revealing how integral
his anthropological hypotheses are to her conception of early forms of human organization
and their longstanding implications on women's oppression.

7. Lévi-Strauss, *The Elementary Structures of Kinship*, 481.

8. This sentiment concerning the intermediate status of women is derived in part from Lévi-Strauss's assertion that women are the most precious possession belonging to a society because they mark the point of transition between nature and culture, or stimulant and sign (ibid., 62–63).

9. *The Second Sex*, 80.

10. Ibid. Offering further proof of this claim, she directly quotes Lévi-Strauss's *The Elementary Structures of Kinship*: "'The relationship of reciprocity which is the basis of marriage is not established between men and women, but between men by means of women, who are merely the occasion of this relationship.'"

11. The necessity of communal relationships in the expression of freedom appearing in *The Ethics of Ambiguity* (1947) was most fully developed in her novel, *The Mandarins* (1954), thus showing the profound impact the Nazi Occupation of France had on Beauvoir's philosophical development.

# A REVIEW OF *THE ELEMENTARY STRUCTURES OF KINSHIP* BY CLAUDE LÉVI-STRAUSS

TRANSLATION BY VÉRONIQUE ZAYTZEFF

AND FREDERICK MORRISON

French sociology has been dormant for a long time. Lévi-Strauss's book must be greeted as an event heralding a spectacular awakening. The efforts of the Durkheim school to organize social facts in an intelligible manner proved to be disappointing since they relied on questionable metaphysical hypotheses and on equally doubtful historical postulates.[1] In reaction, the American school tried to abstain from any speculations; it confined its work to collecting facts without elucidating their apparent absurdity. Heir to the French tradition, but trained in American methods, Lévi-Strauss sought to resume his masters' attempts while guarding against their flaws. He too assumes that human institutions are endowed with signification; but he seeks the key in their very humanity. He exorcizes the specters of metaphysics, but refuses to accept that this world is only contingence, disorder, and absurdity. His secret will be to try to *think the given* without introducing [*faire intervenir*] a thought that would be foreign to it: at the heart of reality he will discover the spirit which inhabits it. Thus he gives us back the picture of a universe that does not need to mirror heaven in order to be a human universe.

It is not for me to critique—and thus to assess—this work as a specialist, but it is not aimed solely at specialists. Let not the reader, who opens the volume at random, be intimidated by the mysterious complexity of the diagrams and tables. In truth, even as the author discusses in minute details the matrimonial system of the Murngin or the Kachin,[2] it is the mystery of society as a whole, the mystery of man himself that he endeavors to penetrate.

The problem he takes on is the most fascinating and the most disconcerting of all those that have attracted ethnographers and sociologists, namely the enigma posed by the prohibition against incest. The importance of this fact and its obscurity result from the unique situation it occupies in the ensemble of human facts, which are divided into two categories: facts of nature and facts of culture. Certainly, no analysis will permit us to discern the exact point of passage from one category to the other, but a reliable criterion distinguishes them: the first are universal while the second are governed by norms. The incest prohibition is the sole phenomenon escaping this classification for it appears in all societies without exception, but it is nevertheless a rule. Various attempts at its interpretation have all endeavored to conceal this ambiguity. Some scholars have invoked both aspects of the law—the natural and the cultural—, but they have established only an extrinsic[3] relation between the two. They assume that a biological interest has engendered the social interdiction. Other scholars have seen in exogamy a purely natural fact, dictated by an instinct. Finally, other scholars, Durkheim among them, consider it exclusively a cultural phenomenon. These three types of explanations result in impossibilities and contradictions. In truth, the incest prohibition is of such great interest because it represents the very moment of the passage from nature to culture. "It is the process by which Nature surpasses itself."[4] This singularity follows from the singular character of sexuality itself; it is normal that the junction between nature and culture is encountered in the field of sexual life, since sexual life, while a matter of biology, immediately involves others [autrui]. This duality is encompassed in the phenomenon of [marital] *alliance*, for while kinship is given, nature imposes the [marital] alliance but does not determine it. Hence, it is possible to grasp directly from life the manner by which man, assuming his natural condition, defines his humanity. The fundamental structures on which human society as such is founded are expressed and accomplished through the incest prohibition.

First of all, exogamy shows that there could be no society without the acknowledgment of a Rule. Contrary to the myths and lies of liberals, the intervention is not solely linked to certain economic regimes; it is as original as humanity itself.[5] The distribution of values between members of the collectivity has always been and could only be a cultural phenomenon. As the food with which she is moreover closely associated, the woman is a scarce product that is essential to the life of the group; in many primitive civilizations, the bachelor is a pariah economically and socially. The very first concern of the collectivity will be thus to prevent the establishing of a monopoly of women. This is the underlying meaning of the incest prohibition, which affirms that women should not receive a social usage based on their natural distribution. Men are forbidden from choosing their [marital] allies among their female relatives, and women are "frozen" to the bosom of the family so that the distribution takes place under the control of the group and not in the private sphere. Despite its negative appearance, the Rule really has a positive meaning, for the interdiction immediately implies an organization. In order to renounce his female relatives, the individual must be assured that a symmetrical renunciation by another male promises him female [marital] allies; that is to say, that the Rule is the affirmation of a reciprocity. Now reciprocity is the immediate way of integrating the opposition of self and other: without such an integration, there would be no society. However, such a relation would have no existence if it remained abstract. Its concrete expression is the exchange: the transfer of values from one individual to another makes them partners; a human "mitsein" can only be established under this condition. The fundamental character of these structures clearly emerges from the study of child psychology. The child's apprenticeship about himself and the world comes in learning to accept the arbitration of others, i.e., the Rule, which reveals reciprocity to him, a discovery to which he immediately reacts with the gift and the demand. This notion of exchange—whose importance Mauss had already established in his essay on the gift and which envelops the notions of rule and reciprocity[6]—provides us with the key to the mystery of exogamy: to forbid a woman to members of a certain group is to immediately put her at the disposition of another group. The prohibition doubles as an obligation of giving his daughter, his wife to another man. [A man] offers the female relative whom he refuses for himself. The sexual act, instead of closing in on itself, opens a vast system of communication. The incest prohibition merges with the institution of human order. Everywhere men have sought to establish a matrimonial regime in which women figure among the gifts by which the relation of each [man] to the others is expressed and social existence, as such, is affirmed.

An extremely important note is necessary here: relations of reciprocity and exchange do not appear between men and women; they are established between men *by means of women*. A profound asymmetry between the sexes exists and always has existed. The "Reign of women" is an outdated myth. Whatever the mode of filiation may be, whether children are included in the father's group or the mother's, women belong to the males and are part of the various prestations they grant each other.[7] All matrimonial systems entail that women are given by certain males to other males.

There is one case where the connection between marriage and exchange appears clearly: that of dual organizations. These organizations present such striking analogies with each other that at times one has been tempted to assign them a single origin. According to Lévi-Strauss, their convergence is explained by the identity of their functional character. The dual system does not give rise to reciprocity, but rather it expresses it in a concrete figure. This same perspective will allow us to explain more complex forms of society. They are not the result of historical and geographical chance; they all manifest the same underlying intention: to prevent the group from solidifying in upon itself and to maintain itself in opposition to the other groups with which exchange is possible.

The author seeks the confirmation of his ideas through a thorough analysis of given social realities. This study constitutes the most important part of his work. There is no question in the present review of going back over its complicated twists and turns. I will simply try to indicate the method used, for the fertility of a hypothesis is demonstrated by its methodical application.

The form of marriage providing the true *experimentum crucis* of the study of matrimonial prohibitions is the marriage between cross-cousins. In a very large number of primitive societies marriage is forbidden between parallel cousins—children of two brothers or two sisters—but it is recommended between cross-cousins—children of a brother and a sister. The extreme interest in this custom comes from the fact that biologically equivalent degrees of kinship are considered, from a social point of view, as being radically dissimilar, making it patently obvious that nature does not dictate its laws to society; and if one understands the origin of this asymmetry, one has the explanation for the prohibition against incest. Marriage between cross-cousins entails a dual organization of the collectivity: they are distributed in fact as if they belonged to two different moieties. However, one must not believe that this division is what defines the rules of exogamy. Primitives do not begin by establishing classes: class is an analytical element, like concept; man thinks before the logician formalizes thought. Thus society is organized prior to defining the separate elements that will appear in this organization.

Where classes meet—and this is not everywhere—they are conceived less as a group of extended individuals than as a system of positions in which only the structure remains constant and where the individuals can move about as long as the relation is respected. The principle of reciprocity acts in two complementary ways: by constituting classes which delimit the extension of the range of spouses, or by determining a relationship that allows one to say whether the individual in question is or is not a possible spouse. In the case of cross-cousins, these two aspects of the principle overlap; however, their affiliation to two different groups is not what destines them to form alliances between them; on the contrary the possibility of an exchange is the raison d'être of the system that brings them into opposition. Women are automatically seen as destined to be exchanged, and this perspective immediately creates an opposition between two types of women: the sister or daughter who must be handed over, and the spouse who is acquired, i.e., the relative and the [marital] ally. Here it is not a question, as Frazer believed,[8] of the solution to an economic problem: economic processes are not isolable. An indivisible act of primitive consciousness recognizes the daughter and the sister as a value that is offered, and the other's daughter and sister as a value that is due. Even before the thing to be exchanged is present, the relation of exchange is already given: before his daughter's birth, the father knows that he must give her to the man—or the son of the man—whose sister he received in marriage. Cross-cousins come from families that are in an antagonistic position and in a dynamic imbalance that can be resolved solely by [marital] alliance. On the contrary, two sisters or two brothers, because of the groups to which they belong, find themselves in a static relation and their children will be considered as part of a same set; in relations with each other they do not bear the sign of alterity which is necessary for establishing [marital] alliances.

Yet, if one restricts himself to viewing the exchange in this limited form—that is as long as it establishes a reciprocity between a certain number of pairs of exchanger units, classes, sections, or subsections—one notices that it does not take all the facts into account. This is what emerges, for example, from the analysis of the Australian data. In its generalized form, the idea of exchange can serve as the key to the study of all societies. Generalized exchange is the one that establishes relations of reciprocity among any number of partners. So one is in the presence of a generalized system of exchange if a man in group A must marry a woman from B, while a man in B marries a woman in C, a man in C a woman in D, and a man in D a woman in A. This is what takes place, among other things, in the case where the marriage is matrilateral, that is to say where the young man must marry the daughter of his maternal uncle. This rule establishes the course of an open cycle to which each individual must conform. When group A gives a woman away to group B, it is a long-term speculation since it has to bank on the fact that B will give a woman away to C, C to D, and D to A. Such a calculation entails risks and this is why new formulas of [marital] alliance are often superimposed on generalized exchange, such as marriage by purchase, which allows one to integrate irrational factors into the system without destroying it.

The application of these guiding principles allows Lévi-Strauss to bring out the signification of matrimonial systems which up to now appeared both contingent and unintelligible. The conclusion of these analyses which take us to Australia, China, India, and both Americas, is the existence of two essential types of exogamy. Direct exchange corresponds to bilateral marriage, meaning that the individual can marry the daughter of his maternal uncle or of his paternal aunt. Indirect (or generalized) exchange corresponds to the matrilateral marriage that authorizes [marital] alliance exclusively with the daughter of the maternal uncle. The first system is only possible in disharmonic regimes, that is to say where residence follows the lineage of the father and filiation follows the lineage of the mother. The second system appears in harmonic regimes where residence and filiation go together. The first one is very fruitful as to the number of systems it is likely to found, but its functional fecundity is relatively weak. The second one, to the contrary, is a fecund-regulating principle leading to a greater organic solidarity within the group. In the case of restricted exchange, the inclusion within or the exclusion outside the class is the deciding factor. In the case of indirect exchange, the degree of kinship, that is to say the nature of the relation, is of prominent importance. Thus disharmonic systems have evolved toward organizations with matrimonial classes while the contrary has taken place in harmonic systems. The latter constitute an open cycle, a long cycle; the former a short cycle. Bilateral marriage is a more secure operation, but matrilateral marriage offers unlimited potentialities, the length of the cycle being in inverse proportion to its security. This is why a foreign factor is almost always added to the simple forms of generalized exchange. Among the groups that embarked on this great sociological adventure, not one of them could entirely free itself from the anxiety generated by the risks of the system, and they have kept a certain ratio or even a symbol of patrilaterality. No system is pure: it is both simple and coherent and yet beset by other systems.

It should be added that the structure of the exchange is not a binding requirement for a preferred spouse. Among other things, the purchase of a wife in substitution for his claim on the [female] cousin allows him to be freed from the elementary forms of the exchange. However, whether indirect or not, global or specific, concrete or symbolic, the exchange is always found at the basis of matrimonial institutions. The idea that exogamy aims to insure a total and continuing circulation of women and girls is thus confirmed. Its value is not negative, but positive. The idea is not that a biological peril is attached to consanguineous marriage, but rather a social benefit results from exogamous marriage. The incest prohibition is the law of the gift par excellence: it is the institution of culture in the heart of nature.

"Any marriage is a dramatic encounter between nature and culture, between [marital] alliance and kinship, . . . Since one must yield to nature in order that the species may perpetuate itself, and concomitantly for social alliance to endure, the very least one must do is to deny it while yielding to it."[9] In a sense, any marriage is a social incest since the husband absorbs a specific possession into himself instead of escaping toward the other. Society demands that within this selfish act, communication with the group be at least maintained: this is why, even though the woman is something more than a sign, she is still like the word, something to be exchanged.

The relation of the man to the woman is fundamentally also a relationship to other men—and other women. Lovers are never alone in the world. The most intimate event for everyone, the sexual embrace, is also a public event: it calls into question at the same time the individual and the whole society. This is the origin of its dramatic character. Those who are scandalized by the burning interest that today's men attach to it display a remarkable ignorance: the extreme importance attached to sexual taboos shows us that this concern is as old as the world and it is far from being superfluous, for man defines his humanity by the manner in which he assumes his sexuality.

Certainly, this choice he makes on his own is not the fruit of a well-thought-out deliberation. However, the premier merit of this study by Lévi-Strauss is precisely to challenge the old dilemma: either human acts are intentional or they are devoid of signification. The author defines them as structures whose whole precedes the parts and whose regulating principle possesses a rational value even if it is not rationally conceived. From where do structure and principle come? Lévi-Strauss abstains from venturing into the philosophical field, and he never departs from a rigorous scientific objectivity; his thought, however, obviously belongs to the great humanistic movement which considers that human existence brings with itself its own reason. One can not read his conclusions without remembering young Marx's words: "The relation of man to woman."[10]

Yet, the book does not awaken only Marxist echoes; it often gave me the impression of successfully reconciling Engels and Hegel, for man originally appears to us as an antiphysis, and what his intervention realizes is the concrete position in front of me of another self [*moi*] without which the first would not be able to be defined. I have also been especially impressed by the similarity between certain descriptions and the theses upheld by existentialism: in positing itself, existence posits its laws in a single movement; it does not obey any internal necessity, yet it escapes contingency of fact because it assumes the conditions of its upspringing.[11] The incest prohibition is both universal and normative because it reveals an original attitude of the existant: to be man is to choose oneself as a man by defining one's possibilities on the basis of a reciprocal relationship with the other. The presence of the other is never an accident, and exogamy, far from restricting itself to recognizing this presence, on the contrary, constitutes it. Through the presence of the other, man's transcendence is expressed and realized: it is the refusal of immanence, the demand for a surpassing. Through communication and exchange, matrimonial regimes provide man with a horizon toward which he can project himself; under their baroque appearance they assure him a human hereafter.

However, attempting to confine such an impartial book to one system of interpretation would betray the book: its fecundity comes specifically from the fact that it invites every reader to think it over in his own way. This is also the reason that no single review can do it justice. A work that delivers facts, establishes a method, and proposes speculations, deserves to be rediscovered individually: it ought to be read.

## NOTES

This review was published in *Les temps modernes* in October 1949, VII (49), 943–49; © Sylvie Le Bon de Beauvoir. Earlier that year, Claude Lévi-Strauss's *Les structures élémentaires de la parenté* was published by Editions des Presses Universitaires de France; hereafter we refer to this title as SEP. A revised edition with the same title was published in France by Mouton and Co. and Maison des Sciences de l'Homme in 1967. The revised edition was translated into English by James Harle Bell, John Richard von Sturmer, and Rodney Needham, with the title *The Elementary Structures of Kinship*, hereafter referred to as ESK. It was published in 1969 by Beacon Press, Boston.

1. Emile Durkheim (1858–1917) was a French sociologist who pioneered the methodology and theoretical framework of rigorous social science.

2. The Murngin are Australian aborigines, and the Kachin are a tribal people occupying parts of northeastern Myanmar and contiguous areas of China and India.

3. This word is "intrinsèque" in the *Les temps modernes* article, but should be "extrin-sèque," as is apparent in the following passage from Lévi-Strauss's SEP, paraphrased in Beauvoir's review: "[C]ertains ont invoqué le double caractère, naturel et culturel, de la règle, mais se sont bornés à établir entre l'un et l'autre une connexion extrinsèque, con-stituée par une démarche rationnelle de la pensée" (28). This passage was translated as "Some put forward the natural and cultural duality of the rule, but could only establish a rationally derived and extrinsic connection between the two aspects" in ESK (24).

4. Beauvoir quotes Lévi-Strauss's SEP: "C'est le processus par lequel la Nature se dépasse elle-même" (29), which is translated as "The prohibition of incest is where nature transcends itself" in ESK (25).

5. The "intervention" Beauvoir refers to here is the incest prohibition, where society inter-venes on the desires of individuals by dictating who is to marry whom.

6. Marcel Mauss (1872–1950) was a French sociologist and anthropologist who studied forms of exchange and contract of peoples of Melanesia, Polynesia, and northwestern North America. He authored "Essai sur le don: Forme et raison de l'échange dans les sociétés archaïques" (The gift: The form and reasons for exchange in archaic societies), *Année soci-ologique*, n.s., I (1925): 30–186, and, later, *Sociologie et anthropologie* (Sociology and anthropology) (1950).

7. In structural anthropology, "prestations" is a technical term involving social exchanges of goods and money between individuals and groups in the establishment of society.

8. Sir James George Frazer (1851–1941) was a Scottish classicist and anthropologist who is especially known for his masterpiece, *The Golden Bough* (1890).

9. Quoted from SEP (561) and ESK (489–90).

10. Beauvoir is probably referring to the passage from Marx's *Philosophical Works*, vol-ume 6, that she quoted in the conclusion of *The Second Sex*: "'Le rapport immediat, naturel, nécessaire, de l'homme à l'homme est le *rapport de l'homme à la femme*' a dit Marx" ("The direct, natural, and necessary relation of person to person is the relation of man to woman," said Marx.) *Le deuxième sexe*, II (Paris: Gallimard, 1976), 526; *The Second Sex* (New York: Knopf, 2010), 766.

11. "Upspringing" (*jaillissement*) comes from Henri Bergson's *Creative Evolution*, trans. A. Mitchell (1907; New York: Modern Library, 1911), 181.

**4**

Short Feminist Texts
from the Fifties and Sixties

# INTRODUCTION

*by Karen Vintges*

Beauvoir's short feminist texts from the 1950s and 1960s follow up on the main themes of her study *The Second Sex*, which was published in 1949. In this voluminous work, Beauvoir had already outlined all the major issues of the second feminist wave of the late sixties and early seventies, namely the issues of economic autonomy for women, women's control over their own bodies, and the liberation of female sexuality. Two decades after its publication, *The Second Sex* was "discovered" by second-wave feminists. However, Betty Friedan's *Feminine Mystique* (1963), which is generally seen as the book that set in motion the feminist movement in the United States, was highly influenced by Beauvoir's study, as Friedan herself acknowledged only later.[1]

Greater availability of contraception and access for women to jobs and higher education are generally seen as the prime initiators of the second feminist wave. The tensions between these new conditions on the one hand and the old patterns of "femininity" on the other formed the social and cultural backgrounds of this movement. From 1968 onward, it spread quickly, from the circles of the new left—where white middle-class women from a variety of oppositional movements began to protest against their own subordination to their male companions—to women in other social strata and classes. Control by men of female sexuality and fertility was seen as central to the oppression of women, and free contraception and abortion on demand became the key issues. However, after a few years the new women's movement shifted toward identity politics, stressing the difference between men and women and arguing for a female "identity." Beauvoir's *The Second Sex* then was openly criticized as representing a "male"—since Sartrean—view of women that had to be superseded by the new, "real" feminism.

The new "identity" feminism, which started with a lot of energy and passion, soon turned into a kind of fundamentalism. Instead of open and experiential, women's identity came to be seen as fixed and pre-given: second wave's "identity" feminism presupposed an *essential* difference between men and women, and it claimed to know the real nature of women, their unconscious, and their desire. As is well known, Beauvoir was skeptical about the idea of a female nature. But not so well known is her statement in the last pages of *The Second Sex* that there will always be "certain differences" between man and woman, since their sexual worlds have special forms. However, for Beauvoir these differences are not a set of fixed characteristics. She concludes: "new carnal and affective relations of which we cannot conceive will be born between the sexes." She adds: "friendships, rivalries, complicities, chaste or sexual companionships that past centuries would not have dreamed of are already appearing."[2] For Beauvoir, sexual difference is never a matter of pre-given identities but rather involves a continuous work of invention. Her feminist texts of the fifties and sixties also express this original voice of a feminism without blueprints. In these texts, we find Beauvoir once more advocating women's control over their own bodies and lives as well as arguing for new forms of love between men and women. Wanting to reach an audience as wide as possible, she moreover published in popular magazines, like the American fashion magazine *Flair* and the women's magazine *McCall's*.

*Flair* was a spectacular style magazine that lasted for only one year. It published on art, intellect, and fashion. Jean Cocteau, Tennessee Williams, Gloria Swanson, Eleanor Roosevelt, Salvador Dali, and Margaret Mead were among its contributors. In an article entitled "It's About Time Women Put a New Face on Love" (1950) Beauvoir elaborated on the first and the last pages of *The Second Sex*. In the introductory pages of this work, she had criticized the idea that love would vanish with the arrival of emancipated women. Her 1950 text as well starts by criticizing this idea: "A thousand prophets mutter that they will drag love to its ruin, and with it all poetry, illusion, and happiness." Men tend to think of love in terms of inequality and submission. Therefore they fear that the obedient woman (symbolized in Boccaccio's story of the patient Griselda) shall be replaced by the praying mantis that kills her male partner. But a new kind of love in which both partners are equal is possible, since love has other roots than a societal structure.

Beauvoir then goes into her concept of the ambiguity of the human condition. We are conscious builders of the world, an aspect that we share with our fellow humans. But we are a unique life as well, an irreplaceable being "bounded only by irreparable death." A human being in other words is an incarnated consciousness, and this double condition (ambiguity) is what love is all about. Love is to see the other both in his impersonal activity and as a finite creature. It can be platonic as well as sexual. But it is sexual desire "that most often gives the physical presence of the beloved its matchless value." As in the final pages of *The Second Sex*, she in this context points to certain differences between men and women that will always remain. "I believe that what fascinates each in the other is the discovery of a human world like its own but *different*: the *other* sex has the fascination of an exotic country; it is a treasure, an Eden, simply because it is different." The bodies and sexuality of men and women are not the same; the sexes differ "in their sensuality, their sensibility, their relation to the world." When they accept each other as ambiguous beings, as consciousness incarnated in flesh, the mutual magic is always there. We cannot predict the forms these new relationships between men and women will take. It may be that certain forms of sensibility are bound to disappear but others will be born. Beauvoir concludes by explicitly arguing for the attitude of invention: "rather than grimly hanging on to what is dying, or repudiating it, would it not be better to try to help invent the future?"

In her prefaces to two books by Marie-Andrée Lagroua Weill-Hallé, from 1959 and 1960, respectively, Beauvoir goes into the theme of women's control over their own bodies. Until the sixties, family planning was still taboo and the sale of contraceptives was restricted all over the world (the birth control pill was approved for sale in the United States in 1960; in France, the sale of contraceptives, including the pill, was not legalized until 1967). Through her experiences as a doctor, Lagroua Weill-Hallé was convinced of the need for family planning. Together with sociologist Evelyne Sullerot, she had started the MFPF, the French Movement for Family Planning in 1956. In the same year, the communist journalist Jacques Derogy published *Des enfants malgré nous* (Children in spite of us) in which he investigated the dramatic reality of clandestine abortions in France—a book that provoked a debate in the French press, and for which he was expelled from the Communist Party by chairman Maurice Thorez.

In her preface to Lagroua Weill-Hallé's *Le planning familial* (Family planning) (1959), Beauvoir points to the strange contradiction between the overall conquering of nature by man on the one hand and the "laissez faire" politics on such an important issue as natality on the other. Because contraceptives were prohibited, the number of illegal and often very dangerous abortions matched the number of newborn children in France every year (between 400,000 and 500,000). Birth control is the only solution. In *La grand'peur d'aimer* (The great fear of loving) (1960), Lagroua Weill-Hallé reported the heartbreaking stories of the women who consulted her but whom she could not help due to the ban on contraceptives. In her short preface to this book, Beauvoir again emphatically argues for the availability of adequate birth control for all women who want it, so that love in the family may survive—a love which for millions of women is their unique recourse against the world's harshness.

In an essay for the journal *La NEF* (*La nouvelle équipe française*), entitled "La condition féminine" (The condition of women), Beauvoir elaborates on women's overall condition in France. *La NEF* published two special issues on this topic and asked Beauvoir for a concluding article. The first special issue, on women and work, *La femme et le travail* (1960), contained sixteen articles, by among others Gisèle Halimi, Colette Audry, and Andrée Michel—whose article "La Française et la démocratie" (Frenchwomen and democracy) Beauvoir refers to twice. The second special issue, on women and love, *La femme et l'amour* (1961), contained another seventeen articles, by among others Madeleine Chapsal and Suzanne Lilar, as well as a cynical letter from the French writer Jean d'Ormesson, which Beauvoir also refers to and in which he criticizes the board of *La NEF* and Beauvoir for denying "the little difference" between men and women.

Beauvoir starts her article by claiming that the condition of women in France has not improved since 1919. Especially women's working conditions have not improved, whether they are working inside or outside the house. The housewife is still socially isolated and without an income of her own. But the woman who works outside the house and earns a salary also has reason to complain. Even for men, working conditions are far from rewarding in this world of capitalist exploitation and individualistic solitude. But women's careers often stagnate because of a lack of support from male colleagues. The working woman moreover is still not allowed to decide when to procreate, due to lack of birth control. She is neither supported by widespread nurseries and day-care facilities nor given easy access to services of domestic help. The cooperation of the father being still secondary, she often lacks enough sleep to recuperate: women in these conditions suffer from chronic fatigue. All in all, women constantly interrogate themselves: working mothers anxiously wonder if they should stop working; housewives ask themselves if they were wrong to give up their occupations. The majority of women throughout the world nevertheless prefer to have jobs. The only possibility for the time being is to struggle and move on until this period of transition is over. If a national economy requires women to work, then the government creates laws and institutions to facilitate the combination of work and raising children, as it has happened in China. If one day in France the economical conditions demand full entry of women in the job market, all the obstacles for women's success would disappear. Men then would take it for granted that women work and would adapt their sensibility and sexuality to it. As for the children, little conformists as they are, they easily would adjust to the new situation. But this takes a reversal in the system of production: socialism is a necessary condition for the many changes that must take place on the level of ideology and myth, as well as relationships between spouses and between parents and children.

Beauvoir wrote another, very short, preface to the book *The Sexually Responsive Woman* (1964) by Phyllis and Eberhard Kronhausen, a study of female sexuality, based on laboratory experiments as well as womens' autobiographies. Beauvoir expresses her sympathy for the Kronhausens' views on overcoming the myths about female sexuality and their efforts to call into question the notion of women's "physiological destiny." In contrast to male prejudices, "the authors grant women an autonomy—both physiological and psychological—equal to that of men."

In 1965, Beauvoir again goes back to the topic of love in an essay in the American women's magazine, *McCall's*. In this essay, she once more celebrates love as a joy and a gift. Why do we fall in love? There are too many reasons. But almost always it has to do with a certain feeling of emptiness. "You do not fall in love when you are completely happy or on the crest of the wave. . . . It is when the monotony of the world becomes apparent that you begin to dream of new horizons." Through another person a new world is revealed and given. The artist, the ambitious man, and the man of action can change their relation to the world or even the world itself. But very often women are not in that position, and even if they are, they often prefer to find a new world through love. To fall in love takes an Other: it takes someone who escapes me and who can introduce me into another world. We experience "the unexpected and wonderful joy of receiving everything without so much effort."

The last text, entitled "Amour et politique" (Love and politics) (1969), is in line with the first in that Beauvoir deals here with a love in which both partners are equal. The text is from an interview Beauvoir did for Radio Luxembourg in which she was asked to react to the novel, *L'aveu* (*The Confession*) by Artur London. The novel dealt with the Stalinist show trial in which he had been prosecuted (a novel that was made into a film by Costa-Gavras in 1970, with Yves Montand in the role of London). The Stalinist show trials, which were meant to underline Stalin's hegemony, were all about confessing crimes: once the confession was made—of course under torture—proof of the crime was accepted and the victim was sentenced. Arthur London's wife, Lise London, asked for a divorce immediately after hearing the news of her husband's confession, but once she heard from him the full facts of the case she ceaselessly fought for his release.

When asked about Lise London's first reaction, Beauvoir reflects on how she is to be understood. Rather than seeing her as unfaithful to her husband, we should realize that she was a woman with a political conviction as unconditional as his. Lise London was a heroine of the French Resistance movement. During the Second World War, she once stood up in public and called for women to participate in the French Resistance. Her political passion was as deep as her husband's. They both loved each other "through politics." Beauvoir thus sided with Lise London, a gesture for which Lise London recently expressed her gratitude.[3]

Discussing Lise London's absolute faith in communism, Beauvoir added this remark: "I myself have never had a political conviction as unconditional as hers." And if we take these short texts together, we indeed find that they emphasize openness to the future and do not suggest any belief in blueprints. Beauvoir advocated the freedom for women to create their own lives and to put new faces on love, in open orientation to the future. She argued for thorough social economic change that would diminish women's burdens in the family and allow the couple to equally share these tasks. The theme of the chronic fatigue of women, caused by the combination of new responsibilities of work and education and traditional conditions of women, including motherhood, remains with us today. Standing up for family planning and contraceptives on behalf of women is still necessary in large parts of the world. The effects of the Vatican's ban on contraceptives are dramatic for women in the third world, especially in relation to the wide spread of HIV. Whereas, among others, the Vatican accused feminism of wanting to break up the family, Beauvoir's feminist texts of the fifties and sixties show that her aim on the contrary was to make it possible for love within the couple to survive. Her articles on love are moving in that they show how she conceives of love as "mutual magic" and as a joy and a gift, a view that keeps its urgency in today's oversexualized, not to say pornographic, society.

## NOTES

1. Sandra Dijkstra, "Simone de Beauvoir and Betty Friedan: The Politics of Omission," *Feminist Studies* 6, 2 (Summer 1980): 293–94.

2. Simone de Beauvoir, *The Second Sex* (Paris: Gallimard, 1949), trans. Constance Borde and Sheila Malovany-Chevallier (New York: Knopf, 2010), 765.

3. Lise London, "Amour et politique, le soutien de Beauvoir" (Love and politics: Beauvoir's support), *Cinquantenaire du deuxième sexe* (Fifty years after *The Second Sex*), ed. Christine Delphy and S. Chaperon (Paris: Éditions Syllepse, 2002), 376–79.

# IT'S ABOUT TIME WOMEN
# PUT A NEW FACE ON LOVE

*by Simone de Beauvoir*

NOTES BY MARYBETH TIMMERMANN

It's about time women put a new face on love. They are becoming both in-dependent and responsible, active builders of the world. But this metamor-phosis still causes dismay. A thousand prophets mutter that they will drag love to its ruin, and with it all poetry, illusion, and happiness. Until now our civilization has never known a love that was not founded on inequality. Women capable of genuine passion kneel worshipfully before their master, sovereign, god. This idea is so deeply rooted in men's hearts that if a woman does not lie prostrate at their feet, they fear that they may themselves be forced to play the ignominious slave. The myth of the patient Griselda has been replaced by that of the praying mantis. The one gives, the other ex-ploits. The gifts that the first showers upon him are a burden, and the second succeeds in wringing profit from the male only through submission to him; both are parasites who camouflage, each in her own way, their dependence. Is it not possible to conceive a new kind of love in which both partners are equals—one not seeking submission to the other? Or in the society of the future will there only be room, as so many claim, for a comradeship in which sex occurs only at absolute need?

It seems to me that the privileged role of love does not depend on this or that superficial structure of society. A much more fundamental explanation may be found in the ambiguity of human nature. Every human being has a double nature. One he shares with his fellows. It is the one that spurs him on; it looks to the future, it defines his ambitions, builds, acts. The go-getter, it stands out from what others have done through results obtained. But each of us possesses another, singular nature: it is locked within an envelope that belongs to no other, within a unique life bounded only by irreparable death. Humanity is only worth its salt when it brings together these two natures. Deprived of mass effort and ambition, man would be no more on this earth than one animal among others, an insignificant accident. Humanity, the sum of these zeros, would itself equal zero. Yet if one were to prize only acquisitiveness and a far-off future, if one were to attach no meaning to the individual, the value of man as a whole would be canceled out. In order to believe in the importance of the world and his own place in it, each must find himself in his work and in his individuality, as a minute particle of humanity and as an irreplaceable being. And it is love given and love received that will be the most powerful aid in bringing about this paradoxical synthesis.

There is a love denounced by every age as sterile: the one that freezes lovers in mutual absorption. Separated from those around them, indifferent to the future, the pair sinks into an egotistical and empty solitude. Legend has it, and quite naturally so, that their end is nearly always death. For if each devours the other, they are devoured in turn by inaction, immobility, boredom: they are already dead. To this emotion, which reveals the folly of lovers who make passion their whole existence, is opposed the ideal of comradeship: comrades united by aims which they pursue together; each recognizing in the other a like freedom and activity. They merge their wills; they dispense with what is individual: all is leveled out, and their deaths, like their lives, might be interchanged. That sex enters at need into this comradeship between man and woman does not alter its essentially impersonal character: doubtless only in the act of sex do they ever physically possess each other, but then merely in what is general. To cherish in the individual what gives him his difference and still accord him the universal rights that are every human being's; to stand united with him through all his impersonal drives and ambitions and still be filled with wonder at what is unique and matchless in his nature: that is the miracle achieved by love alone, in its highest form.

Men like Nietzsche, Tolstoy, and D. H. Lawrence well understood that a true and fruitful love should encompass both the immediate physical presence of the beloved and the beloved's aims in life. But only to the woman did they propose this ideal, since according to them she has no other purpose; man has only to find in her his complacent reflection. I believe that in an equalitarian love, she will not renounce this fine role as ally, but that the man will also be willing to take it on. It is understood that this reciprocity is possible only when the two share the same aims in life or can reconcile them: the love we describe here presupposes friendship; but how much more fruitful it would be than a one-sided devotion. The woman would then be able to bring to the man the confidence, the support that he demands so concretely, but she would also be giving herself to an effort that would put her shoulder to shoulder with him: otherwise, her docility is blind and servile. The man, instead of seeking a kind of narcissistic exaltation in his mate, would discover in love a way of getting outside himself, of tackling problems other than his own. With all the twaddle that has been written about the splendor of such generosity, why not give the man his chance to participate in such devotion, in the self-negation that is considered the enviable lot of women? Let each partner think simultaneously of the other and self: the woman will be rescued from the timidity which so often holds her down, and the man will be healed of his egotistical pride: each will benefit by a taste of virtues that up to now have been reserved for the other sex.

However, this harmonious entente still does not constitute love. Love places each for the other as an ally, a fellow being, in the bosom of the human community, as it sets each overwhelmingly and incomparably apart. Together the lovers face the world and the future; but each is also astonished to see an accomplice looking out from those cherished eyes; there can be no other like the beloved in life, no replacement in death. It is this love that is the most complete relationship possible with another person: to see him both in his impersonal activity and in his irreplaceable reality; as builder and as object; as all that transcends himself and as finite creature. If woman becomes for man his veritable equal, she will feel no less the need to be thus marvelously confirmed within and to confirm with her love the one whose love crowns her.

As we have defined it here, love may be platonic as well as sexual: it suffices that the presence of the beloved be revealed in what is unique, contingent, and pathetically perishable; this revelation may operate in more than one way. Nevertheless, the fact remains that sexual attraction is the more usual instrument. It is desire that most often gives the physical presence of the beloved its matchless value. Therefore it would be dangerous to the future of love if women as they advance their state were to lose their allure in men's eyes. At this point the prophets of woe wail most loudly, "Femininity will be lost, femininity will be lost!" This catastrophe has been announced as imminent for so long that we are entitled to our skepticism: it may be that the attraction of one sex for the other has profounder causes than the rustling of a petticoat, the shape of a boot. I believe that what fascinates each in the other is the discovery of a human world like its own but *different*: the *other* sex has the fascination of an exotic country; it is a treasure, an Eden, simply because it is different. Yet here again men persist in regarding this difference as another aspect of inequality; but nothing proves this is not capable of change. The two sexes can become equals, allies, without abolishing the distance between them that renders each desirable to the other. To tell the truth, I cannot possibly conceive how this desirability could ever be destroyed, since the body and sexuality of the man and the woman are different, and therefore different in their sensuality, their sensibility, their relation to the world; and since the physical need that each has for the other will maintain their mutual magic. That consciousness and freedom should find incarnation within a flesh that is my biological destiny—this will always be for me, whether man or woman, an overwhelming miracle: perhaps all the more awe-inspiring, to the contrary, for the spiritual powers—the thought, the will—that assert themselves with greater brilliance. The man who manifests these virtues, in the midst of humanity, seems in women's eyes to be endowed with virile qualities; it may be that one day the human virtues of women will enhance her femininity in men's eyes.

Conjectures would be rash at this point: the future does not belong to us. And that is why no one has the right to condemn the future in the name of the present. In every age there have been those who lament the world of the future simply because it promised to be different from the past. We must avoid falling into this trap: our lack of imagination discredits, depopulates these times beyond our ken; but there are others for whom they will one day be real and assuredly richer than we wish to suppose. Doubtless there are forms of sensibility which are bound to disappear as have many others before them: but others will be born. Rather than grimly hanging on to what is dying, or repudiating it, would it not be better to try to help invent the future? Today, too many women fight off love because it evokes ancient slaveries, and too many men refuse to believe in it because they fail to know it by its ancient face. Let both men and women overcome their distrust, and they will find that it is possible to restore, in freedom and in equality, the human pair.

## NOTES

"It's About Time Woman Put a New Face on Love," *Flair*, 1, 3, April 1950, 76–77; translator unknown; © Sylvie Le Bon de Beauvoir. This article was originally published in English, and the original French text has not been found, but given Beauvoir's rejection of essentialism, we have changed singular "Woman" to plural "Women" in the title and in certain cases where Beauvoir means all women or women in general in order to avoid essentialist connotations that Beauvoir would not have intended and to maintain consistency throughout the volume.

The following appeared at the end of the original publication of this article in *Flair* magazine: "Co-ruler with Sartre of France's intellectual avant-garde, Simone de Beauvoir spent her youth in Paris, took her Ph.D. at the Sorbonne. In 1943 she gave up teaching for writing: novels, a play, problematic essays that have become a feminine testament for existentialists. Her recent book *The Second Sex*, which explores the role and destiny of women, will be published in America this year."

# PREFACE TO *FAMILY PLANNING*

*by Simone de Beauvoir*

TRANSLATION AND NOTES BY MARYBETH TIMMERMANN

The idea of "family planning" has only hesitantly begun to make its way into France, even though it is common practice in four-fifths of the world. Dr. Lagroua Weill-Hallé's book shows the benefits gained by the countries that put it into practice, and by contrast, brings attention to the outrageously backward legislation to which French families are subjected.[1]

The figures are enough to prove that "Planning" does not mean Malthusianism. It is not a matter of restricting the increase in population, but of bringing it into balance, reconciling the interests of Society with those of families and individuals. At a time when man's conquest of nature is making more and more stunning progress, it seems aberrant that, when it comes to something as important as the birth rate, the official motto in our country is still, "let nature run its course."

No one today can continue to ignore the disastrous consequences of such an obscurantism. Each year the number of abortions is approximately equivalent to that of births; they estimate that there were between 400,000 and 500,000 in 1956. Most of those who get abortions are mothers who already have a family of two or three children. For the immense majority of young households, their limited resources and insufficient lodging radically prevent them from having any more children. Since the methods that are currently used to limit fertility provide uncertain results at best, many women who are pregnant against their wishes have no other recourse than to get an abortion.

Correctly performed, the operation is benign. Of course this is not true if it is performed illicitly as is the case in France, where basic precautions are neglected out of poverty, urgency, and despair. Sometimes the result is death, sometimes permanent infertility, oftentimes serious physiological or psychological problems. The indictments against this specifically French curse are abundant, but denouncing it is useless if people refuse to prevent it. When illegality has permeated morality to this point, repression is powerless; we would be better off honestly admitting that the law is the sin and must be changed. There exists only one way to eliminate abortion and its ravages, and that is to authorize women to protect themselves effectively from pregnancies that their life conditions or their health do not allow them to bring to term. The opponents of Birth Control object that some women are hesitant or fail in their attempt to abort, but would they dare to congratulate themselves if they considered the fate of those "children in spite of us" of whom Derogy has so eloquently spoken?*[2] Newspapers relate the most wrenching cases of beaten or abandoned children, but no one talks about those who waste away due to the lack of nourishment and care, and those who become psychologically or morally deficient adults.

I find it monstrous that a law forces women to bring into the world beings destined to hardship and misfortune.

The drama of women forced into too many closely spaced pregnancies is no less tragic. Their health is depleted; they are exhausted by a workload that exceeds their strength, and their lives become nothing more than a dismal struggle against despair. They become an intolerable burden for the men already obsessed with the worry of so many mouths to feed. The fear of a new pregnancy poisons conjugal relations, resulting in frustrations for both spouses that end up destroying their equilibrium. This is how so many households become living hells after a few years of marriage. Because planning out their lives is forbidden to men and to women, it is impossible for them to correctly manage the entirety [*ensemble*] of their existence. Prematurely overwhelmed with children, the woman must give up working, and the man must give up gaining a higher professional, intellectual, or technical level. The future is barred to them, so they settle for facing urgent needs as they arise day by day. A society which condemns itself to this stagna-

---

* *Des enfants malgré nous* [Children in spite of us], Éditions de Minuit.

tion is seriously handicapped in comparison to those that liberate human energies.

If the increase of a population is paid for by a decrease in its health, its intellectual level, and its possibilities, then nothing is gained, quite the contrary.

Certainly "Family Planning" is not sufficient to guarantee an equilibrium. The inclination to have children, which is natural for young couples if nothing inhibits them, must be encouraged as well. This presupposes the construction of a world where they will find reasons to live and propagate life. But if they find none, forced procreation would only be more abominable.

On the ground where Dr. Lagroua Weill-Hallé situates her book, all that she demands, and what those who are associated with her efforts demand, is the abolition of an anarchy harmful to each one of us and to all of us, in favor of a reflective freedom [*liberté réfléchie*]. In every domain, man today refuses to abandon himself to the hazards of fate; he organizes, rationalizes, takes his destiny once again into his own hands. Why would he leave things to fate when his family life is at stake? The favorable results of "Family Planning" in the countries that practice it clearly show that none of us should hesitate any longer to engage ourselves on this path.

## NOTES

Simone de Beauvoir, "Préface" to *Le "planning" familial*, by Dr. Lagroua Weill-Hallé (Paris: Maloine, 1959); © Sylvie Le Bon de Beauvoir.

1. Dr. Marie-Andrée Lagroua Weill-Hallé (1905–94) was a noted French gynecologist and founder of the French Family Planning movement. All forms of contraception were explicitly illegal in France until 1967.

2. The French journalist and writer Jacques Derogy (pseudonym of Jacques Weitzmann) (1925–97) was a pioneer in the field of investigative reporting. He wrote *Des enfants malgré nous* (Paris: Minuit, 1956) in an effort to expose the horrors of illegal abortions.

# PREFACE TO *THE GREAT FEAR OF LOVING*

*by Simone de Beauvoir*

TRANSLATION AND NOTES BY MARYBETH TIMMERMANN

"How do other women do it?" This heart-wrenching leitmotiv is repeated all throughout the collection of testimonies given to us today by the honorable Dr. Weill-Hallé. The exhausted, harassed, frightened, and hounded women who come to ask her for help believe themselves to be the victims of some singular and obscure malediction. To them their despair seems too absolute to not be abnormal. Each one imagines that surely other women know of ways to escape the traps into which they have fallen and the insidious danger that incubates in their blood. But alas, this is far from true. Dr. Weill-Hallé recounts individual cases in a deliberately terse style; each one of these stories makes us feel the throbbing of a unique life, and yet the tremendous and painful import of her book comes from the fact that it gives us a sampling of tragedies that are repeated a thousand times each day. Each year in France, there are at least five hundred thousand abortions, but how many unwanted pregnancies are endured in anguish? How many children are born unwanted, unloved, or mistreated? How many households are devastated by excessive burdens and how many couples are torn apart for fear of another pregnancy? How many women's careers have been shattered and loves been lost? How many women are tortured by obsessive fears or pushed into depressions and neuroses? What a waste! But a hypocritical conspiracy conceals it even from the women concerned; they endure their fate in a solitude that is oftentimes mixed with shame or even remorse. No one shows them that their misery is in no way accidental but instead comes inevitably from the situation created by a legislation that stubbornly persists in obscurantism. Today in France, limited salaries and insufficient lodging prevent young couples from raising more than two or three children in a healthy environment. Yet truly effective methods of contraception are forbidden to them. Both spouses suffer from this contradiction, but the woman suffers much more than the man. It is her body that experiences the exhaustion of pregnancy and birth; the man can escape from the domestic hell while she is consumed by it. Day by day, hour by hour, she struggles to complete impossible tasks; if she fails, her husband sees it as her fault, and in the majority of cases, he considers it up to her to avoid inopportune pregnancies. "How? How do other women do it?" This anxious refrain never gives her a rest; her blood runs cold, panic fills her heart, and her thoughts spin around in circles.

People readily proclaim, in this day and age, that "the woman question" is settled. The women who write advice columns assert that women find complete satisfaction in the blossoming of their femininity. Women, say men, now have the same rights and the same possibilities as us; if they don't take advantage of them, it's their own fault. Optimists exalt feminine nature and pessimists denounce its incurable faults, but they all agree to keep silent about the real issue that women have to confront: How, in the current economic circumstances, can you succeed in a career, build a happy home, joyfully raise children, be of service to society and achieve self-realization, if at any moment the crushing burdens of a new pregnancy can come upon you? "For women, freedom begins with the womb," wrote one of my correspondents. The confidences received by Dr. Weill-Hallé confirm that this elementary freedom—the freedom of conception—is not only demanded by egoists who are avid to "live their own life," but much more frequently by women who are devoted to endeavors in which they have engaged their entire raisons d'être. A young graduate thinks that her existence is a distressing failure if a third child prevents her from completing her studies and pursuing the career to which she aspired. A mother wants to assure happiness for her husband and children, but if a new baby comes along, poverty and overcrowding will rear its ugly head and her household will risk falling apart. And what about love? For millions of women it is the unique recourse against the harshness of the world. It fades away slowly or dies brutally if the couple is haunted by the fear of a child. No one helps these women who resist and fight blindly against a destiny that they see as unacceptable. The most painful pages of the indictments brought together by Dr. Weill-Hallé are perhaps those in which she describes—without being able to find the reason for it—the indifference and even the hostility of men with regards to their partners in distress. One, who would later become a good husband, abandons his pregnant girlfriend; another young husband only says, "figure something out" to his dismayed wife. In bourgeois households, where lies are the rule, a woman doesn't even dare to confide in other women, and if she consults her doctor his answer to her terrors will be a lesson in morality. Even if he sympathizes, what can he do for her? Nothing. By telling us the tragedies of all those desperate women who came to her office, Dr. Weill-Hallé is also quietly and very discreetly evoking her own personal drama: "I closed the door and never saw her again. . . . I never saw Miss X again either . . . I regret only being able to listen to Mrs. S." A few well-placed words of advice here and there are all a doctor can provide without falling into illegality; his hands are tied.

But Dr. Weill-Hallé does not just accept her helplessness, and that is why she has written this book. She is not trying to write literature; she paints a picture of the harsh condition of French women today so that we may collaborate with her in order to find a remedy for it. For many years she has been trying to convince France to embrace the idea of "family planning." In a short book, not nearly well enough known, she showed the benefits of this method for the countries that put it into practice, which include four-fifths of the world. The statistics she cites prove irrefutably that when it comes to controlling the birth rate, individual free choice can be perfectly reconciled with demographic progress. The majority of young women who spoke with Dr. Weill-Hallé wanted children; they simply asked to freely choose the date of their next pregnancies. Young couples are naturally inclined to propagate life, if they look around and find reasons to live. A healthy society should take care to furnish them with some of these reasons, and then it would have no need to rely on "forced procreation." In reality, this system of constraint, far from benefiting the increase in population, is paid for by a decrease in its health, its intellectual level, and its possibilities. At a time when man's conquest of nature is making more and more stunning progress, it seems aberrant that, when it comes to something as essential as the birth rate, the official motto in our country is still, "let nature run its course." Dr. Weill-Hallé rightly asks for the abolition of this anarchy which is harmful to each one of us and to all of us in favor of a reflective freedom [liberté réfléchie].

Those who read her book will be shocked no doubt that the painful disorder she denounces has not caused more public outrage; it is monstrous that in such a large number of cases, the arrival of a child spells catastrophe. The explanation of this passivity is the silence that shrouds this taboo subject. Only a handful of psychiatrists, a few doctors, and some social workers are aware of the extent of the damage, and almost no one speaks of it. Dr. Weill-Hallé has chosen to speak out, and I hope that a very great number of women and men hear the tragic confessions she has transcribed for us, for I am sure that they will then desire with all their heart to support her efforts. So much useless suffering must be eliminated as rapidly as possible. We must respond with more than a shrug of the shoulders to the anxious plea, "How do other women do it?"

## NOTES

Simone de Beauvoir, "Préface" to *La grand'peur d'aimer*, by Dr. Marie-Andrée Lagroua Weill-Hallé; first published by Éditions Julliard-Sequana (Paris, 1960); republished by Éditions Gonthier (Paris, 1961); reprinted in *Les écrits de Simone de Beauvoir*, ed. Claude Francis and Fernande Gontier (Paris: Gallimard, 1979), 397–400; © Éditions Gallimard, 1979.

# THE CONDITION OF WOMEN

by *Simone de Beauvoir*

TRANSLATION AND NOTES BY MARYBETH TIMMERMANN

The conclusion that strikes the reader at the end of this study is that in France, things are not going well for women.[1] They are not going well for adolescents either, or the elderly, or children, or male adults. The country is sick and all its members bear witness to this infirmity. It is impossible to heal any of them by amending the law, however considerably [*par des amendements importants*]; the entire body must be treated. Because the structures of our society have not budged, the condition of women has not improved since 1919 and, as Andrée Michel has clearly shown, has even degraded at the same time as democracy has regressed.*[2] The only hope permissible to Frenchwomen today is that France might change.

Women suffer even more than men do from the turmoil, injustice, and anachronism in which we live. It is in men's interest to affirm that the second sex has never been better off, and certain women whose first concern is to please men agree. "Well," they say, "statistics show that 39.6% of women are wage-earners, while about two-thirds stay at home, which means that

---

* Andrée Michel, "La Française et la démocratie," [Frenchwomen and democracy] *La NEF* 4, October–December 1960: 20–36.

88

each one is free to choose according to her aspirations between those two lives. Men are not as lucky; they are obliged to work whether they want to or not." It takes a good deal of bad faith to let oneself be taken in by this sophism. First, in the immense majority of cases, women do not have a choice, and for the very rare ones to whom a choice is given, it does not represent an advantage but a predicament. Certainly neither of these two paths results in a satisfying situation. I have received a large number of letters from women during the last ten years and have spoken with many women, and recent studies confirm my personal experience: their difficulties have only increased and are essentially due to the current conditions of women's work.

Except for a privileged few, all women work. Some—housewives, peasants, laborers or employees in a family business—are not remunerated; others earn a salary. All have serious reasons to complain.

As for the life of the housewife, my opinion has not changed. To varying degrees, according to her monetary resources and the number of her children, she is exhausted by infinite and conflicting tasks that no social legislation regulates and that gain her no marketable skills. If the husband of a woman who has slaved away for twenty years in the house dies, or leaves her, or if she wants to leave him, she will have nothing to show for it, not even a certificate that helps a cook find a job, and as she gets older, she will see her economic value diminish. No one willingly hires a forty-year-old woman with no specialized skills. She is indeed as indissolubly attached to the home as the serf was to the glebe in the days of old. Socially, she is reduced to isolation; the vague exchanges between neighbors are no substitute for the professional solidarity that is created in the factory, office, or labor union. The only group into which she is integrated is the family, which reinforces her dependence with regards to her husband. Psychologically, dependence is still her lot, for she receives no other compensation than the gratitude and affection of her spouse and children—a precarious reward that is often lacking—which turns her life into a series of arid chores to which she submits with a growing resentment. In general, for a few years the "housewife" finds a certain equilibrium in accepting her mutilations[3] and getting carried away by devotion; and then resignation turns into rancor. If she can, she decides to work outside the home and deplores the lost years; she would have gotten a better position if she had continued her studies or started earlier in her career. Many do not have the opportunities or the courage necessary to tear themselves away from their stagnation,[4] but when feelings are laid bare, domestic slavery is experienced as a degradation. Then conjugal hatred flourishes, and the couple struggles in one of those hells so numerous and so common that it is hardly noticed, and yet is one of the worst blights of our society.

However, women wage-earners can hardly congratulate themselves on their fate either. Even for men, in this world of capitalist exploitation and individualistic solitude, work is generally nothing but an unrewarding necessity; it rarely possesses an intrinsic interest. But at least men are stimulated by a double ambition: to make money and to assert themselves socially through professional success. Women have practically no recourse against the monotony of the job. From the start, girls are offered many fewer possibilities than boys. Andrée Michel reports that for boys, technical schools offer 392 occupations; for girls only 174 are available, and these are specifically feminine: sewing, fashion, etc. They are doomed to tasks that are monotonous, very poorly paid, and with no future. In her book on the *Promotion of Women*, Célia Bertin notes that, concerning the professions, parents are willing to make a considerable investment for the education and training of their son but would consider it unwise to invest in a girl; she will get married and in any case[5] will not climb very high. A situation as secretary or nurse is enough for her; it's useless to make sacrifices to train her as a lawyer or a doctor. Then the barriers come into play, and on this point, all the testimonies are in agreement. I personally have gathered some gripping ones. All other things being equal—work, zeal, capacities—women remain confined to inferior positions while their masculine counterparts rise; the clientele does not have confidence in a woman lawyer or a woman doctor, and their colleagues do not support them. In the spirit of competition, men very deliberately maintain the myth of feminine inferiority, and this propaganda is effective. Women contribute to making the barriers insurmountable by their certainty in having to face them. "In any case,[6] a woman can not *make it to the top* [*arriver*], so it is useless to struggle." She gets comfortable in the mediocrity that is imposed upon her, and by her example and words she encourages other women to the same resignation. But this way she gains almost no benefit from her efforts. Her mediocre tasks in themselves provide her with no joy; they don't permit her to happily fill her pockets and they don't flatter her pride. Only the real but austere satisfaction of earning one's daily bread remains.

What is still more serious is that this autonomy is very costly. The wage-earning woman obviously does not renounce love, and love brings about children. And besides, she wants children; but in order to smoothly reconcile her occupation with motherhood, she must, thanks to birth control methods, be able to decide when to procreate. Nurseries, day-cares, domestic help and all those elements effectively organized by States that encourage working women must exist on a large scale. In our country, children are born by chance, the mother raises them with no help, and conventions require that she assume the responsibility almost exclusively; the cooperation of the father is secondary even if she works and earns as much as him. With two or three children and modest resources, she can not continue to pursue her profession without performing exhausting acrobatics. A woman doctor, employed by a large Parisian factory, was telling me that the workers who were also mothers of a family constantly lived on the verge of a nervous depression. "They sleep only five hours; they are always sleepy and tired; they never make it up. All it takes is a trifle—a sickness, an unexpected expense, a big worry—and everything comes apart; they collapse." Even in the better-off strata of society, a woman who works and raises children experiences chronic fatigue, an imbalance that often leads to a *break-down*.[7] Three days ago, I received a letter from a woman engineer who is thirty-five years old and who is just now coming out of one of these crises. In her letter she told me:

> Yes, I thought that it would be possible to lead several lives at the same time: the life of a wife, a mother, a professional, and a participant in the world around me. I felt I would be able to coordinate them. Well, due to lodging and personal conditions, I led the life of a tightrope walker, and I struggled against getting bogged down by household chores. Was trying to keep my mind alive worth the resulting trepidations of the heart and the impossible schedules? If I had simply been the mother of a family who believed in her household activities, wouldn't I have been more balanced? Or if I wanted a professional life, should I have refused to have children, children being acceptable only in a future world "made of great communities [*ensembles*] with parks and nurseries"? It is the same thing for the other women I know. Marriage has sorted the intellectual girls into the many who returned to the traditional life of housewife and the few who sought to live for marriage with children and at the same time for the intellect. None of this latter group has serenity (they are engineers, college professors, fashion artists, etc.).

What struck me the most in this letter is the anxious interrogation: "Was I wrong?" I have often heard this; the housewife overwhelmed by her slavery moans, "If only I had an occupation!" while she who has an occupation murmurs, "If only I didn't need to work!" or if the need is less pressing, she hesitates, "Wouldn't it be better if I gave this up?"

In truth, with only a few rare exceptions, women do not choose their kind of life. Single or married to a man who earns little, women laborers and employees could not live without their pay. In a negative way, therefore less visible but just as imperious, domestic confinement is inflicted upon the housewife; for two-thirds of Frenchwomen there are no career prospects outside of the home. However, due to the fact that a double life is opening up to women—while men know only one—each woman thinks she sees a sort of contingence at the heart of her destiny, which renders it more unbearable. A malcontented man blames the very foundations of society; he thinks that in this world as it is, things could not have happened otherwise for him. Women—because they are victims of a carefully orchestrated mystification and because, due to their situation as secondary beings, they are less solidly integrated into the collectivity—give much more importance to occasional causes. They think they are dealing not with a system, but with people; those responsible for their troubles are their parents, a certain boss, their husbands, or themselves. They repeat, "It's his fault," or "It's my fault." Rancor as well as remorse can easily turn into neurosis, and even more than fatigue, the perpetual rethinking of their fate leads to an imbalance in women. Those who had the freedom of a choice react to failure with feelings of guilt; they reproach themselves for having sacrificed their home, their children, or on the contrary for having shirked in their work. They reproach themselves for living as a parasite instead of bringing money home. They end up deciding to change their path; the domestic woman seeks a job and the lawyer closes her office; and they run into new obstacles. Some wear themselves out in this coming and going. Far from giving an advantage to women, the mirage or the existence of another possibility feeds her dissatisfaction.

Yet between the two situations I have just described, there is no equivalence; studies have shown that the majority of women aspire to a paid job. I spoke with some female employees in the Hispano-Suiza factories one evening; none of them would have agreed to give up her job. They all emphasized the feeling of *dignity* that they derived from it, and they vigorously protested when a man objected that they were neglecting their duties as mothers. "Our children are as well brought up and as happy as any others. We take care of them." In September of [19]58, during the referendum campaign, I knew some young women who found ways to hold meetings until midnight, and who at six in the morning distributed fliers and hung posters, who woke their children at seven and gave them breakfast, and who had to be at their office by eight thirty; they seemed serene. Perhaps they wore themselves out in the long run. But the nervous depressions caused by this type of overexertion, as dramatic as they might be, can be cured. The slow wasting away of the domestic slave is not as noticeable, yet the mutilations she endures, the disgust and rancor which consume her, are incurable. The most painful letters I have received come from housewives.

So there is no question of going backward. Besides, history never goes back to where it used to be. Throughout the entire world, women are becoming emancipated. The only solution for them is to forge ahead; women today suffer from being pulled in all directions, but that will come to an end when this transition period is over.

The most well-balanced women I have met are in China, among high-ranking professionals: doctors, and engineers. They were lucky to have participated through their work in a great collective endeavor: the construction of the New China, for which they cared passionately. But what was especially interesting to me was that their private life was troubled by no conflict. In their eyes, working was a given. Practically, everything was put into place so that they could, like men, devote themselves to their families and to their occupation at the same time, and within their profession, no discrimination worked against them. Ideologically, they were victims of no prejudice, no myth; the Chinese jumped from the feudal family to the conjugal family without passing through paternalism. But during this same period in the Occident, men internalized, in the form of a superiority complex, traditional values, which remain engraved in their hearts, whereas the Chinese man rejected traditions and values in one fell swoop. In any case,[8] ideology *is* practice insofar as it is articulated in words; treated as equals, women are thought of as equals. The State needed her, which gave rise to her promotion; high-ranking professionals were lacking, and mobilizing the elites of both sexes led to treating them with perfect equity.

If one day the French economy, in a similarly ingenious way, were to make an appeal to French women to work, we would see all the objections brandished by the antifeminists crumble. The government would create laws and institutions necessary for the reconciliation of factory and home; the barriers, victimizations, and roadblocks that hinder women's success would be abolished. The so-called psychological problems that reflect, in truth, an objective situation would immediately disappear; there would no longer be scruples, rancor, remorse, doubts, neuroses. If men found it natural for their wives to work, they would see themselves obligated to take on the consequences of this situation and adapt their sensibility and sexuality to it. Women would be freed from the fear of displeasing in accomplishing themselves. And the children? They supposedly require the constant presence of their mother and complain, "The neighbor lady across the way stays home all day. Why do you work? Is it because Papa doesn't earn enough money?" One forgets that a child is not an innocent spontaneity, nor the voice of nature; he is conditioned by his entourage, and no one is more conformist than a child. It is only the anomaly of the situation that is shocking; he would accept it unquestioningly if it were taken for granted.

And the "*petite différence*"?[9] The physiological givens will still remain, remarks Mr. d'Ormesson in his article in this issue.[10] We know that physical strength loses its importance with the progress of automation. As for resistance and skill, women have plenty of those. A well-organized economy would easily make room for maternity leaves; if they are planned and accepted, they will hinder neither production nor the worker. The only thing left is the menstrual cycle, wherein, according to Mr. d'Ormesson, lies the specificity of women's destiny. Let us reassure him: if they have mental health and good hygiene, the majority of women take care of it very well. Masculine mythology makes it into a distressing and somewhat shameful sign of our weakness; if it were imposed upon men, they would find the monthly gift of their blood superbly virile. As long as women remain an underdeveloped sex economically speaking, any masculine singularity will symbolize, to the males, their own superiority.

Everything would change—ideologies, myths, relations between spouses and within each person, between parents and children, and between everyone and society—if society were to be transformed. Inversely, only an economic upheaval can finally make women into full-fledged individuals. It is in the best interests of a regime based on exploitation to maintain discriminations between individuals; equality cannot appear without the coming of a socialism. This condition, although necessary, is not immediately satisfying. Historically, the second sex has gotten off to a bad start because, during the times of elementary technology like hunting and fishing, and in the context of scarcity, the physiological difference between men and women worked in favor of men. These past millenniums may continue to condition us for a long time.[11] In order for women to obtain this professional equality upon which all the rest depends, there must be work for everyone. This implies a great increase in earthly prosperity and a rationalization of production on a universal scale. In vain do we speculate over these tomorrows of our prehistory. What is certain is that this march toward abundance and reason can happen only if there is an overthrow of the system of production. If women do not want to content themselves with finding individual solutions to their singular problems, they must fight alongside the men who want to hasten this overthrow.

## NOTES

"La condition féminine," *La NEF* (*La nouvelle équipe française*) 5, January–March 1961, 121–27; reprinted in *Les écrits de Simone de Beauvoir*, ed. Claude Francis and Fernande Gontier (Paris: Gallimard, 1979), 401–9; © Éditions Gallimard, 1979. This article served as the conclusion to *La NEF*'s multivolume series on "The Frenchwoman Today" (*La Française aujourd'hui*). There were a few minor changes made to the original article in the *Écrits* version that have been noted here.

This article was preceded by the following editorial introduction:

> We have come to the end of the study undertaken by *La NEF* on the situation of "the Frenchwoman today." In the first issue, appearing in October of 1960, *La NEF* studied the relationship between French women and work. In this current issue, *La NEF* covers the problems of "women and [love]." We do not claim that this study is complete and definitive. We are aware that there are many aspects of "the Frenchwoman today" that we were not able to tackle and have not included here. However, we think that the articles published in these two issues of *La NEF* provide new research and information to the study of a question that one might think is well-known, but in reading these articles, one will see that in reality it is very poorly understood. This picture of the condition of women in France in 1960 needed a conclusion, which we have asked Simone de Beauvoir to write.

1. Beauvoir is referring to the inquiry into the current situation of Frenchwomen, undertaken by the French periodical, *La NEF*, and published in their October–December 1960 and January–March 1961 issues. The articles in the October–December issue focused on the questions of women and work, while the January–March 1961 issue focused on women and love. The editors invited Beauvoir to write the concluding article for this special series.

2. The following note appeared in the *Écrits* edition of this article: "Andrée Michel and Geneviève Texier, *The Condition of the Frenchwoman Today*, 2 vol. (Paris: Denoël-Gonthier, 1964)."

3. This is "mutilations" in *Écrits*, apparently a correction of "mutalisations," which is how it appears in the *La NEF* article.

4. In *Écrits*, this reads "s'arracher à leur marasme"; this is apparently a correction of how it appears in the *La NEF* article, which reads "s'accorder à leur marasme" (to consent to their stagnation).

5. In *Écrits*, this appears in the singular ("de toute façon"); in the *La NEF* article, it is plural ("de toutes façons").

6. Ibid.

7. "break-down" is in English in Beauvoir's text.

8. In *Écrits*, this appears in the singular ("de toute façon"); in the *La NEF* article, it is plural ("de toutes façons").

9. In *La NEF*, the grammatical article is also inside the quotation marks ("la petite difference").

10. Jean d'Ormesson (1925–present) is a French writer and member of the Academie Française since 1973. His letter to the editors of *La NEF* was included in the January–March 1961 issue of their series on "The Frenchwoman Today." See Jean d'Ormesson, "Lettre à *La NEF* sur la 'petite différence' entre les hommes et les femmes" (Letter to *La NEF* on the "little difference" between men and women), *La* NEF 5 (January–March 1961): 29–32.

11. In *Écrits*, it reads "continueront peut-être longtemps à nous conditionner"; in the *La NEF* article, it is "continueront peut-être longtemps de nous conditionner."

# PREFACE TO *THE SEXUALLY RESPONSIVE WOMAN*

*by Simone de Beauvoir*

NOTES BY MARYBETH TIMMERMANN

The Doctors Kronhausen have written a forthright, courageous, and highly rigorous study on the difficult problem of women's sexuality, about which so little is known. They have gone further and called into question even that which has hitherto been regarded as an unalterable fact of Nature: women's "physiological destiny." In this realm as in so many others, male prejudice insists on keeping women in a state of dependency. In contrast to this, the authors grant women an autonomy—both physiological and psychological—equal to that of men.

I am not qualified to pass definite judgment on all the findings and conclusions of the Doctors Kronhausen. On the whole, however, the wide range of documentation as well as their precise and subtle analyses are thoroughly convincing.

Quite aside from this, I have found *The Sexually Responsive Woman* truly absorbing and fascinating reading. I can only hope that a piece of work such as this will be widely read and stimulate many more analyses aimed at overcoming the myths and clichés with which we are only too easily satisfied.

The authors have done much to set the facts in their true light. My personal sympathies and best wishes are on their side.

## NOTES

Simone de Beauvoir, "Préface" to *The Sexually Responsive Woman* by Phyllis and Eberhard Kronhausen (New York: Grove Press, 1964); translator unknown; © Sylvie Le Bon de Beauvoir. This article was originally published in English, and we do not have access to the original French text, but given Beauvoir's rejection of essentialism, we have changed singular "woman" to plural "women" in cases where Beauvoir means all women or women in general in order to avoid essentialist connotations that Beauvoir would not have intended and to maintain consistency throughout the volume.

# WHAT LOVE IS—AND ISN'T

*by Simone de Beauvoir*

NOTE BY MARYBETH TIMMERMANN

Why do you fall in love? Nothing is more simple. You fall in love because you are young, because you are growing old, because you *are* old; because spring is fading, because autumn is beginning; from excess energy, from fatigue; from gaiety, from boredom; because someone loves you, because he does not love you. . . . I find too many answers: perhaps the question is not so simple, after all.

The experience of love is so universal that it seems to have no mystery. Everywhere, at every hour, even at this very moment, thousands of men and women are saying to each other with astonishment or awe, "I love you. I am in love." They are saying it loudly or softly, with these words or others, but they are saying it—for otherwise it would not be love. "I need you. I will suffer without you. I can no longer live without you." Time and space hang in the balance, immobilized before a face that holds the essence of everything that is precious in this world.

Since we no longer believe in the myth of predestined lovers, how can we explain these exclusive choices? To the lovers, they are self-evident. Yet friends ask one another, "What does he find in her? What does she see in him?"

Stendhal has described this process as a "crystallization" that can transform anyone at all into a unique being. Today, psychoanalysts speak of it as an "investment." But why have Paul and Paulette begun to "invest," to "crystallize" precisely with Pierrette and Pierre? The choice amazes their friends.

It has been said that "lovers are alone in the world." No statement is more false. According to Freud, the love relationship involves not two people but four. Actually it goes much further than this and involves the whole of society. "You are different. You are an exception. You are not like anybody else." Everyone who has been in love has said these words, and when they do, they are saying that their beloved has been chosen in comparison with all others and *against* all others. A person who is too harmoniously adjusted to society may never know love. In the past, and even in the present, there have been entire civilizations that were unaware of romantic love.

The first great romance in the West, Tristan and Isolde, is the story of a revolt. You love in defiance of a husband or a wife, in defiance of your parents, in opposition to friends and surroundings, in defiance of all those who in some way have thwarted you. Suddenly you deny their importance; you even forget their existence. Lovers isolate themselves; but their solitude has not been given to them; they have seized it with defiance. Love would not have its somber violence if it were not always, at first, a kind of revenge: revenge against a closed society to which you can suddenly belong; against a foreign country in which you can suddenly take root; against a provincial circle from which you suddenly escape.

Love often takes us by surprise. It is only when we meet the man, the woman, who fulfills our expectations that these expectations are revealed to us. But even before this, we had in us, masked or disguised, that emptiness, that need. You do not fall in love when you are completely happy or on the crest of the wave; it is only when life has lost its flavor. Nor do you fall in love on the eve of a long voyage, but rather in strange surroundings and especially in the letdown of the journey's end.

However, extreme unhappiness, an impending catastrophe destroying all hopes, all plans, may also make love impossible. Boredom, on the other hand, is singularly suitable for love. It is when the monotony of the world becomes apparent that you begin to dream of new horizons. Love does not appear when life fulfills you, nor when it crushes you, but only to those who openly or secretly wish to change. For it is then that you anticipate love and what love brings: through another person, a new world is revealed and given to you.

This kind of experience can be captured by other means. The ambitious man, the man of action, the artist can change his relationship with the world or even the world itself. If he throws himself body and soul into his project, love has no hold over him. But not everyone is in a position to impose his will in this way, and that is why women today are particularly predisposed to love. They rarely possess the implements—an art, a profession—that will permit them to enlarge or overturn the universe without the help of someone else. Love is their only opportunity. But even the most privileged often prefer the unexpected and wonderful joy of receiving everything without so much effort. To explore an unfamiliar country is work, but to possess it through the love of an appealing foreigner is a miracle. In this case, as in many others, love is a marvelous shortcut.

Still, the shortcut must present itself. You must, in order to fall in love, encounter an attractive object. What is attractive differs, understandably, for each individual. Values that are socially acceptable—beauty, fortune, intelligence—do not in every case give rise to love. What you expect in a lover depends on your childhood, your past, your plans, on the whole context of your life. You may be looking for something very specific: a father, a child, a kindred spirit; security, truth; an exalted image of yourself. Or your need may be ambiguous, indefinite or even infinite. You may want something else, no matter what, just as long as it is something you do not have.

Whatever the values, the symbols or the role may be, however, no one will awaken my love unless I see him basically as The Other. If he annexes himself to me, he loses the power to take me into another world. This is why envy so often gives birth to love. The very fact that a man or woman escapes you may be enough: you find yourself projecting onto him all the qualities you are looking for in The Other. However, if he holds back too stubbornly, then you cease to expect anything from him; love is aborted.

You may, on the other hand, be fascinated by the fascination you hold for someone else, by the dazzling image that he gives you of yourself. This is the pitfall of the narcissists. The masochists and all those who have chosen defeat fall into another trap: loving those who are indifferent to them. For you can love not only for the joy of loving or the glory of being loved, but also sometimes for the poignant bitterness of not being loved.

And here I come back to my point of departure. Why do you fall in love? Nothing could be more complex: because it is winter, because it is summer; from overwork, from too much leisure; from weakness, from strength;

a need for security, a taste for danger; from despair, from hope; because someone does not love you, because he does love you. . . .

## NOTES

"What Love Is—and Isn't," *McCall's*, August 1965, 71, 133; translator unknown; © Sylvie Le Bon de Beauvoir. The article was preceded by "A Celebrated Frenchwoman explains . . ."

# LOVE AND POLITICS

*by Simone de Beauvoir*

TRANSLATION AND NOTES BY MARYBETH TIMMERMANN

I think that Lise London cannot be understood if one also does not understand what communism is and what having an absolutely unconditional faith in communism is.[1] Lise London is a heroic woman. She is the one who, during the Occupation, got up on the counter in a store at the corner of the rue Daguerre and the avenue de la Porte-d'Orléans, and launched an appeal to all the women of France, telling them that they must resist and help their husbands to resist in every possible manner. Incidentally, it was an organized demonstration: they sang "la Marseillaise," and there were FTP there to defend Lise London.[2] When the Germans arrived, the FTP fired on them, and there were deaths on both sides. Lise London managed to escape, but later, she was arrested, tortured, and deported. Before the war, she had gone to fight in Spain, and had been an activist for her entire life.

Communism was her faith, her unconditional belief in the USSR and in Stalin. After the victory, she kept her faith absolutely intact. She believed in two things that were merged into one: her husband and communism. She herself had wondered what it would be like, for a militant, to realize that her husband is a traitor since, during the Rajik trial,[3] she had said to her husband, "that must be terrible to be the wife of a militant communist whom you love and admire, and to realize that he was a traitor and that your children have a traitor for a father."

[ ... ]⁴ When her husband was arrested, she thought she was in that situation. So she fought as much as she could to refuse to believe it, but what finally was more convincing than her conviction was that she heard her husband admit to it. So, insofar as she had confidence in him—which is exactly why the dilemma is terrible—she believed in his confession. As long as he had not confessed, she said, "No, it is not possible," even when their comrades, even when everyone else was murmuring, "Something is not quite right."

When she heard him confess, she thought, "He never said anything to the Gestapo; he never had a weakness in his character; he is a sincere and honest man; therefore, if he confesses, it must be true!"

## "Therefore, he is guilty."

It was a bit like a religious temptation. She thought, "It is my love for him that prevents me from believing him guilty, but I must be a good communist and vanquish what comes from my love for him. Therefore, he is guilty."

I think that it was to resist what her love was pushing her to believe that she did what was perhaps even a bit more than was necessary, and wrote that letter in which she completely dissociated herself from him.

But what is touching also, is that the first time she was able to see him alone, in his prison, her children were distracting the guard's attention and London told her, "I am not guilty; everything is rigged; everything is false. This trial is a complete fabrication!" And she immediately believed him, withdrawing her request for divorce that very day.

And after that, she fought ceaselessly for him with all possible conviction and energy and efficiency too, I might add. So much so that London also immediately found himself closely united with her and they lived *together* the entire imprisonment in the most harmonious way, and ever since they continue to live in an absolutely perfect harmony. [ ... ] I feel absolutely no right to criticize this woman. I myself have never had a political conviction as unconditional as hers. I do not understand her completely from the inside—I can not put myself exactly in her shoes—but I can understand, from the outside, that given her political faith and given that neither she nor her husband ever doubted the legality of the trials, she was upset and had believed for a moment that her husband was guilty.

It must be understood that they loved each other through politics and that for them it was not true, it is not true that "love excuses everything"— an expression, incidentally, that is a cliché without much sense.

## NOTES

Simone de Beauvoir, "Amour et politique," *Le nouvel observateur* 222, February 10–16, 1969, 23; © Sylvie Le Bon de Beauvoir.

The magazine article was preceded by the following editorial introduction: "Many who read the admirable 'Confession' by Artur London (one of the fourteen accused in the Slansky trial that took place in Prague in 1951), asked themselves how his wife Lise could have believed, for one single instant, that her husband was guilty. She knew him since she was fifteen years old as a man and as an activist in the [Communist] Party. Artur London, former combatant in the Spanish Civil War and hero of the French Resistance, had been arrested by the Gestapo, tortured and then deported; he had resisted everything. When he was arrested again in 1951—this time by his "friends"—he was Deputy Minister of Foreign Affairs in Czechoslovakia. Denounced as a traitor, he ended up admitting it. At first consumed by doubts, his wife Lise London eventually ended up believing that the accusation was well-founded. What led her to that conclusion?

Interviewed by Jean Carlier of Radio Luxemborg, Simone de Beauvoir responds to that and other questions."

1. Lise London (1916–2012), a militant Communist throughout her life, was the widow of Artur Gerard London (1915–86), who was a high-ranking Czechoslovak Communist official. In 1951, he was falsely accused of treason and became one of the victims in the Slansky show trial, which was part of a Joseph Stalin–inspired purge of "disloyal" elements in the national Communist Parties in Central Europe, as well as a purge of Jews from the leadership of Communist Parties. After his release and rehabilitation, Artur, in collaboration with Lise, wrote a powerful autobiographical account of his ordeal. See *L'aveu* (Paris: Gallimard, 1968), and *Le nouvel observateur* 217 (January 6, 1969). *L'aveu* was translated as *The Confession* by Alastair Hamilton (New York: Morrow, 1970).

2. "La Marseillaise" is the French national anthem, which originated in the French Revolution, and whose lyrics are a call to battle against invading oppressors; the *Francs Tireurs et Partisans* (FTP) was the military wing of the French Communist Party and became an active military Resistance organization.

3. Lánszló Rajik was a Hungarian Communist and politician, serving as Minister of Interior and Minister of Foreign Affairs. In 1949, he was falsely accused and tortured into confessing to treason at his show trial in Budapest. Rajik, along with Dr. Tibor Szönyi and András Szalai, was sentenced to death.

4. These ellipsis points enclosed in brackets appear in the original article; *Le nouvel observateur* apparently printed only excerpts of the longer interview that was broadcast on Radio Luxemborg. This occurs one other time, in the second to last paragraph.

## 5

# Brigitte Bardot and the Lolita Syndrome

# INTRODUCTION

*by Elizabeth Fallaize*

Brigitte Bardot seems at first sight an odd choice of subject for the author of *Le deuxième sexe*.[1] Yet Beauvoir had displayed an enthusiasm for film throughout her life; references to films and to film actresses abound in the memoirs, and in *Le deuxième sexe* actresses often serve as examples in Beauvoir's consideration of female narcissism and of mythical ideals of female beauty. In the late 1950s and the 1960s Beauvoir was far from the only intellectual, or even the only female intellectual to interest herself in Bardot: Marguerite Duras had published an article on Bardot the previous year, in 1958; the French critic François Nourissier was to publish a study in 1960, and even the heavyweight British critic Bernard Levin was sufficiently interested to write a review of Beauvoir's study in *The Spectator* in 1960.[2] More recently, numerous film and cultural studies critics have undertaken studies of "BB."

Beauvoir, then, was in the vanguard of an impressive array of commentators, and her reading of the Bardot myth—for she is quite clear that it is a constructed image that Bardot's films and publicity machine project—is an extremely interesting one. It centers on her contention that Bardot is the supreme example of a new model of woman as erotic object: the *garçon manqué* or tomboy child-woman, whose ambiguous androgyny manages to suggest childhood innocence and sexual availability simultaneously. The new model is nevertheless built on old myths. The childlike naturalness with which Bardot is presented, her adolescent style of self-presentation—tousled hair accompanies jeans and sweater—and the casual attitude to sex that her characters adopt, is identified by Beauvoir as a new twist on the traditional myths of femininity that she had examined at length in *Le deuxième sexe*. Allying woman to nature, which requires taming, the myth invites the male spectator to see himself as the master and savior of a sexually available but weaker vessel. However, Beauvoir also perceives a more subversive element to the new model: the Bardot figure demystifies sex, stripping the sexual encounter of the hypocrisy with which society is wont to surround it, and evoking the unaccustomed image of a woman in charge of her own sexuality. Bardot becomes a sexual predator, operating on equal terms with men, substituting an active sexuality for the passive magic trap of the vamp. This, suggests Beauvoir, is the reason why Bardot is so unpopular in France. The average Frenchman is unable to cope with a woman operating sexually on equal terms. He prefers to be able to patronize her and assert his superiority by reducing her to a passive object. The American male, on the other hand, is better able to cope with equality. Even he is nevertheless likely to fear the adult independent woman, and this is why he is so easily charmed by the nymphet figure of Bardot, who does not yet resemble the more threatening figure of wife or mother.

Beauvoir's analysis of this model of male desire is fueled by her recent reading of Nabokov's novel *Lolita*, which she not only mentions in the article, and highlights in the title of her piece, but which she also discusses in *La force des choses* (*Force of Circumstance*).[3] The novel had been published in France in 1955, after Nabokov had been unable to find an American publisher; when the novelist Graham Greene drew attention to it in the British press, the book was banned in France for two years, and it was then published in the United States in 1958, where it became an immediate best seller. Beauvoir describes it in *La force des choses* as a book that cuts through some of the hypocrisy of attitudes to sexuality, a theme that she had pursued in *Le deuxième sexe*. In the penultimate chapter, "La femme indépendante" (The independent woman), Beauvoir lays out with some force the difficulty for women of establishing an independent sexual life, and denounces the confusion so often made in France between "*femme libre*" and "*femme facile.*"[4] The same equation is raised here, but on a more positive note, when Beauvoir asserts that a free woman is the very contrary of an easy woman. A comparison of the two texts suggests that Beauvoir is more confident about the future for women's sexuality in 1959 than she had been in 1949. Nevertheless, many of the beauty myths that she analyzes in *Le deuxième sexe* are shown in this piece to remain in force. Even if the image is of "naturalness," the alienation remains for the woman represented in a false image of herself. Long sections of "Mythes" (Myths) had deconstructed the myths surrounding women and nature, and the section on dress in "La vie de société" (Social life) had discussed the balance between "naturalness" and "artifice" which women's clothing and makeup depend on in the construction of an alienated self-as-object.

The role of the film director in the construction of Bardot's self-as-object is placed center stage by Beauvoir. Roger Vadim, whom Bardot married when she was eighteen, directed the film that first brought the two to fame, *Et Dieu créa la femme* (*And God Created Woman*) (1954); he is credited by Beauvoir with manipulating the Bardot image to achieve the demythologizing of sexuality of which she so approves. However, she is critical of Vadim's reproduction of myths of male superiority and dislikes his dehumanization of sexual relationships. Via a comparison with *African Queen* (1951), directed by John Huston with Humphrey Bogart and Katharine Hepburn, and with Ingmar Bergman's *Sommarlek* (1951), Beauvoir elaborates a theory of situated eroticism, which allows her to analyze why Vadim's presentation of sexuality turns spectators into voyeurs.[5] She is much more enthusiastic about the radical turn that Bardot's image takes under the direction of Claude Autant-Lara, widely considered to be a dangerously antiestablishment figure in the 1950s. In *En cas de malheur* (*Love Is My Profession*) (1958), Bardot plays an amoral heroine on the margins of society who refuses to be recuperated. Beauvoir's admiration for this film, in which Jean Gabin costars and on which her friend the novelist and screenwriter Pierre Bost had collaborated, is clearly one of her principal motivations for writing a study of Bardot.[6]

Presciently, Beauvoir writes that Bardot is unlikely to continue to occupy the radical posture that this film constructs, and she sketches out with considerable humor a series of possible futures for the actress. Bardot's actual evolution into an animal rights activist and extreme right-wing commentator, found guilty by the French courts on more than one occasion of incitement to racial hatred, would no doubt have led Beauvoir to revise her admiration of Bardot, though she is careful to stress in her article that she is not concerned with Bardot the person, but only with her image.

How far would Beauvoir's admiration of the Bardot myth be shared by feminist film critics today? Ginette Vincendeau, in her 1992 article "The Old and the New: Brigitte Bardot in 1950s France," examines the Bardot persona to conclude that her films largely "encouraged conservative views of women."[7] However, her reading shares a surprising amount of common ground with Beauvoir's, including a deconstructive analysis of the "naturalness" of Bardot, and Vincendeau argues, like Beauvoir, that male fears of adult female sexuality are defused by the childish innocence of the persona. What Vincendeau sees, though, and Beauvoir does not, is the way in which the camera repeatedly isolates and fetishizes parts of the actress's body, a mise-en-scène that reproduces the conventions of pinup photography and is often at odds with the way in which the narrative of the film tends to adopt the character's point of view. Film criticism—and feminist criticism in particular—has of course developed out of all recognition since 1959, and Beauvoir's enthusiasm for the innovations in the realm of sexual independence, which the Bardot persona implies, has to be seen in the context of the repressive sexual standards for women operating in the 1950s.

Vincendeau has another interesting point to make about context: she argues that women viewers' hostility to Bardot in the 1950s was less likely to have been motivated by jealousy of their husbands' interest in Bardot than by jealousy of the flaunted image of a female sexual liberation that could have no reality for all but a privileged few from the Parisian bohemian-bourgeois milieu.[8] As a member of this milieu, Beauvoir, like Marguerite Duras, who similarly approved of Bardot, was in a position to identify with Bardot's representation of sexual liberation. And this, in the end, is what Beauvoir argues Bardot represents; nowhere in the article does she suggest that sexual liberation is in itself a substitute for women's liberation. In *La vérité* (*The Truth*), a film made in 1959, Bardot's lifestyle is deliberately linked to Beauvoir's when the Bardot character is criticized for having read *Les Mandarins* (*The Mandarins*). To my knowledge there is no record of Beauvoir's reaction to this turning of the tables that sees the Beauvoir myth of independent female sexuality deployed to shore up the Bardot myth. One might speculate that she would have been deeply flattered.[9]

## NOTES

1. A number of commentators begin their analysis with the same remark, including Catherine Rodgers whose article "Beauvoir piégée par Bardot?" (Beauvoir taken in by Bardot?) in *Simone de Beauvoir Studies* 17 (2000–2001): 137–48, a helpful source.

2. Marguerite Duras, "La reine Bardot" (Queen Bardot), *France observateur*, 1958. Reprinted in *Outside* (Paris: P.O.L., 1984): 246–49; François Nourrissier, *Brigitte Bardot* (Paris: Grasset, 1960).

3. *La force des choses*, vol. 2 (Paris: Gallimard, 1963), 252.

4. *Le deuxième sexe*, vol. 2 (Paris: Gallimard, folio, 1949), 610.

5. Beauvoir's development of this theory has been seen as an early model of the branch of feminist film criticism, which sees the spectator's gaze as voyeuristic. See Sylvie Blum-Reid, "Simone de Beauvoir and Visual Pleasure," *Simone de Beauvoir Studies* 14 (1997): 140–48.

6. Interestingly, Marguerite Duras also declares this her favorite Bardot film. See "La reine Bardot," 247.

7. Ginette Vincendeau, "The Old and the New: Brigitte Bardot in 1950s France," *Paragraph* 15 (1992): 73–96, 93.

8. Ibid., 88.

9. Vincendeau suggests that the use of Beauvoir's name acts on the level of a guarantee of glamorous cultural myths and as an emblem of new sexual attitudes. See ibid., 89.

# BRIGITTE BARDOT AND
# THE LOLITA SYNDROME

*by Simone de Beauvoir*

On New Year's Eve, Brigitte Bardot appeared on French television. She was got up as usual—blue jeans, sweater, and shock of tousled hair. Lounging on a sofa, she plucked at a guitar. "That's not hard," said a woman.[1] "I could do just as well. She's not even pretty. She has the face of a housemaid." The men couldn't keep from devouring her with their eyes, but they too snickered. Only two or three of us, among thirty or so spectators, thought her charming. Then she did an excellent classical dance number. "She *can* dance," the others admitted grudgingly. Once again I could observe that Brigitte Bardot was disliked in her own country.

When *And God Created Woman* was shown in first-run houses on the Champs-Elysées, the film, which cost a hundred and forty million francs, brought in less than sixty. Receipts in the USA have come to $4,000,000, the equivalent of the sale of 2,500 Dauphines. BB now deserves to be considered an export product as important as Renault automobiles.

She is the new idol of American youth. She ranks as a great international star. Nevertheless, her fellow-countrymen continue to shy away from her. Not a week goes by without articles in the press telling all about her recent moods and love affairs or offering a new interpretation of her personality, but half of these articles and gossip items seethe with spite. Brigitte receives[2] three hundred fan letters a day, from boys and girls alike, and every day indignant mothers write to newspaper editors and religious and civil authorities to protest against her existence. When three young n'er-do-wells of reputable families murdered a sleeping old man in a train at Angers, the Parent-Teachers' Association denounced BB to Mr. Chatenay, the deputy-mayor of the city. It was *she*, they said, who was really responsible for the crime. *And God Created Woman* had been shown in Angers; the young people had been immediately perverted. I am not surprised that professional moralists in all countries, even the USA, have tried to have her films banned. It is no new thing for high-minded folk to identify the flesh with sin and to dream of making a bonfire of works of art, books, and films that depict it complacently or frankly.

But this official prudery does not explain the French public's very peculiar hostility to BB. Martine Carol also undressed rather generously in her hit films, and nobody reproached her, whereas almost everyone is ready to regard BB as a very monument of immorality. Why does this character, fabricated by Marc Allegret and particularly by Vadim, arouse such animosity?[3]

If we want to understand what BB represents, it is not important to know what the young woman named Brigitte Bardot is really like. Her admirers and detractors are concerned with the imaginary creature they see on the screen through a tremendous cloud of ballyhoo. Insofar as she is exposed to the public gaze, her legend has been fed by her private life no less than by her film roles. This legend conforms to a very old myth that Vadim tried to rejuvenate. He invented a resolutely modern version of "the eternal feminine" and thereby launched a new type of eroticism. It is this novelty that entices some people and shocks others.

Love can resist familiarity; eroticism cannot. Its role in the films dwindled considerably when social differences between the two sexes diminished. Between 1930 and 1940 it gave way to romanticism and sentimentality. The vamp was replaced by the girl friend, of whom Jean Arthur was the most perfect type. However, when in 1947 the cinema was threatened with a serious crisis, filmmakers returned to eroticism in an effort to win back the public's affection. In an age when women drive cars and speculate on the stock exchange, an age in which they unceremoniously display their nudity on public beaches, any attempt to revive the vamp and her mystery was out of the question. The films tried to appeal, in a cruder way, to the male's response to feminine curves. Stars were appreciated for the obviousness of their physical charms rather than for their passionate or languorous gaze. Marilyn Monroe, Sophia

Loren, and Lollobrigida are ample proof of the fact that the full-blown woman has not lost her power over men. However, the dream-merchants were also moving in other directions. With Audrey Hepburn, Françoise Arnoul, Marina Vlady, Leslie Caron, and Brigitte Bardot they invented the erotic hoyden. For a part in his next film, *Dangerous Liaisons*, Vadim has engaged a fourteen-year-old girl. The child-woman is triumphing not only in the films. In *A View from the Bridge*, the Arthur Miller play, which has been a hit in the United States and a bigger one in England and France, the heroine has just about reached the age of puberty. Nabokov's *Lolita*, which deals with the relations between a forty-year-old male and a "nymphet" of twelve, was at the top of the best-seller list in England and America for months. The adult woman now inhabits the same world as the man, but the child-woman moves in a universe [that] he cannot enter. The age difference reestablishes between them the distance that seems necessary to desire. At least that is what those who have created a new Eve by merging the "green fruit" and "*femme fatale*" types have pinned their hopes on. We shall see the reasons why they have not succeeded in France as well as in the United States.

Brigitte Bardot is the most perfect specimen of these ambiguous nymphs. Seen from behind, her slender, muscular, dancer's body is almost androgynous. Femininity triumphs in her delightful bosom. The long voluptuous tresses of Mélisande flow down to her shoulders, but her hairdo is that of a negligent waif. The line of her lips forms a childish pout, and at the same time those lips are very kissable. She goes about barefooted, she turns up her nose at elegant clothes, jewels, girdles, perfumes, make-up, at all artifice. Yet her walk is lascivious and a saint would sell his soul to the devil merely to watch her dance. It has often been said that her face has only one expression. It is true that the outer world is hardly reflected in it at all and that it does not reveal great inner disturbance. But that air of indifference becomes her. BB has not been marked by experience. Even if she has lived—as in *Love Is My Profession*—the lessons that life has given her are too confused for her to have learned anything from them. She is without memory, without a past, and, thanks to this ignorance, she retains the perfect innocence that is attributed to a mythical childhood.

The legend that has been built up around Brigitte Bardot by publicity has for a long time identified her with this childlike and disturbing character. Vadim presented her as "a phenomenon of nature." "She doesn't act," he said. "She exists." "That's right," confirmed BB. "The Juliette in *And God Created Woman* is exactly me. When I'm in front of the camera, I'm simply myself." Brigitte was said not to bother to use a comb, but to do up her hair with her fingers.

She was said to loathe all forms of worldliness. Her interviews presented her as being natural and unpretentious. Vadim went even further. He painted her as naïve to the point of absurdity. According to him, at the age of eighteen she thought that mice laid eggs. She was moody and capricious. At the gala performance of her film, *Please, Mr. Balzac,* the producer waited in vain for her to show up. At the last minute, he informed the audience that she was not coming. She was described as a creature of instinct, as yielding blindly to her impulses. She would suddenly take a dislike to the decoration of her room and then and there would pull down the hangings and start repainting the furniture. She is temperamental, changeable, and unpredictable, and though she retains the limpidity of childhood, she has also preserved its mystery. A strange little creature, all in all; and this image does not depart from the traditional myth of femininity. The roles that her scriptwriters have offered her also have a conventional side. She appears as a force of nature, dangerous so long as she remains untamed, but it is up to the male to domesticate her. She is kind, she is good-hearted. In all her films she loves animals. If she ever makes anyone suffer, it is never deliberately. Her flightiness and slips of behavior are excusable because she is so young and because of circumstances. Juliette had an unhappy childhood; Yvette, in *Love Is My Profession,* is a victim of society. If they go astray, it is because no one has ever shown them the right path, but a man, a real man, can lead them back to it. Juliette's young husband decides to act like a male, gives her a good sharp slap, and Juliette is all at once transformed into a happy, contrite, and submissive wife. Yvette joyfully accepts her lover's demand that she be faithful and his imposing upon her a life of virtual seclusion. With a bit of luck, this experienced, middle-aged man would have brought her redemption. BB is a lost, pathetic child who needs a guide and protector. This cliché has proved its worth. It flatters masculine vanity; it reassures mature and maturing women. One may regard it as obsolete; it cannot be accused of boldness. But the spectators do not believe in this victory of the man and of the social order so prudently suggested by the scenario—and that is precisely why Vadim's film and that of another French director, Autant-Lara, do not lapse into triviality. We may assume that the "little rascal" will settle down, but Juliette will certainly never become a model wife and mother. Ignorance and inexperience can be remedied, but BB is not only unsophisticated but dangerously sincere. The perversity of a "Baby Doll" can be handled by a psychiatrist; there are ways and means of calming the resentments of a rebellious girl and winning her over to virtue. In *The Barefoot Contessa,* Ava Gardner, despite her licentiousness, does not attack established values—she condemns her own instincts by admitting that she likes "to walk in the mud."

117

BB is neither perverse nor rebellious nor immoral, and that is why morality does not have a chance with her. Good and evil are part of conventions to which she would not even think of bowing.

Nothing casts a sharper light on the character she plays than the wedding supper in *And God Created Woman*. Juliette immediately goes to bed with her young husband. In the middle of the banquet, she suddenly turns up in a bathrobe and, without bothering to smile or even look at the bewildered guests, she picks out from under their very noses a lobster, a chicken, fruit, and bottles of wine. Disdainfully and tranquilly she goes off with the loaded tray. She cares not a rap for other people's opinion. BB does not try to scandalize. She has no demands to make; she is no more conscious of her rights than she is of her duties. She follows her inclinations. She eats when she is hungry and makes love with the same unceremonious simplicity. Desire and pleasure seem to her more convincing than precepts and conventions. She does not criticize others. She does as she pleases, and that is what is disturbing. She does not ask questions, but she brings answers whose frankness may be contagious. Moral lapses can be corrected, but how could BB be cured of that dazzling virtue—genuineness? It is her very substance. Neither blows nor fine arguments nor love can take it from her. She rejects not only hypocrisy and reprimands, but also prudence and calculation and premeditation of any kind. For her, the future is still one of those adult inventions in which she has no confidence. "I live as if I were going to die at any moment," says Juliette. And Brigitte confides to us, "Every time I'm in love, I think it's forever." To dwell in eternity is another way of rejecting time. She professes great admiration for James Dean. We find in her, in a milder form, certain traits that attain, in his case, a tragic intensity—the fever of living, the passion for the absolute, the sense of the imminence of death. She, too, embodies—more modestly than he, but quite clearly—the credo that certain young people of our time are opposing to safe values, vain hopes and irksome constraint.

That is why a vast and traditional-minded rear guard declares that "BB springs from and expresses the immorality of an age." Decent or unwanted women could feel at ease when confronted with classical Circes who owed their power to dark secrets. These were coquettish and calculating creatures, depraved and reprobate, [and] possessed an evil force. From the height of their virtue, the fiancée, the wife, the great-hearted mistress, and the despotic mother briskly damned these witches. But if Evil takes on the colors of innocence, they are in a fury. There is nothing of the "bad woman" about BB. Frankness and kindness can be read on her face. She is more like a Pekingese than a cat. She is neither depraved nor venal. In *Love Is My Profes-*

*sion* she bunches up her skirt and crudely proposes a deal to Gabin. But there is a kind of disarming candor in her cynicism. She is blooming and healthy, quietly sensual. It is impossible to see in her the touch of Satan, and for that reason she seems all the more diabolical to women who feel humiliated and threatened by her beauty.

All men are drawn to BB's seductiveness, but that does not mean they are kindly disposed toward her. The majority of Frenchmen claim that women lose their sex appeal if they give up their artifices. According to them, a woman in trousers chills desire. Brigitte proves to them the contrary, and they are not at all grateful to her, because they are unwilling to give up their role of lord and master. The vamp was no challenge to them in this respect. The attraction she exercised was that of a passive thing. They rushed knowingly into the magic trap; they went to their doom the way one throws oneself overboard. Freedom and full consciousness remained their right and privilege. When Marlene displayed her silk-sheathed thighs as she sang with her hoarse voice and looked about her with sultry eyes, she was staging a ceremony, she was casting a spell. BB does not cast spells; she is on the go. Her flesh does not have the abundance that, in others, symbolizes passivity. Her clothes are not fetishes and, when she strips, she is not unveiling a mystery. She is showing her body, neither more nor less, and that body rarely settles into a state of immobility. She walks, she dances, she moves about. Her eroticism is not magical, but aggressive. In the game of love, she is as much a hunter as she is a prey. The male is an object to her, just as she is to him. And that is precisely what wounds masculine pride. In the Latin countries, where men cling to the myth of "the woman as object," BB's naturalness seems to them more perverse than any possible sophistication. To spurn jewels and cosmetics and high heels and girdles is to refuse to transform oneself into a remote idol. It is to assert that one is man's fellow and equal, to recognize that between the woman and him there is mutual desire and pleasure. Brigitte is thereby akin to the heroines of Françoise Sagan, although she says she feels no affinity for them—probably because they seem to her too thoughtful.

But the male feels uncomfortable if, instead of a doll of flesh and blood, he holds in his arms a conscious being who is sizing him up. A free woman is the very contrary of an easy woman.[4] In her role of confused female, of homeless little slut, BB seems to be available to everyone. And yet, paradoxically, she is intimidating. She is not defended by rich apparel or social prestige, but there is something stubborn in her sulky face, in her sturdy body. "You realize," an average Frenchman once said to me, "that when a man finds a woman attractive, he wants to be able to pinch her behind."

119

A ribald gesture reduces a woman to a thing that a man can do with as he pleases without worrying about what goes on in her mind and heart and body. But BB has nothing of the "easygoing kid" about her, the quality that would allow a man to treat her with this kind of breeziness. There is nothing coarse about her. She has a kind of spontaneous dignity, something of the gravity of childhood. The difference between Brigitte's reception in the United States and in France is due partly to the fact that the American male does not have the Frenchman's taste for broad humor. He tends to display a certain respect for women. The sexual equality that BB's behavior affirms wordlessly has been recognized in America for a long time. Nevertheless, for a number of reasons that have been frequently analyzed in America, he feels a certain antipathy to the "real woman." He regards her as an antagonist, a praying mantis, a tyrant. He abandons himself eagerly to the charms of the "nymph" in whom the formidable figure of the wife and the "Mom" is not yet apparent. In France, many women are accomplices of this feeling of superiority in which men persist. Their men prefer the servility of these adults to the haughty shamelessness of BB.

She disturbs them all the more in that, though discouraging their jollity, she nevertheless does not lend herself to idealistic sublimation. Garbo was called "The Divine"; Bardot, on the other hand, is of the earth.[5] Garbo's visage had a kind of emptiness into which anything could be projected—nothing can be read into Bardot's face. It is what it is. It has the forthright presence of reality. It is a stumbling block to lewd fantasies and ethereal dreams alike. Most Frenchmen like to indulge in mystic flights as a change from ribaldry, and vice versa. With BB they get nowhere. She corners them and forces them to be honest with themselves. They are obliged to recognize the crudity of their desire, the object of which is very precise—that body, those thighs, that bottom, those breasts. Most people are not bold enough to limit sexuality to itself and to recognize its power. Anyone who challenges their hypocrisy is accused of being cynical.

In a society with spiritualistic pretensions, BB appears as something deplorably materialistic and prosaic. Love has been disguised in such falsely poetic trappings that this prose seems to me healthy and restful. I approve Vadim's trying to bring eroticism down to earth. Nevertheless, there is one thing for which I blame him, and that is for having gone so far as to dehumanize it. The "human factor" has lost some of its importance in many spheres. Technical progress has relegated it to a subordinate and at times insignificant position. The implements that man uses—his dwelling, his clothes, etc.—tend toward functional rationalization. He himself is regarded by politicians, brains-trusters, publicity agents, military men, and even educators, by the entire "organization world," as an object to be manipulated. In France, there is a literary school that reflects this tendency. The "new novel"[6]—as it calls itself—is bent on creating a universe as devoid as possible of human meanings, a universe reduced to shiftings of volumes and surfaces, of light and shade, to the play of space and time; the characters and their relationships are left in the background or even dropped entirely. This quest is of interest only to a small number of initiates. It has certainly not influenced Vadim, but he, too, reduces the world, things, and bodies to their immediate presence. In real life, and usually in good novels and films, individuals are not defined only by their sexuality. Each has a history, and his or her eroticism is involved in a certain situation. It may even be that the situation creates it. In *African Queen*, neither Humphrey Bogart nor Katharine Hepburn, who are presented as aged and worn, arouses desire beforehand. Yet when Bogart puts his hand on Katharine's shoulder for the first time, his gesture unleashes an intense erotic emotion. The spectators identify themselves with the man, or the woman, and the two characters are transfigured by the feeling that each inspires in the other. But when the hero and heroine are young and handsome, the more the audience is involved in their history, the more it feels their charm. It must therefore take an interest in it. For example, in Ingmar Bergman's *Sommarlek*, the idyll which is related is not set in the past arbitrarily. As a result of this device, we witness the revels of two particular adolescents. The young woman, who has moved us and aroused our interest, evokes her youthful happiness. She appears before us, at the age of sixteen, already weighed down with her entire future. The landscape about her is not a mere setting, but a medium of communication between her and us. We see it with her eyes. Through the lapping of the waters and the clearness of the nocturnal sky, we merge with her. All her emotions become ours, and emotion sweeps away shame. The "summer trifling"—caresses, embraces, words—that Bergman presents is far more "amoral" than Juliette's adventures in *And God Created Woman*. The two lovers have barely emerged from childhood. The idea of marriage or of sin does not occur to them. They embrace with hesitant eagerness and unchaste naïveté. Their daring and jubilation triumphantly defy what is called virtue. The spectator does not dream of being shocked because he experiences with them their poignant happiness. When I saw *And God Created Woman*, people laughed during scenes. They laughed because Vadim does not appeal to our complicity. He "de-situates" sexuality, and the spectators become voyeurs because they are unable to project themselves on the screen. This partially justifies their uneasiness. The ravishing young woman whom they surprise, at the beginning of the film, in the act of exposing her nakedness to the sun, is no one, an anonymous body. As the film goes on, she does not succeed in becoming someone. Nonchalantly combining convention and provocation, Vadim does not deign to lure the audience into the trap of a convincing story. The characters are treated allusively; that of BB is loaded with too many intentions for anyone to believe in its reality. And the town of St-Tropez is merely a setting that has no intimate connection with the lives of the main characters. It has no effect on the spectator. In *Sommarlek*, the world exists; it reflects for the young lovers their confusion, their anxious desire, their joy. An innocent outing in a boat is as erotically meaningful as the passionate night preceding it and the one to follow. In Vadim's film, the world is absent. Against a background of fake colors he flashes a number of "high spots" in which all the sensuality of the film is concentrated: a strip-tease, passionate lovemaking, a mambo sequence. This discontinuity heightens the aggressive character of BB's femininity. The audience is not carried away once and for all into an imaginary universe. It witnesses without much conviction, an adventure which does not excite it and which is broken up by "numbers" in which everything is so contrived as to keep it on tenterhooks. It protects itself by snickering. A critic has written that BB's sexuality was too "cerebral" to move a Latin audience. This amounts to making BB responsible for Vadim's style, an analytical and consequently abstract style that, as I have said, puts the spectator in the position of a voyeur. The consenting voyeur who feeds on "blue films" and "peep shows," seeks gratifications other than the visual. The spectator who is a voyeur in spite of himself reacts with annoyance, for it is no fun to witness a hot performance cold-bloodedly. When BB dances her famous mambo, no one believes in Juliette. It is BB who is exhibiting herself. She is as alone on the screen as the strip-tease artist is alone on the stage. She offers herself directly to each spectator. But the offer is deceptive, for as the spectators watch her, they are fully aware that this beautiful young woman is famous, rich, adulated, and completely inaccessible. It is not surprising that they take her for a slut and that they take revenge on her by putting her down.[7]

But reproaches of this kind cannot be leveled against *Love Is My Profession*, the film in which BB has displayed the most talent. Autant-Lara's direction, Pierre Bost's and Aurench's scenario and dialogue, and Gabin's performance all combine to grip the spectator. In this context, BB gives her most convincing performance. But her moral reputation is none the better for it. The film has aroused furious protests; actually it attacks the social order much more bitingly than any of her early ones. The "amoralism" of Yvette, the heroine, is radical. She prostitutes herself with indifference, organizes a holdup, and has no hesitation about striking an old man. She proposes to a great lawyer a deal that threatens to dishonor him. She gives herself to him without love. Then she falls in love with him, deceives him, and artlessly keeps him informed of her infidelities. She confesses to him that she has had several abortions. However, although the scenario indicates for a moment the possibility of a conversion, she is not presented as being unconscious of the nature of her behavior and capable of being won over to Good, as defined by respectable folk. Truth is on her side. Never does she fake her feelings. She never compromises with what seems to her to be obviously true. Her genuineness is so contagious that she wins over her lover, the old unethical lawyer. Yvette awakens whatever sincerity and dynamism still remain in him. The authors of this film took over the character created by Vadim, but they charged it with a much more subversive meaning: purity is not possible in our corrupt society except for those who have rejected it or who deliberately cut themselves off from it.

But this character is now in the process of evolving. BB has probably been convinced that in France nonconformity is on the way out. Vadim is accused of having distorted her image—which is certainly not untrue. People who know BB speak of her amiable disposition, her kindness, and her youthful freshness. She is neither silly nor scatterbrained, and her naturalness is not an act. It is nevertheless striking that recent articles which pretend to reveal the "real BB," "BB seen through the keyhole," "the truth about BB," mention only her edifying traits of character. Brigitte, we are told again and again, is just a simple girl. She loves animals and adores her mother. She is devoted to her friends, she suffers from the hostility she arouses, she repents of her caprices, she means to mend her ways. There are excuses for her lapses: fame and fortune came too suddenly, they turned her head, but she is coming to her senses. In short, we are witnessing a veritable rehabilitation, which in recent weeks has gone very far. Definitive redemption, for a star, comes with marriage and motherhood.

Brigitte speaks only faintly about getting married. On the other hand, she often declares enthusiastically that she adores the country and dreams of taking up farming.* In France, love of cows is regarded as a token of high morality. Gabin is sure of winning the public's sympathy when he declares that "a cow is more substantial than glory." Stars are photographed as much as possible in the act of feeding their chickens or digging in their gardens. This passion for the soil is appropriate to the reasonable bourgeoise that,

---

* Written before Mademoiselle Bardot became Madame Charrier.

as we are assured, Brigitte is bent on becoming. She has always known the price of things and has always gone over her cook's accounts. She follows the stock market closely and gives her broker well-informed instructions. During an official luncheon, she is said to have dazzled the director of the Bank of France with her knowledge. To know how to place one's money is a supreme virtue in the eyes of the French bourgeoisie. A particularly imaginative journalist has gone so far as to inform his readers that Brigitte has such a passion for the absolute that she may enter upon the paths of mysticism. Wife and mother, woman farmer,[8] businesswoman, Carmelite nun, BB has a choice of any one of these exemplary futures. But one thing is certain: on the screen she is already beginning to convert. In her next film, *Babette Goes to War*,** she will play a heroine of the Resistance. Her charming body will be hidden from us by a uniform and sober attire. "I want everyone under sixteen to be able to come and see me," she has been made to say. The film will end with a military parade in which Babette acclaims General de Gaulle.

Is the metamorphosis definitive? If so, there will still be a number of people who will be sorry. Exactly who? A lot of young people belong to the old guard, and there are older ones who prefer truth to tradition. It would be simpleminded to think that there is a conflict of two generations regarding BB. The conflict that does exist is between those who want *mores* to be fixed once and for all and those who demand that they evolve. To say that "BB embodies the immorality of an age" means that the character she has created challenges certain taboos accepted by the preceding age, particularly those which denied women sexual autonomy. In France, there is still a great deal of emphasis, officially, on women's dependence upon men. The Americans, who are actually far from having achieved sexual equality in all spheres, but who grant it theoretically, have seen nothing scandalous in the emancipation symbolized by BB. But it is, more than anything else, her frankness that disturbs most of the public and that delights the Americans. "I want there to be no hypocrisy, no nonsense about love," BB once said. The debunking of love and eroticism is an undertaking that has wider implications than one might think. As soon as a single myth is touched, all myths are in danger. A sincere gaze, however limited its range, is a fire that may spread and reduce to ashes all the shoddy disguises that camouflage reality. Children are forever asking why, why not. They are told to be silent. Brigitte's eyes, her smile, her presence, impel one to ask oneself why, why not. Are they going to hush up the questions she raised without a word? Will she, too, agree to talk lying twaddle? Perhaps the hatred

---

** Written before this film was released.

she has aroused will calm down, but she will no longer represent anything for anyone. I hope that she will not resign herself to insignificance in order to gain popularity. I hope she will mature, but not change.

## NOTES

"Brigitte Bardot and the Lolita Syndrome," trans. Bernard Frechtman, *Esquire*, August 1959; reprinted as *Brigitte Bardot and the Lolita Syndrome* (New York: Reynal & Co, 1960); also appeared in *Les écrits de Simone de Beauvoir*, ed. Claude Francis and Fernande Gontier (Paris: Gallimard, 1979), translated from English original; © Sylvie Le Bon de Beauvoir. This article was originally published in English, and we do not have access to the original French text, but given Beauvoir's rejection of essentialism, we have changed singular "woman" to plural "women" in cases where Beauvoir means all women or women in general in order to avoid essentialist connotations that Beauvoir would not have intended and to maintain consistency throughout the volume.

1. This appears as "the woman" in the *Esquire* article, but makes more sense as "a woman" since there were thirty or so spectators and presumably more than this one woman.

2. This appears as "received" in the past tense in the *Esquire* article, but makes more sense in the present tense in this context.

3. Marc Allegret (1900–1973) was a French screenwriter and film director for whom Roger Vadim worked as assistant director and cowriter. In 1954, Roger Vadim (1928–2000), whom Bardot married when she was eighteen, directed the film that first brought the two to fame, *Et Dieu créa la femme (And God Created Woman)*.

4. This appears as "a light woman" in the *Esquire* article, but we have changed it to "easy woman" because Beauvoir surely wrote *"femme facile"* here in keeping with her thoughts on this matter expressed in *Le deuxième sexe*. There, as Elizabeth Fallaize points out in her introduction to this piece, "In the penultimate chapter, 'La femme indépendante' (The independent woman), Beauvoir lays out with some force the difficulty for women of establishing an independent sexual life, and denounces the confusion so often made in France between *'femme libre'* and *'femme facile.'"* *Le deuxième sexe*, vol. 2 (Paris: Gallimard, folio, 1949), 610.

5. This appears as "of the earth earthy" in the *Esquire* article, so we have corrected this apparent typo.

6. This appears as "the young novel" in the *Esquire* article, but surely Beauvoir was referring to the "new novel" or *"nouveau roman,"* which was a literary movement that emerged in the late 1950s challenging the traditional conventions of the novel with a new conception of time, plot, and character.

7. This appears as "running her down" in the *Esquire* article, but we have changed it to the more common expression "putting her down."

8. This appears as "farmerette" in the *Esquire* article, but we have changed it to the more standard "woman farmer."

## 6

# The Situation of Women Today

# INTRODUCTION

*by Debra B. Bergoffen*

In 1966, when Simone de Beauvoir and Jean-Paul Sartre visited Japan at the invitation of the University of Keio and their Japanese editor Mr. Watanabe, their books had been translated, were well known and highly regarded. Though Beauvoir and Sartre knew this, neither realized how powerfully their work resonated with the Japanese. They were unprepared for the more than one hundred journalists and crowds of mostly young people waiting to greet them when they arrived. The existential difference between East and West was not, it seemed, as great as the geographic distance.

However impressed she may have been by this powerful welcome, Beauvoir was not misled by it into thinking that an affinity for her work in Japan meant that her world and that of Japanese women were the same. This lecture "The Situation of Women Today" makes it clear that she takes the question of social, cultural, and existential differences seriously but that she does not see these differences as barriers to the project of fostering women's solidarity.

Beauvoir situates this lecture within two contexts: (1) her hopes for *The Second Sex*; and (2) the social, economic, and political realities of Japan,

129

France, and the United States. Speaking of *The Second Sex*, Beauvoir expresses the hope that it will become outdated. She tells her audience that once women achieve concrete social, political, and economic equality, *The Second Sex*'s analyses of women's alienation will no longer be relevant. It is important to note that the lecture does not tie Beauvoir's vision of the end of women's exploitation to the end of sexual difference. Instead it suggests that the existential situation of women will be lived differently. Once women are no longer the second sex, their sexual difference(s) will be lived neither as the difference between the autonomous sex, the masculine subject, and the dependent one, the inessential feminine other, nor under the direction of the myth of femininity. More than that she cannot say.

In addressing the social, economic, and political realities of Japan, France, and the United States, Beauvoir foregrounds her Marxist commitments. Sounding very much like Rosa Luxemburg, the early-twentieth-century Marxist-feminist, Beauvoir accepts the political importance of breaking the suffrage barrier but argues that the right to vote without meaningful access to public life and concrete economic opportunities leaves women depoliticized. As depoliticized, they will end up supporting the bourgeois status quo against their own best interests. Arguing that playing a role in public life is essential for developing a sense of solidarity, Beauvoir argues that lacking this experience of solidarity women will fail to see the connection between their inferior status, whatever their class, and larger questions of social inequality.

What is especially interesting about this lecture, given the feminist critiques of Beauvoir's so-called essentialism, is the way that Beauvoir attends to the specific situations of Japanese, French, and American women. She notes the differences in the ways that these bourgeois democracies live the democratic contradiction between their idealizations of equality and their structural inequalities. Noting that each of these societies is undoing the work of the feminist movement, she also notes the different ways that each society accomplishes its regressive work. The situation of women in these countries may be analogous. It is not, however, the same. Thus the women in each of these countries will have to find contextually specific ways of opposing the particular cultural myths of motherhood, femininity, and marriage that delegitimize their public status. They will also have to engage in situated materialist analyses to understand the specific economic forces served by their particular mode of subordination. One way of marking the effect of this lecture on Japanese women and of registering the impact of *The*

*Second Sex* in Japan is to note that in 1969, after it was published in paperback, *The Second Sex* appeared on the best-seller list in Japan.

If Beauvoir was unhappy to discover that in 1966 women's inequality remained a stable feature of bourgeois democracies, she would surely be unhappy today. The backlash is alive and well. The contradictions of bourgeois democracy remain intact. For all the efforts of global feminist movements, neither women's solidarity nor a solidarity between women and men based on seeing the connection between the cause of women's rights and the cause of social justice exists on a scale large enough to be politically effective. If unhappy, however, Beauvoir would not be without hope. This lecture shows us that her hope would be grounded in her analyses of the effects of the changes that have occurred and in her expectation that concrete assessments of the analogous but diverse circumstances of women's lives can and will produce the solidarity necessary to develop effective liberatory strategies.

# THE SITUATION OF WOMEN TODAY

TRANSLATION BY DEBBIE MANN

I am going to speak to you about the condition of women today: that does not mean that I am addressing only half of this gathering for I consider this to be a problem which concerns men as much as it does women. I will speak to you particularly about the condition of French women, because I know it best, but I believe that what I will say to you applies to your country just as much as mine, for the problems of women in France and in Japan are very similar. In fact, in both countries just after the war, women, who until then had no political rights, were accorded all of these rights: the right to vote, the right to be elected to office, etc., etc. Moreover, there has been a great surge [*élan*] of women into the world of work. There already were in France—fewer, I think, in your country—women who exercised the liberal professions, but there were many more who started at that time. We saw the number of women lawyers, doctors, and engineers increase; some of them became very actively involved in political struggles and there are even some who successfully embarked upon political careers. We saw more women writers than before. In short, in every domain, there was what has been called in my country a veritable "advancement of women." And this élan was so considerable that in 1950 when I wrote *Le deuxième sexe* [*The Second*

*Sex*] in which I was fighting against the alienation of women and for their liberation, I expressed, at the end, the hope that this book would soon be outdated. And I thought that it would be. I mean that I was expecting that in the ten, fifteen years which were to follow, the "woman problem" would be posited completely differently and women would attain that concrete, real, and total equality that I wished for them.

In fact, it was completely otherwise. In some ways, in France today, it is thought in certain circles that *Le deuxième sexe* is outdated. But not at all for the reasons that I had imagined. People feel, on the contrary, that women today have understood their true vocation as being only a homemaker wife, mother, shut away in her home. This is a rather startling phenomenon in France. As for me, I find it unfortunate and depressing because I see in it a real regression. I am well aware that not everyone is in agreement on this point for there is a very strong antifeminist movement in France and, I believe, in the world as a whole.

I explained at length in *Le deuxième sexe* why the condition of a woman confined within her private life, reduced to the status of a relative being, appears to me to be inferior to that of the woman who accomplishes herself through a job, through a career, through social or political action. I am going to briefly repeat my reasons to you since it is precisely this point which is controversial. First, I think that the woman who accepts living in total economic dependence on a man—which is the fate of the traditional wife—also accepts living in moral and psychological dependence, in total inner dependence. And I think that no human being should accept this. The dependent woman accepts it, because the material condition of a life is the underpinning of that entire life. If a woman is incapable of supporting herself, she is obliged to comply with the wishes of the man. And in particular if—and this happens frequently—a marriage turns sour, and a woman stops loving her husband, she finds herself obligated, for material reasons, to make many compromises. She is incited to moral trickery, to bad faith, to self trickery, in short to a whole set of behaviors that I judge deeply reprehensible. At the same time her happiness is at stake: it is dependent on the freedom of the other, on the freedom of the man. I have seen many heartbreaking examples of this: if the man stops loving his wife, if he chooses to leave her, she very often finds herself without resources of any kind, whether material or moral, because she had wagered everything on her husband's love. She was, in her most inner being and in the deepest part of herself, entirely dependent to the point that she no longer even knows who she is or why she is alive, when she is no longer loved.

133

Moreover, women today, like men, live much longer than before, and a forty-year-old woman still has a long existence ahead of her. Now, a forty-year-old woman who has raised her children, who has lived only for them and for her husband, finds herself in an often tragic state of distress and forlornness. She really no longer knows what to do with herself. She tries to take an interest in the families of her daughters and sons, which is not at all the same thing as attending to her own life. Her lack of autonomy is expressed at that point by the feeling of her own uselessness and by a deep unhappiness. Thus, from the standpoint of what I will call her personal dignity, from the standpoint of her happiness and equilibrium, a woman cannot accomplish herself if she limits herself to being a wife and mother. People sometimes counter with the example of American women who, while they are materially dependent on man, might manage to dominate him psychologically and morally so to speak. In actual fact, this is untrue. My own experience during my travels in America has been confirmed by conversations with American feminists who acknowledged that the situation of their compatriots was exactly the same, fundamentally, as that of French women. Insofar as it is the man who, by his profession determines the household budget and the place of residence, the woman is dependent. She spends what her husband gives her to spend; the vacation destination is ultimately chosen according to the amount of money the husband has at his disposal. She can only make a few variations on this foundation as a consumer. She can bother her husband about little things; this is the revenge of American women. But making a man's life unbearable at home is not a genuine way of being free. And, consequently, in my opinion, this example confirms what I am saying to you instead of invalidating it.

Furthermore, if we consider the social and public life of a woman, she gives this up by accepting to be closed up in her home. We, French women, and you, Japanese women, have the right to vote, but it is a completely abstract right if it does not go along with activities outside the home. Real participation in social life is helping to build the world in which we live. It is helping to build it by a job which, one way or another, is integrated with one's social life.

Moreover, the only real political influence one can have, the only practical, concrete connection to this world in which we live, is the connection one has through labor union struggles or by belonging to a certain special interest group, in any case by being linked with others in an active and concrete solidarity. Now the woman who is shut away in her home works a great deal and even sometimes more than the woman who exercises a profession.

But she works in a way that does not give her economic independence since she earns no salary. Comparing her lot to that of an unskilled laborer, one woman said to me bitterly, "At least at the end of the day *he* has the satisfaction of knowing that he has earned his own living while *I* work eight or ten hours per day and at the end of the day I haven't earned a cent. I still have to ask my husband for money if I want to buy something for myself or the children." And furthermore, the woman who lives like this inside the home is cut off from others instead of being linked with them; she has no hold on the world which would permit her to change either her own condition or the state of society in general.

There is thus a double renunciation: on the plane of personal autonomy on the one hand, and on the other, accomplishment as a human being who has a social and political role to play. This is why I consider the passage from the status of a working woman to that of a housewife as a regression. I will not linger any longer on these ideas because I developed them at length in *Le deuxième sexe*. Rather, I would like to explore why women today are victims of this regression.

The first reason is the setbacks they meet with on a professional level. Careers in the liberal professions have become open to them and many people claim that today their opportunities are equal to those of men. But this is absolutely untrue. If we consider—and I keep coming back to France, but I think that there are analogies with what is taking place here—if we consider first the professional training of women, a large number of surveys and statistics have shown that parents are not at all disposed to make the same investments when it is a question of the education of a girl and that of a boy. Raising a child, pushing the child to go far in his studies, let's say for example as far as a residency in medicine, requires of parents expenditures which are often quite large and which can even represent a real sacrifice. Parents make these sacrifices for a son, not for a daughter, for a number of reasons. First, people think that the daughter can always get by in another way: she can always get married; it is really foolish to spend so much money, to do without, when a daughter may settle afterward for becoming a wife and mother.

Moreover, it is understood—precisely because we do not yet live in a world in which there is equality between men and women—that parents do not disgrace themselves by setting up their daughter in a very subordinate profession. It is quite alright that the daughter be a secretary or a nurse; whereas in certain milieus it would not be acceptable for a son to be only a secretary or a nurse. He must be a doctor or a lawyer; he must shine for the honor of his parents.

All people internalize what is taking place around them in the world: women therefore find it natural to be sacrificed to either their brother or their fiancé; on this point I have many examples I could give you. There is a couple who particularly attracted my attention because the husband and the wife have realized a quasi-equality in their daily life, but on the basis of a radical inequality. It is a question of a young woman and a young man, both students, who met when they were twenty years old and who fell in love. They decided to get married. But this wedding and setting up housekeeping required financial sacrifices which did not allow both of them to continue their studies: costly medical studies. They decided that the young woman would settle for a nursing degree and the man would complete medical school, which is what they did. They formed a couple which is not unhappy but in which there is a profound inequality which is painfully felt by the woman.

From the start it was understood: if one of the two ought to continue his studies while the other did not, it was the boy. If one thinks of the liberal professions, one immediately encounters this segregation of the two sexes. If we now consider working women who belong to the proletariat, we are going to find an analogous differentiation. In France, there are very few vocational training schools open to girls: around thirteen, I think, while there are about fifty of them for boys. There are about fifty areas in which boys can do their apprenticeship, which means around 300 trades that they can choose to take up, whereas the choice for a girl is going to be limited to about thirteen areas. And this is not the only difference between the two: the trades that are open to a girl are generally dead ends. She will be only a dressmaker's assistant all her life; she will not get out of this station in life [condition], whereas for the boy who works as a mechanic or an electrician, there are many possibilities, and he can advance in his trade; the girl cannot. Thus in the bourgeois class as in the working class, the opportunities given to boys and girls are very unequal from the start. As a result, I have just said that for working class women the question of advancement does not come up. In theory, however, in the liberal professions, a woman attorney or a young female doctor can succeed more or less brilliantly. But actually, their opportunities are unequal in the very exercise of their profession. Many women have told me so, in France as in Japan: there are terrific barriers which condemn women—except a few extremely rare exceptions—to mediocrity.

First, she will be hired much less easily than a man. I know a young female chemist who did extremely well in her studies, and who tried very early, therefore with all likelihood of success, to get a job in dye factories or in the foods industries. But she always got the same reception from the managers: "What do you expect, Miss? When qualifications are equal we prefer to hire a young man because, after all, you might get married and give up your job. All the costs that I will have incurred in these early years when you are still lacking necessary skills will not be compensated. If you do not give up your job when you have your first child I will be obligated to pay you maternity leave. All in all, I much prefer to deal with a man who will not cause me to incur this type of expense." A woman has much more difficulty getting hired than a man. Once she is finally started in a career, people will put much less trust in her. In the case of women as well as men, there is a mistrust with regard to a female lawyer or doctor; as soon as one is faced with a case that is a bit difficult one says to oneself, "Oh, in any case I much prefer to consult a man." Because there is a certain antipathy on the part of women who do not work with regard to those who do, male and female clients will go much more willingly to see a man even if the competence of the woman is in reality exactly the same.

Since she will never have to handle the truly difficult cases she will always remain at the very bottom of the ladder. For example, in France we have a lot of female attorneys, but in general they are only assistants in practices belonging to men. They do small, secondary tasks and earn very trifling amounts of money. It is their male colleagues who run the practices, argue all the big cases, and settle all the interesting affairs. Likewise, women doctors generally restrict themselves to gynecology or pediatrics. They have a limited clientele; they do not become the owners of a large practice; they do not have a glittering clientele like their male colleagues. If we consider women who are in administration, they come up against a barrier that their male colleagues, bosses, and superiors automatically put up; one can say that in this case a veritable masculine freemasonry is systematically and deliberately opposed to women's progress. They are not granted responsibilities analogous to those of men because people mistrust them a priori: therefore they cannot prove that they would be capable of assuming them. If, by chance, they are given an important assignment this importance will not be recognized; they will actually be doing the work of an office manager and they will be treated like an assistant clerk. I spoke with one of my former students, a woman who has been working at Shell for twenty-five years and has done a very good job. She has no family problems, since she is married but has no children, and everyone recognizes her ability. However, after a certain point, at a certain level, she saw all of her male colleagues of the same

137

age and experience promoted ahead of her. She never rose above a certain rank. And yesterday I saw a young Japanese woman who told me the same thing. "I work as well as a man, but I will never go beyond [*dépasserai*] a certain level. The organization of the company for which I work is absolutely opposed to it." This brings about a disparity in salary; moreover, there are countries where this disparity is accepted. To get back to France, there was a time when the principle of inequality was accepted on the pretext, people said—and it is an admirable argument—that women have fewer needs than men. Consequently, for the same work, the same number of hours, and the same results women were paid two-thirds of what men were paid. Today, this is absolutely prohibited by law. But there are many ways to cheat. And, for example, as I was telling you, a woman is given the work of an office manager and she is paid as an assistant clerk. In all domains, whether it be in the liberal professions or in the working class one sees exactly the same thing happen. Very recently in England there were major proclamations by female workers who set as their primary goal the struggle for equal pay for men and women. But their spokeswoman added that there was no hope at all of attaining it for ten or even fifteen years. Three or four months ago there was also a very gripping movement in Belgium: female workers gathered, held mass demonstrations, and marched in the streets calling for equal pay. By their protests and strikes, they obtained it in certain firms. This victory represents a hope, an example; but it is the exception. In this respect, a woman is generally at a great disadvantage compared to a man. She will not have a brilliant career, she will not have a level of success which will satisfy her, and she will be paid less than he.

Furthermore, a woman must reconcile this work, which is in itself not very satisfying, with her life as a wife, mother, and homemaker. In France, nothing is done to facilitate this reconciliation.

There is one thing that you Japanese women have obtained that we French women have not: in your country, contraception is very widely used and abortion is allowed if you have a valid reason for seeking it. In our country, on the contrary, contraception is limited to very small groups; we do not have the right to inform people widely on this problem; as for abortion, it is strictly forbidden. A woman therefore often has a child that she does not want, and which forces her to stop working. This greatly limits the accomplishments of a woman in any career or profession. Furthermore, it is expected that the household tasks are accomplished almost exclusively by the woman. Now, these tasks are very demanding. As there is no day care, child care, or other outside help given to the woman, it is she who must be totally responsible for taking care of the children, the housework, the shopping, the laundry, etc., etc., which consumes, when she has two or three children, something like four or five hours of her time.

If a woman has put in an eight-hour day at work and works five or six hours more at home, at the end of the week she finds herself in an absolutely terrifying state of exhaustion. It is not yet at all customary for the man to really help the woman; sometimes he helps her a little bit, and there is even a certain tendency taking shape in that direction. But in fact, in the most positive case that I have seen, that of the couple I spoke to you about earlier, in which the young woman is a nurse and her husband is a doctor, she marvels that he does about a third of the household chores. In general, she told me, the man does at most a fifth or a tenth of these tasks; and quite often none at all. And this is a profound, completely concrete inequality which results in the woman being more worn out than the man at the end of the workday. I must add that a psychological wrenching goes along with this physiological fatigue because, especially in the current context, given the campaign mounted today in favor of women staying home, the woman who works outside the home is ravaged by guilt [*mauvaise conscience*]. People explain to her that her children would be better cared for and happier if she spent all day with them, and that her husband, too, would prefer that she do nothing other than take care of him.

So she thinks that her household is not run as well as her neighbor's across the street. She compares herself to women who are only housewives; she finds herself less well dressed, she feels bad. She tries to succeed in all areas at once; she will take care of her home as well as the neighbor who does nothing else, while at the same time striving to shine in her profession. This is how heartbreaks, obsessions, and neuroses, which are more and more numerous in French women today, are born. This problem is so serious in our country that in the last two years, a great deal has been written about it. It has given rise to much reflection, many meetings and discussions; measures have been proposed in order to bring relief to the working woman, in order to help her improve her condition. But all the measures which are proposed today more or less unofficially lead to reducing women's participation in the workforce and lowering women's productivity, thereby limiting their chances of realizing themselves as working women; people do not seek to relieve them of their household tasks. For example, something called the principle of recycling of women [*recyclage de la femme*] has been proposed. A woman would work, let's say until she was twenty-five, then when she got married and had children, she would give up her profession for ten or fifteen years; at the end of this time, she would have to be rehired and given the same promotion as a woman who had pursued her career for those fifteen years. One can see the danger right away: if, when hiring a woman, someone thinks that she is going to work for four years and then she will have to be rehired fifteen years later when she has lost her professional skills, he will prefer not to hire her. But what has been discussed above all is the shortened workday. A bill was unofficially considered providing that a woman would receive the same salary as man for a workday that was only three-quarters as long. Many meetings have been devoted to this problem and, for tactical reasons, the French Communist Party maintained that it was necessary to obtain for women the same salary as men even though the woman would only be working three-quarters of the day.

I must say that, for now it was very heartbreaking, during those meetings, to see women like those about whom I have spoken to you, come to explain: "I work like a man. I put in a very hard eight hours per day; and then there is the time that I must spend doing the cooking, the laundry, taking care of the children. I am exhausted; I am worn out; it would be fair that I be paid the same for working three-quarters of the day and not a whole day." This demand is very understandable and it may seem fair. Nevertheless, it is very dangerous because, in the long run, it would end up maintaining the segregation between men and women. To adopt this measure would be to undermine the opportunities for women in the professional sphere. Indeed, even with a state-controlled economy and a state-controlled job market, it would be very dangerous to establish a priori a distinction between men and women with respect to work. In a society like ours, a free enterprise society, it is completely foolish to imagine that any businessman would be as much of a philanthropist to agree to pay a certain price for three-quarters of a workday when he could have a whole day for the same price. The result would be that getting hired, which, as I have said, is already difficult for women, would become completely impossible. Consequently, taking such a step would, in the long run, be absolutely disastrous for the condition of women.

And I am dwelling on this because in our country, the debate has been and remains extremely impassioned. Really, the only thing that needs to be done to improve the lot of the working woman is not to reduce her work but to reduce, on the contrary, her family and household responsibilities. In order to do this, we would need day-care centers for infants and children, public services and also a change in habits such that men would agree to really share equally with women all the household work. This is not at all impossible in itself: it is a question of mentality, a tradition to be fought.

Unfortunately, this is not at all the direction that French society today is taking. On the contrary, there is clearly a will to oppose women working and to bring women back to the home. For about ten years there has been a considerable campaign in this direction in the United States. An American feminist, Betty Friedan, has written an excellent book entitled *The Feminine Mystique* in which she describes the very deliberate undertaking by American business to transform the woman into the ideal consumer. The American market seeks to increase the number of consumers or at least to multiply the number of objects purchased by each person. Statistics have shown that the ideal consumer is *not* the working woman because she buys quickly, according to her needs, without taking care in selection; nor is it the traditional housewife, because she buys the same thing that her mother bought and makes do with what she bought two years before: the ideal consumer is she who was educated to have a life of freedom, a career, an intellectual life, and who is confined in the home. In her, there is a kind of restlessness, a dissatisfaction that she is going to express by repeatedly buying refrigerators, television sets, by changing cars every three months and vacuum cleaners every week, which suits those who sell cars and vacuum cleaners just fine. Molding such women has been work carried out both by advertising agencies and all the big firms: they have succeeded in increasing Americans' needs for consumption through the ideal consumer, which is this woman.

A whole propaganda results: the woman can only realize herself [*s'accomplir*] in her home by fulfilling her household tasks which, moreover, as explained to American women, are creative tasks: in the way she prepares a dish, cleans the house, etc., she can demonstrate, so she is told, as much creative power as if she were writing Shakespeare's plays. Thus there is a major campaign orchestrated in this direction. In France, we are seeing a very similar one developing; for reasons that are a little different, we extol all of the traditional values, all of the values of femininity, and in particular, motherhood. We declare that a woman must first of all, fulfill her "woman's job," [*métier de femme*] that being a woman is in itself a profession, that a woman maims and betrays herself if she does not give herself over entirely to homemaking. And this is why I said to you that many women nowadays, and even women who at the time had liked *Le deuxième sexe*, declare today that they have changed, that they have understood that there is women's work to be accomplished which is not at all the same as men's work. But it is interesting to understand the answer to this question: why has the progression in the situation of women, which began to take shape in your country in 1945, stopped? Why are we seeing a regression in France?

I believe that in both cases we have the same explanation: we belong to bourgeois democracies and there is at the heart of bourgeois democracy a contradiction which can be noted in many domains and among them in that of women. On the one hand, bourgeois democracy calls itself a democracy, that is to say, a system of government in which there is perfect equality among all the citizens. There is no discrimination whether on the basis of race or, of course, on the basis of sex. Consequently, women are equal to men. It is in order to demonstrate this that we were given political rights just after the war—the right to vote in particular—and it was deemed that we were to be satisfied with this, that by granting us these rights we were really being recognized as equal to men. But on the other hand, bourgeois democracy is bourgeois, which implies that the leadership of the country rests with a certain class; this class naturally wants to retain its privileges, its leading role, i.e., the established order. We are touching on an extremely important point here. It is a question of giving the impression that we are living in a democracy while at the same time maintaining the established order which is based on inequality. In particular, women will be kept in a state of inferiority.

There are several very precise reasons for this. First, there are economic reasons. In France we have about 26% of women in the workforce. I believe that in your country the figure is about 45%, which is higher, but in both cases not all women work and in our country it is even a clear minority. Obviously, if only 26% of women work in France, it is because our society of today does not call for more. Otherwise, there would be an appeal, pressure, and the number of working women would increase. This is what happened in France just after the First World War: many men had died in the war; women were needed, and the female workforce was called upon. This is what helped women to become emancipated. But today, one cannot increase the female labor force. In order to give work to all women, one would be forced to "take" as they say, positions from men; a society which would like to have women work in equal numbers with men today would be required to put some of the men out of work. No society consents to this, because male unemployment is considered an anomaly, proving that society is not doing well, whereas we find it absolutely normal that the majority of women do not work. A society that is healthy can have a high percentage of women who are not employed. So there can be no question of taking jobs from men in order to distribute the work to be accomplished to men and women equally. The élan of women toward careers and professions will be discouraged: women will be urged to stay at home and not seek employment.

Along with these economic causes and linked to them, there is a cause that I will call a political one. As I was saying earlier, politics does not consist of simply going to put a ballot in a ballot box. Being truly politicized is taking part in social struggles, and the only way to have a hold on society, to really integrate oneself into it, in such a way as to be able to act effectively, is to belong to labor unions or pressure groups, to demonstrate solidarity with others. If a woman is deprived of these possibilities she is also deprived of all political effectiveness. And the fact is that in France, barring some exceptions of course, women on the whole are depoliticized. Yes, they vote, but what is a vote which is not grounded in convictions, in participation in public life? It takes on the appearance of an abdication. And indeed, often women vote in order that they will not have to concern themselves with politics, which means that they vote for the established power. It is not at all a fluke that in our country there is a regression in the status of women and the existence of a personal power.[1] Personal power is all the better established when the nation as a whole is more depoliticized. It is therefore fitting that women are depoliticized, and that they constitute a component of depoliticization, therefore a guarantor of the stability of the established power. Thus, for economic and political reasons, society finds it advantageous to keep women in the home.

There is a third reason: of course the ruling class wants to make its values, morals, and traditions prevail. Now, our modern bourgeoisie, which is industrial and technocratic, is returning to the values of the traditional bourgeoisie: these are, among others, the values of motherhood and the subordination of women to men. They are taken up again on the level of the superstructure at the same time as in the infrastructure of society; the relegation of women to a subordinate role is very useful for keeping the bourgeois world as it is. Therefore, you see that there is a strong link between the status of women and that of society. That is why I began by telling you that in my opinion, in talking about the condition of women, I was speaking to men as well as to women. Because the fact that women are subjugated to men leads to an enslavement of men to society.

This is very striking in America. People have perpetuated the myth that the American man is subjugated by the American woman. This is not true at all—as certain American feminists have pointed out in some excellent books. Men are enslaved to the organization by means of women; for example, if a man is compelled by his social status to give a mink coat to his wife, it is not she who compels him to give her this coat. But together, they both crave this proof of their affluence; they owe it to themselves to maintain their status. And by the

143

expenditures which this exigency requires of him, the man is at the mercy of the organization: he must obey the demands of the society to which he belongs. This is very striking in America with regard to consumption. In France, the problem is a little different and above all political; the apolitical attitude of women brings about that of men. If the woman shuts herself away in the home she is also going to shut the man in with her. Today, men are much less interested in labor union struggles or social struggles; instead of militating, they gladly spend the evening watching television, which extols to them in an entirely concerted fashion respect for the established order or which entertains them with escapist films. The man finds himself shut inside the home by his wife and with his wife. He becomes more and more depoliticized.

Inversely, one can see that in all the great periods of women's emancipation there was also a progressive effort within society. The best example is perhaps that of the emancipation of American women in the nineteenth century, before the abolition of slavery. Some very courageous women led in concert the struggle for their own emancipation and for that of Blacks. Some of them began to go from city to city speaking out against slavery. They were attacked; they were advised, "You are women, you must stay at home." They were led, in speaking out for Blacks, to also speak out for themselves. And conversely, there were some who began by defending their own cause and who then came to understand that they had to widen their struggle: since they were calling for the emancipation of a certain group of human beings, they ought to call for that of all those who were oppressed. And so, the feminist struggle and the abolitionist struggle were carried out in the United States in a single movement. One could find many other examples. Always and everywhere the struggle for the emancipation of women is linked to the struggle for progressivism in general. And I would say conversely that there is no possibility of women's emancipation—there cannot be a true change in the condition of women—without a transformation of the economic structures.

I do not mean that socialism is a sufficient condition for women to be truly equal to men. I know of no country in which this equality has been realized. In the USSR, in Poland, the status of women is clearly inferior to that of men. There are no women who are important political leaders, highly placed administrators, or high-level civil servants; one can barely cite two or three exceptions. However, in the USSR, 95% of women work. They do not have the highest level situations but nevertheless they have achieved a kind of dignity, of participation in public life, of self rapport [*rapport à soi*] that I have not encountered in other countries.

If socialism is not a sufficient condition, it is certainly a necessary one. Women will all work beginning the day there is work for everyone, when there is a need for their work, not before. But this work will only be needed, the full use of human efforts will only be needed the day we see a complete restructuring of the world of production.

I will conclude therefore by saying that in my opinion feminism is far from being outdated [*dépassé*] and that, on the contrary, we must keep it alive. Opposing something or denying it is not a surpassing, but rather a regression. I think that feminism is a cause that is common to men and women, and that men will only come to live in a more just, better-organized world, a more decent world, when women have a more just and more decent status. The acquisition of equality between the sexes is the business of both. Moreover, women must not confine themselves to specific demands. They must widen their scope and they must also struggle side by side with men for an overall change in society because they will only manage to bring about the triumph of their own cause by aiding in the progress of all humanity.

## NOTES

"Situation de la femme d'aujourd 'hui," *Les écrits de Simone de Beauvoir*, ed. Claude Francis and Fernande Gontier (Paris: Gallimard, 1979), 422–39; © Éditions Gallimard, 1979. This is the transcript of a September 20, 1966, lecture by Simone de Beauvoir in Tokyo, Japan, the first of her three lectures presented in Japan in September 1966.

1. "Personal power" refers to the government of Charles de Gaulle, who, as President of France (first elected in 1958 and reelected in 1965), had personal control of government policy.

**7**

# Women and Creativity

# INTRODUCTION

*by Ursula Tidd*

"Women and Creativity" is an important text in Simone de Beauvoir's corpus of nonfictional writing. It develops her arguments on gender and creativity first expounded in the second volume of *The Second Sex* and offers an oblique reflection on her own experience and "situation" as France's most well-known woman intellectual and writer in the mid-1960s. Beauvoir delivered her lecture on "Women and Creativity" on September 22, 1966, the second in a series of three lectures she gave during a visit to Japan with Jean-Paul Sartre.[1] The same title, "Women and Creativity," was used as the generic title to her lecture series. This lecture and her final lecture, entitled "My Experience as a Writer," focusing on her own engagement with writing, in effect constitute a somewhat ironic commentary on Sartre's own lectures in Japan on the function of the (implicitly male) universal intellectual, which were later to be published as "Plaidoyer pour les intellectuels" (A Plea for intellectuals).[2] In "Women and Creativity," there is still, nevertheless, a universalism that haunts Beauvoir's discourse concerning the relationship between gender and creativity. Her predominant focus on literature here and in her final lecture, "My Experience as a Writer," was of particular interest in Japan at this time. As she explains in *All Said and Done*, by 1966 Japan was

149

the third largest producer of books in the world and Japanese society was highly literate. At the time of her visit, all of Beauvoir's books were available in Japanese, including *The Second Sex*, which had been a runaway best seller the previous year.

An important intertext for Beauvoir's reflections on gender and creativity here is Virginia Woolf's groundbreaking essay, *A Room of One's Own* (1929), which started life as two lectures on "Women and Fiction" delivered to an audience of Cambridge women undergraduates. Woolf's essay, which has been described as "the first sustained essay in feminist literary theory," addresses several of the same questions as Beauvoir's lecture, although the latter also extends to a discussion of women's creativity in the domain of the visual arts.[3] Both Woolf and Beauvoir emphasize the material constraints on women's creativity in patriarchal society and reject any notion that women might be "naturally" less capable of accomplishing great works. In this contention, both women fundamentally challenge the patriarchal humanist notion of an essential self—as a result of their recognition of the importance of psychoanalysis and feminism as interpretive tools to understand selfhood. The (successfully fulfilled) creative self is hence viewed as the locus of an interplay of forces: talent, opportunity, hard work, and self-belief, validated and sustained by society, past and present.

Beauvoir endorses here Woolf's call for "a room of one's own" and "five hundred [pounds] a year" as the means to facilitate women's production of great literature. Beauvoir argues that the room in question is both a reality and a symbol, for a woman needs to belong to herself and to have material freedom in order to write and to accomplish creatively. Woolf's hypothetical example in *A Room of One's Own* of Shakespeare's sister, who is prevented by her "situation" from enjoying the same benefits as her brother and is condemned instead to domesticity, pregnancy, and suicide, is taken up in "Women and Creativity" in Beauvoir's example of a woman who tries in vain to lead the bohemian life and accomplish the work of Van Gogh—an example also cited at the end of *The Second Sex*. But here a question arises: do creative women have to live and work "like (solitary, middle-class) men" to fulfill their creative potential or might they choose different modes of creative production? The development, since the 1960s, of women-only, joint and collective modes of creative production would suggest otherwise.

Woolf and Beauvoir both emphasize the negative effect of a perceived lack (at the time) of a women's creative tradition on women writers and artists because, as they see it, no work of genius is produced in a void but is the result of an historical and contemporary dialogue with other writers, artists, and thinkers. Interestingly, they also both cite the celebrated Japanese woman writer, Murasaki Shikibu, author of *The Tale of the Genji*, although Beauvoir argues, rather disparagingly, that despite being an important figure in Japanese literature, her challenge to Japanese court society was minimal. Toril Moi has argued that "Beauvoir's peculiarly Western individualism" is responsible here for diminishing the importance of Murasaki's work.[4]

Referring back to her first lecture, "The Situation of Women Today" delivered two days earlier, Beauvoir assesses women's chances of achieving professional excellence in general, arguing that their overall "situation" in patriarchal society constrains their ambitions and opportunities. Since women must struggle in conditions that are so much less favorable than those enjoyed by men, it is improbable that many could achieve professional excellence of any kind. As Woolf argues, it is not simply that the creative artist has to struggle to overcome the indifference of capitalist society toward her or his work; additionally, creative women face outright hostility (from society, their chosen creative milieu, and their families and male partners, if they have them), rather than the mere indifference sometimes experienced by their male counterparts.

Consequently, women face considerably more material and psychosocial obstacles in their bid to transcend the status quo of creative achievement, especially in the visual arts. Beauvoir cites the examples of Germaine Richier (1902–59), the French sculptor, and Maria Elena Vieira da Silva (1908–92), the Portuguese painter, neither of whom has yet achieved the great renown of male artists such as Alberto Giacometti (1901–66) or Pablo Picasso (1881–1973). Like Woolf, Beauvoir also had a sister, Hélène, who was a painter and so had a detailed knowledge of women's experience in the male-dominated artistic establishment.

Creative writing is hence, according to Beauvoir, an easier field in which women might realize their creative potential for it is more practically viable and demands less financial outlay. But here, too, women face the same psychosocial obstacles as in other fields of creative endeavor. As in *The Second Sex*, Beauvoir draws here on a psychoanalytic account of the development of female subjectivity, arguing that because a girl identifies with her mother who is usually a traditional woman in patriarchal society and subordinate to patriarchal authority, a girl experiences her subjective isolation and emergence into the world in a more nuanced and passive way than a boy. To transcend the given and to realize her potential in the world, she must identify with the father—thereby idealizing the phallus—and hence construct the mother as a rival for his affections and possibly as a negative repository of all that is deemed bad and debilitating. In this process, she internalizes a patriarchal and disempowering image of femininity from both parents (unlike a boy for whom a patriarchal image of masculinity is largely beneficial to the elaboration of his transcendental achievement in the world). This prevents a girl from radically contesting her subjective isolation by means of the production of creative work. She does not feel the existential need to go beyond the given, having been brought up to avoid taking responsibility for the world, and so is less likely to question and reimagine the world at a fundamental level. Where women do experience a creative vocation, it is, however, easily shaken and diverted into more traditional occupations. Creative excellence requires an unshakable faith in one's vocation, a supportive environment, and a certain distance from the world in order that one might be able to question and imagine the world anew. In such circumstances, argues Beauvoir, talent and even genius might then flourish. Given women's precarious access to these conditions, exceptionally creative women are in a tiny minority.

For, as Beauvoir argues, there are exceptions, such as the case of Virginia Woolf, whose father, Leslie Stephen, encouraged her intellectual vocation. As a child, Beauvoir herself was also encouraged by her father to read and write, and she initially took her own vocational inspiration from the British woman writer, George Eliot (1819–80). Early in her life, books provided Beauvoir with an imaginary interlocutor and a future vocation as a writer, relieving her of her existential isolation and offering her the chance to reimagine the world as text.

Reading her analysis of "Women and Creativity" almost fifty years on, one can observe that Beauvoir identifies many of the most important factors that still impinge, though to a lesser extent in certain parts of the world, on women accomplishing outstanding creative work. In many countries, women still do not have equality of status or salary with men in many professions; their access to financial support and patronage is still often ultimately mediated by male gatekeepers in a way that the inverse is simply not the case. In terms of Beauvoir's brief psychoanalytical theorization of gender, genius, and creativity, this has been taken further in recent decades by figures such as Luce Irigaray, Julia Kristeva, and Christine Battersby—in ways that shed light on Beauvoir's own problematic relationship to creativity. Drawing on Kristeva's *Black Sun: Depression and Melancholia*, Toril Moi, for example, has illuminatingly argued that Beauvoir's own writing is at its most challenging and disturbing of the status quo when she confronts and transcends her loss and pain.[5] If, according to Moi's Kristevan reading of

Beauvoir's creative activity, the artistic imagination is always melancholic as it mourns the loss of the archaic mother, when that loss is confronted and accepted, a reparative imaginary object can come into being, thereby propelling the Beauvoirean writing subject into new spaces of heterogeneous subjectivity. But Moi notes that several of Beauvoir's texts fail to engage with and transcend that loss and pain, her creative power thus remaining mired in depression, suspended over the void.

Aspects of Beauvoir's views on creativity have been challenged by both Moi and Battersby, for example, who argue that a masculine universalist and Romantic notion of genius and creativity is operant at times in *The Second Sex* and in "Women and Creativity."[6] It does seem to be the case that Beauvoir has a particular type of creative personality and mode of creative production in mind when she talks of a woman being unable to lead the bohemian lifestyle of a Giacometti or a Van Gogh. An idealization of a masculine solitary creator/genius type does appear to be in play at times to the detriment of the consideration of other forms of creative collaborative production, such as writing partnerships or group artistic projects. The conflation of the concepts of genius and creativity in Beauvoir's discourse fosters this phallic idealization. It is an idealization that is also deeply Romantic in origin, as Beauvoir's description of her writing vocation in *Force of Circumstance* suggests: "The fact is that I am a writer—a woman writer, which doesn't mean a housewife who writes but someone whose whole existence is governed by her writing."[7] Yet in privileging the importance of women's solitary production of creative work, Beauvoir indicates perhaps an awareness of the politics of collaboration and its potential to conceal the extent of women's individual contribution to the creative process—a situation, some have argued, which might have occurred at times in her intellectual dialogue with Sartre.[8] In this way, perhaps, the discursive conflicts apparent in "Women and Creativity" suggest aspects of Beauvoir's own complex relationship to genius and creativity, torn as she is between a certain unconscious phallic idealization and remembering—both literally and figuratively—the loss of the archaic mother.

Yet Beauvoir does try to counter here a naturalistic assumption concerning creativity as a kind of "natural secretion" (and implicitly hitherto associated with male creators) and argues that women can be original creative artists, writers, and geniuses, although in the mid-1960s prevailing gendered roles and spheres of activity restricted most women in patriarchal society from creating highly original work. In 1929, Woolf contended that it would take "another hundred years" as well as a "room of one's own" and "five hundred a year" for women to become poets. Writing almost forty years later, Beauvoir argues that the creative woman of genius is on her way.

## NOTES

1. For an account of Beauvoir's visit to Japan in 1966, see Chapter V of *Tout compte fait* (Paris: Gallimard, 1972), 279–313; *All Said and Done* (Harmondsworth: Penguin, 1977), 273–305; and Asabuki Tomiko, *Vingt-huit jours au Japon avec Jean-Paul Sartre et Simone de Beauvoir (18 septembre–16 octobre 1966)* (Twenty-eight days in Japan with Jean-Paul Sartre and Simone de Beauvoir) (Paris: Langues et Mondes—L'Asiathèque, 1996).

2. Simone de Beauvoir, "My Experience as a Writer," in *"The Useless Mouths" and Other Literary Writings*, ed. Margaret A. Simons and Marybeth Timmermann (Urbana: University of Illinois Press, 2011), 275–301; Jean-Paul Sartre, "Plaidoyer pour les intellectuels," in *Situations VIII, autour de 68* (Paris: Gallimard, 1972); "A Plea for Intellectuals," in *Between Marxism and Existentialism*, trans. John Matthews (New York: Pantheon, 1974).

3. Morag Shiach, Introduction to Virginia Woolf, *A Room of One's Own* (Oxford: OUP, 1992), xii.

4. Toril Moi, ed., Introduction, *French Feminist Thought* (Oxford, U.K.: Blackwell, 1987), 2.

5. Toril Moi, *Simone de Beauvoir, The Making of an Intellectual Woman* (Oxford, U.K.: Blackwell, 1994), 250–51.

6. Christine Battersby, *Gender and Genius, Towards a Feminist Aesthetics* (London: The Women's Press, 1989), 150–54.

7. Simone de Beauvoir, *La force des choses II* (Paris: Gallimard Folio, [1963] 1978), 495; *Force of Circumstance* (Harmondsworth: Penguin, 1968), 664.

8. See Kate and Edward Fullbrook, *Simone de Beauvoir and Jean-Paul Sartre, The Remaking of a Twentieth Century Legend* (Hemel Hempstead: Harvester Wheatsheaf, 1993).

# WOMEN AND CREATIVITY

by *Simone de Beauvoir*

TRANSLATION AND NOTES BY MARYBETH TIMMERMANN

I am going to speak to you today about the condition of women again, because it seems to me that this is just as burning an issue in Japan as it is in
France. I am going to consider it from a particular angle. The question that
I would like to examine is this: All throughout the history of humanity, it is
clear that women's achievements [*réalisations*] in every domain—political, artistic, philosophic, etc.—have been considerably inferior in number and quality to those of men.[1] Why? Could there be, as some antifeminists claim, an
inferiority in women's nature that prevents them from successfully matching
the accomplishments of men? Or does women's condition, as shaped by society, influence their possibilities of achievement [*réalisation*] by keeping them
in a state of inferiority? Of course, the latter opinion is mine, and I would like
to explain to you why. There is a very famous English woman writer whom
I like very much, and with whom some of you are very familiar: her name is
Virginia Woolf.[2] She has responded on a certain level to the question that I
pose, having asked herself why, in the literary sphere, the works of English
women writers were so rare and in general of lesser quality. And in a very
nice little book called *A Room of One's Own*, she has responded in a very
simple and true way, I think. The first condition for writing is having a room

of one's own, a place where one can retire for several hours, without being interrupted, where one can reflect, write, reread what one has done, critique oneself, and be alone with oneself. In other words, the room is at once a reality and a symbol. In order to be able to write and in order to be able to accomplish something, one must first belong to oneself. But traditionally, women do not belong to themselves. A woman belongs to her husband and her children. At any moment, the husband or children can come ask her for an explanation, a helping hand, or a favor that she is obligated to satisfy. She belongs to the family, to the group; she does not belong to herself. Under these conditions, writing is, if not impossible, at least an extremely difficult endeavor. Virginia Woolf took the example of Shakespeare. She imagines what would have happened if an extremely talented little girl had been born in the place of Shakespeare, exactly in his place. She shows that it would have been impossible for her to create anything. She would have stayed at home, cooking and sewing; she would have gotten married and had children. It is impossible to imagine that she would have gotten the education that Shakespeare did, or that she would have become an actress or playwright. She would not have been Shakespeare; she would have been nothing. *I* also attempted, in *Le deuxième sexe* [*The Second Sex*], a similar analysis regarding Van Gogh.[3] I tried to show that a girl born in Van Gogh's place would not have had the chances that he had; his life in Borinage, the social contacts that allowed him to develop his thoughts and his personality, and the entire rest of his existence. In short, I am in complete agreement with Virginia Woolf. We have said the same thing: No matter how gifted a being might be at birth, these gifts will remain sterile if social conditions or surrounding circumstances prevent their exploitation. That is what Stendhal, who was a great feminist, expressed in this striking turn of phrase: "Any genius who is born a woman is lost to all humanity."[4]

Very well, one might say; it has been this way up until now. But for at least twenty years now women have had the same chances as men; they vote, they can choose the professions they want, and yet we haven't seen during these past twenty years any truly great achievements [*réalisations*] by women. That's true. But I would like to show in fact that it is absolutely fallacious to claim that women and men have had equal chances during the last twenty years. I am going to show precisely how they have not.

First let's consider women's careers—I have already spoken a bit about this in my previous lecture, but I want to revisit this topic from a different angle. It certainly is true that there are women lawyers, doctors, engineers, and architects, but the greatest names of lawyers, engineers, doctors, and architects in France are the names of men. Why? Is there something within women that destines them to mediocrity? Let's take a more careful look. First of all, as I was saying the other day, only a very limited number of women exercise these professions. Now a statistical law states that the larger the group, the greater the chances that one of its members will distinguish himself. If, all other things being equal, I randomly selected a group of one hundred medical students and then a group of ten others, and if I were asked which group would produce a great leader or a great researcher who will be illustrious in the field of medicine, I would a priori bet on the group of one hundred. And I would have a ten to one chance of winning. It is a very basic truth, but one that is unfortunately too little known. Women in all these branches are much less numerous than men, so the chances are much greater that it will be a man and not a woman who will achieve [*réalise*] great things. Secondly, women face a barrier in all professions. This barrier stops them at a certain point; they do not earn as much money as men do, they do not attain the same level or title, and what seems even more important to me, they do not succeed in acquiring the same talent. Talent is not a given any more than what is called genius. It is something that is conquered. If you have to confront difficulties and you work to overcome them, you are led to surpass yourself. If you remain in an easy domain, you will stay at an easy level. If, by antifeminist prejudice, one refuses to entrust difficult cases to a woman lawyer or a woman doctor, they will never have the opportunity to really show what they are capable of. To show what you are capable of is always to surpass, in some way, what you are capable of; it is to go even further: to dare, to seek, to invent. That is when a value is affirmed, discovered, and realized. But this chance is denied to women. They themselves hesitate to venture into very difficult domains. First of all, they are subject to all the familial servitudes of which I spoke the other day. They have concerns and are obligated to think of other things besides their careers; they must share their time between their professional work and the work they do at home. So they dare not consider launching themselves down an arduous path. And I think that here I am touching on what is perhaps the most important thing. Women themselves, insofar as they attempt something, do not attempt it with the same audacity and the same hope that men do. They are beaten before they start because they know that society will not give them their chance. What good does it do to aspire to practice general medicine or become a great psychiatrist or great specialist when you know that you will not have the necessary support or the necessary clientele? So, very wisely, you confine yourself to gynecology, pediatrics, or nursing; you accept minor positions that your masculine colleagues don't want, because you think that after all, if you show more ambition you are wasting your efforts. This has indeed happened to many women who serve as a discouraging example to others. Besides, given everything that I have just told you—the small number of women who work, and the fact that working women remain the exception—a woman's ambition finds itself automatically more limited than a man's. I was very struck by the reaction of a young woman film director during a time when women never exercised that profession. I was asking her about her ambitions and her projects. And she answered, "Oh! It's already difficult enough, already exceptional enough to be a woman director in France. If in addition I had to be a great director, it would be too much!" She was completely satisfied to be a director, even a mediocre one. Her ambition was limited for two reasons at the same time: because she didn't think anyone would ever give her the means to make great films, and because it was enough for her, given the situation, to make minor ones.

Finally, there is another reason that persuades women to be contented with little. Given the divided character of women's condition, and given that the woman who works also wants to have a happy life, a successful home and love life, she finds it prudent to be self-effacing on the professional plane. A man has the privilege that the greater a doctor, surgeon, or lawyer he is, the more attractive he is considered to be. His wife admires him and is happy about it. A woman, on the contrary, if too successful, risks discouraging, annoying, and humiliating her husband. She dares not. Twenty years ago, when I visited some women's universities in America, I spoke with students who seemed, judging by their conversations, to be capable of great brilliance and whose professors told me that they only obtained mediocre grades. So I wondered why. Many told me frankly, "Well, our grades must not be too low because then we would look like imbeciles, but if our grades are too high, we appear pedantic and intellectual, and thus will not marry. We want to do well in our studies as long as it won't prevent a man from marrying us." I have seen other cases, between married couples. I had a friend, younger than me, who was preparing for an *agrégation* in philosophy.[5] Her husband was also. My friend had only one fear: that she would pass and her husband would fail. And in the end, even though she was perfectly prepared, she did everything to fail, while her husband passed. They are a happy enough couple, but the young woman still feels some regret because she thinks that she could have succeeded in her professional life better than she has. Many similar cases can be found in France today. It can be said then, that the professional mediocrity of women is explained by a host of circumstances that come, not from their nature, but from their situation.

Now let's consider the domain which is more particularly the subject of this lecture: that of artistic and literary creation. One might say that in this domain one depends much less on others than when one pursues a career. One has no boss or clients. The woman who stays at home has plenty of leisure time. She has much more time for creating and for self-realization than the man who spends his days in an office. Why does she not take better advantage of her freedom?

First let's ask ourselves why, for all time and still today, we see so few women who are painters and sculptors. Let's try to examine their situation in detail. First, we are going to see the same factors in play as those in the course of a career. A boy who wants to become a sculptor or painter finds little support in his family, so he is more or less obliged to fight for some help in his long apprenticeship of painting or sculpture. But for a woman it is worse. She is treated like a madwoman and is redirected to more feminine jobs: stenography or dressmaking. Very, very rare are the women who manage to receive serious training in painting or sculpture. Here again, naturally, statistics play a role: the fewer women there are who attempt sculpting or painting, the fewer there will be who will succeed in producing great works. Next, the barrier of which I have spoken also plays a role here, because these are occupations that require large sums of money. It is costly to have a studio, to have plaster or marble, tubes of paint and canvas. These occupations require considerable financial support. Sometimes friends or family can provide this support. They would provide it for a man, but not for a woman. Consider what Theo Van Gogh did for his brother Vincent, financially supporting him during his entire life and thereby allowing him to become a great painter. It is difficult to imagine a brother or father doing the same for a sister or a daughter. They would lack confidence; the case would seem abnormal to them; there exists no example of such behavior.

Moreover, in order to make money, one must have the backing of art dealers or collectors. Now I am rather familiar with the art world, and I know that an art collector or dealer would not invest in a young woman. He would come up with reasons; he would say, "She will get married and give up painting," or if she is already married, "She will have children and then give up painting," or if she already has children, "She will have more children and give up painting." They always think that one day the woman will give it up; she is therefore a bad investment. In reality this rationalization hides a much less rational thought: the truth is that he thinks, "She is a woman; therefore she has no talent." And by doing this, he denies her the means to acquire it or show that she has some of it, which ends up reinforcing the prejudice: She is a woman; therefore she has no talent.

Moreover, the difficulties that a woman has to confront if at first she doesn't earn a living as an artist are absolutely terrifying. A boy who barely makes a living as a painter and who leads what is called a bohemian lifestyle—poorly lodged, poorly dressed, lacking in social status, hanging out in any old café—is considered an artist. He fits into a category and is accepted; his originality is a sign of his vocation and a promise of talent. If a woman lives in the same manner, she suffers more. Not having a proper house and clothing is much more contrary to the traditional image of herself that has been given to her. It must be understood that every woman, even the most emancipated, is profoundly influenced by her education. A woman would therefore hesitate; many would not have the courage to lead that type of life. And if one among them has the courage, she would be singled out: she would not be an artist, but a madwoman, a monster. Much more courage is needed for a woman to face this kind of life than for a man. In addition, if she gets married and has children, it becomes absolutely impossible for her to continue working. I know many young women who started to paint but who were forced to quit because such an occupation demands eight or ten hours of work each day, and it is not possible to find that kind of time while leading the life of a homemaker, wife, and mother. At most, if the husband has considerable good will, his wife might manage to paint or sculpt, but on the condition of not having any children. Now this is a grave decision for a woman to make; for many women the choice between motherhood and a creative career brings about a bitter conflict. Men do not have to face this choice; they can perfectly well be a father, have a home, a wife, children, and a successful and full affective life, all while being creative.

There are stubborn women who choose to sacrifice everything in order to paint or sculpt. But they dispense so much effort in this struggle, so much energy in confronting public opinion and triumphing over their inner resistances, that they find themselves much less available for their work than a man who is spared these difficulties. Now availability is one of the most necessary conditions for the blossoming of what is called genius. In order to raise oneself up to a noticeably superior level of creation, one must aim uniquely at that goal, in complete freedom and without foreign concerns. There is a very great artist whom I knew well and whom I deeply admire that you surely are familiar with: his name is Giacometti.[6] His manner of living was absolutely extraordinary. Even when he earned a lot of money, he was so indifferent to material contingencies that he lived in a sort of shack that leaked on rainy days; he would collect the water in bowls which themselves had holes, so water ran on the floor and he couldn't have cared less. He had a tiny, uncomfortable studio where he would work all night long, sleeping whenever he felt like it: at five or six o'clock in the morning or at noon. He would toss on any old thing for clothes, wearing a string for a belt to hold up his pants, and his hands covered with plaster. He didn't care one bit, and everyone thought it normal that he lived in such a way; he was an artist; anything he did was accepted. And in particular his wife submitted to this sort of existence. He therefore had absolutely no preoccupations except his sculpting. One need not make a large effort of imagination to see what would be the fate of a woman who tried to imitate Giacometti. She would be put in an asylum, or at least be considered as crazy. One can not suppose that a husband would agree to accommodate such a rhythm of life; any social life would be forbidden to her. And in truth, she herself would refuse this type of existence; she would have no inner knowledge of this supreme freedom that was Giacometti's. And that is why we have women sculptors in France and women painters—there are even some whom I consider as very great artists like Germaine Richier and Vieira da Silva[7]—who nevertheless have not reached the greatness of a Giacometti or a Picasso.[8] And here I come to the essential point that will allow us to understand why in the domain of literature, a domain that seems very accessible to women, they remain, except with rare exceptions, inferior to men. When it comes to explaining the limits of women's achievements [*réalisations*], their interior conditioning is much more important than the exterior circumstances of which I have spoken until now.

With literature, we broach the domain where the antifeminists seem to have the most trump cards. Indeed, although an eighteen-year-old girl has not acquired the rudiments of sculpture or even oftentimes painting, every young woman who belongs to the privileged class has learned the art of writing, and oftentimes in a very extensive manner. Literature is not a domain foreign to her. She has read. She has written papers, essays, and letters. She speaks and expresses herself. In this domain she has had a training as solid as her brother. And it is much easier to sit at the corner of a table with a pen and paper than to have a studio, canvases, and paints.

Yes, on the surface, the situation seems favorable to the woman who wants to write. There are a certain number of them who live in the condition described by Virginia Woolf: they have no room of their own. But there are also those who have some time to themselves, once their children are raised—and even before, in well-to-do families where the woman has help.

Neither the absence of training nor the lack of time prevents them from re-alizing themselves. The best proof is that there are many women who write. Out of the avalanche of manuscripts received each year by French publish-ing houses, a third of them are written by women. I know from experi-ence that women have the time to write, because I personally receive a large quantity of manuscripts coming from women who, having nothing to do, decide to try their hand at literature. Why are there so few of this number that are worth something? And among those that are worth something, why are so few of them really first class?

The first reason is, contrary to what is believed by those women who write because they have nothing to do, one does not haphazardly become a writer. Writing is the result of a vocation; it is the response to a certain appeal, some-thing that generally is heard at a very young age. There are exceptions, voca-tions that come later in life, like that of Jean-Jacques Rousseau,[9] for example. But the majority are rooted in the individual from childhood. Mozart's voca-tion was decided at five years old, Flaubert's at nine, and I could cite many other examples.[10] But on this plane, everything encourages the little boy to be ambitious, while nothing encourages the little girl in that direction. One must have an enormous ambition to want to write, that is, to re-create the world in a certain manner and take charge of it anew [le reprendre en charge] in order to show it to others. The male child is encouraged to be ambitious because he belongs to the superior caste. They tell him right away, "You are a boy; you must not behave like that; you are a boy so you must get good grades in school; you must not cry, etc." This virile ideal is presented to him right away and presupposes that he must always surpass himself. The little boy is taught that he himself must surpass himself. In addition psychoanalysis teaches us that the Oedipus complex in little boys is manifested by his love for his mother and by a very violent rivalry with his father.[11] He wants to equal his father and even surpass him. Ambition is therefore implanted within him by his edu-cation and by his spontaneous affectivity, which means that the roots of his ambition are extremely profound. Now the correlative of this exigency placed upon him by society is a rather tragic sense of forlornness and solitude. He is asked to stand out above all others, to raise himself up above all his peers; he feels alone; he is frightened and overwhelmed. He experiences what ex-istentialism has called forlornness [délaissement].[12] And he experiences it in anguish. And one of the reasons that drive most artists and writers to create is precisely their reaction against forlornness and anguish. Ambitious and at the same time feeling contingent and abandoned [délaissé], the little boy truly has all the reasons for wanting to "do something" and in particular for wanting to create, to write. If we consider the little girl, things happen completely other-wise. Classically, she starts out identifying with her mother, who in most cases is a traditional woman: a relative and secondary being. So she learns to iden-tify herself with a relative and secondary being. In her games and fantasies and myths, she dreams of herself in this way, which is a way of denying and eliminating ambition. Later she identifies herself more or less with her father. But by that time, when the Oedipus complex develops in her and she starts to see her mother as a rival and be more or less in love with her father, she is already eleven or twelve years old; she is already habituated to modesty and loves her father humbly, considering herself as inferior to him. She does not presume to equal him. All she wants is to be his disciple, his reflection, some-thing very modest compared to what he himself was. And since she loves her father, if he, like most men, has a traditional image of women and wants his daughter to become a good wife, a good mother, a society woman, and an accomplished homemaker, she will rein in the little bit of ambition that she might have and choose to become an accomplished mother and housewife. Moreover, due to the fact that she lacks ambition and thinks of herself as a relative being, she feels protected by society. She is not asked to stand out or be self-sufficient, and she thinks that first her family and then a husband will take charge of her throughout her life; she experiences the forlornness and anguish of existing less than the little boy does, and therefore has less need to surpass and re-create this world into which she has been thrown. She feels the need to construct an oeuvre much less than the boy does; she is more conformist than him, and conformism is the very opposite of creation, which starts by questioning the given reality. Therefore, for all these reasons, little girls have a creative vocation much more rarely than do boys. It happens to certain girls, however, and I don't have enough time to expand upon this point, but I think that it would be very interesting to consider the particular conditions under which certain women have had a vocation as a writer at a very young age. By examining a number of cases, one thing struck me: most women who have had the vocation to write were spared the identification with their mother, or at least they had a father who was ambitious for them and who pushed them to become a writer. Virginia Woolf is a striking example. As a very small child she was treated by her father as a boy; all the ambitions he might have had for a boy were transferred to her. She had always been encouraged to write; she became the writer she became in accordance with the paternal wishes. What struck me in studying your great writer Murasaki Shikibu,[13] was encountering the presence of her father in her memories of childhood. She tells that when her brother studied Chinese, he had a lot of trouble learning the Chinese characters while she learned them very quickly. And the father basically said, "What a shame that she is not the boy!" It is only a clue, since she does not relate many details of her childhood, but this clue seems very interesting to me because at the origin of this great oeuvre realized by a woman—the greatest oeuvre in the world, I think, that has been realized by a woman—there is a paternal presence beginning in childhood. But I do not have the time to expand upon it; it would require a very detailed and nuanced study. I simply wanted to make you recognize and understand that talent and genius are the response to a vocation. But such a vocation is not encouraged in women, as a general rule, while on the contrary, everything in the little boy's education spurs him toward it.

Now, let's consider the situation of adult women. We are going to see that it is favorable to a certain point, but only to a certain point, for the realization of a literary oeuvre. In order to create, as I was telling you, one must have the will to give the world to be seen [*donner à voir le monde*]; therefore one must see it, and therefore one must be at a certain distance from it. When one is entirely immersed in a situation, one can not describe it. A soldier can not write about a battle when he is fighting in it. But if one is completely foreign to a situation, one can not write about it either. If someone tries to *recount* a battle *off the cuff*, without having seen one, it would be detestable. The privileged position is that of the person who is slightly marginalized: a war correspondent for example, who shares in part the risks of the combatants, but not completely; he is included, but not fully involved. He is the one who is best placed for describing a battle. Well, women are to some small extent in that situation. Since this is a masculine world, the big decisions, heavy responsibilities, and important actions fall to men; women live in the margins of this world. They access it only through their private lives, through men, in a mediate way, rather than directly. Women have much more leisure time than men, that is to say not only the time but also the inner disposition for watching, observing, and criticizing. They are ready spectators, and that is a privileged position for anyone who wants to write. Here again I will take your great writer Murasaki Shikibu as an example. She was marvelously well placed for writing the great novel she wrote, which gives the most extraordinary picture imaginable of the Court at the beginning of the eleventh century. She lived at the Court; she was what we in France call a lady-in-waiting, very close to the Empress, and yet she herself did not have the responsibilities of a man; she was neither an important government official, nor warrior, nor diplomat; she didn't act. She was included without being involved [*dans le coup sans y être*] which is a privileged position. It is not so amazing, upon reflection, that it was a woman and not a man who wrote *The Tale of Genji*. I would compare her to a woman whose works are much less important, but who is well-loved and means a great deal to us in France: Mme de La Fayette.[14] She too, several centuries later, described in a novel the customs and manners of the French Court. She described them with a very impressive gift of observation, critical sensibility, and much talent. Mme de La Fayette was also tied to the Court without, however, being charged with official duties there. She was admirably placed for giving us a depiction of its manners. As you can see, women, situated somewhat on the margins of society, find themselves well placed for writing literary works. That is why there exists such a large number of successful and important works by women.

However, in the works of the two women I have just compared, something strikes me: they both remain in agreement with the society of their time. Murasaki Shikibu, for example, takes great care to tell us, "I am a woman so I don't speak Chinese," which is false, but she does not want to appear pedantic or as a bluestocking. Occasionally she will also stop and say, "I will not tell this particular story; it is not fitting for a woman." Basically she is playing, in a completely charming manner, incidentally, at being the traditional woman, the woman who doesn't know anything and who tells a story as if by chance, but who is not at all pedantic and doesn't break with the traditional image of women. Similarly, Mme de La Fayette absolutely does not contest the morals and manners that she describes to us. She approves of them. She approves, at least in her novel, of the inequality that exists between men and women in the sexual and conjugal life of her time. This is why I have said that women are well placed for describing the society, the world, and the era to which they belong, but only to a certain point. The very great works of art are those that call the entire world into question. But women do not do that. They critique and contest the details, but in order to call the world completely into question, one must feel profoundly responsible for that world. Yet women are not responsible for the world, insofar as it is a man's world; they do not effectuate this taking charge anew [*reprise en charge*] that characterizes great creators. They do not radically contest the world, and that is why no women in the history of humanity have created a great religious or philosophical system, or even a great ideology. For that, one must in some way make a *tabula rasa* of all the givens—as Descartes made a *tabula rasa* of all knowledge[15]—and start anew. And due to their condition, women are not in a position to do that!

There will be objections that all this is certainly valid when it comes to women in the past, but for women of today, the situation has changed completely. Women should be able to take charge of the world anew and feel as responsible for this world as men do. Therefore they could contest it in the same way, demolishing it in order to rebuild it. But this is not true, because we must not underestimate the importance not only of education, but of the entire context in which a woman's life is inscribed and which remains the same as in the past.

Women are marked, I repeat, not only by the education they receive directly from their parents and teachers, but also by what they read and the myths communicated to them in the books they read—including those written by women. They are marked by the traditional image of woman, and to break from it is something very difficult for them. Oftentimes a woman will write while enclosed in her private world, remaining confined in that little universe of hers. So she writes more or less to kill time, and there is a very unkind expression used to designate this type of book: they are called *ouvrages de dames* [ladies' works]. And indeed very often one has the impression that women write as they would embroider or paint with water colors: to pass the time. Some show talent, that is to say that they are rather good at describing this very closed, very limited little world which is their own. Their books are charming and are read with a certain amount of enjoyment, but they have little impact. In addition, the factors that I mentioned earlier concerning women's careers—the timidity before men and the fear of disturbing the household peace if one is too successful—also play a role in this domain. I remember a young woman who had brought me a manuscript which was not too bad, and I told her that with a little audacity and a bit of confidence in herself, and also work, she would succeed in writing a good book. Her response was, "Yes, I'd like to write a good book, but deep down I don't want to. My husband is very happy that I write in that it keeps me at home. I don't go out, I don't flirt, and that's very well. But if I were successful, I don't know what would become of my marriage." I have seen other women who have written a successful first book, and who have stopped there because their success caused problems between them and their husbands. Obviously those were women whose vocations were not very firm. But who knows how far they could have gone if they hadn't been held back from the start by so many considerations that have nothing to do with literature.

Of course not all women are like that. Some challenge this traditional image and try to author exacting and important works. They stake the essentials of their lives on their writing. In France today, writing is what counts above all for certain women, and everything else is subordinate to it. Their practical life is organized around their writing, and what's more,

166

they are interested in the world; they have social and political activities and are equal to many men writers in their mode of living as well as in their achievements [*réalisations*]. All the same, in none of these women can be found what I would call a certain extremism because they remain haunted by the myths of femininity. Again I take the example of Giacometti; he was a bit crazy when he said he wanted "to wring the neck of sculpture." It was an inordinate ambition and could have seemed arrogant if it weren't at the same time an act of faith and an exigency. When Giacometti spoke of wringing the neck of sculpture, it was beautiful because it meant several things: "I believe that I will be able to produce statues that no one has ever made before and resolve problems that have never before been resolved, and if not, then neither sculpting nor painting is worth it. I will be able to eliminate that portion of failure contained in any work." But this act of faith was at the same time the statement of an exigency, which meant: "I will be content with none of the busts or statues that I have made up until now, even if everyone else admires them and even if someone pays me millions for them. That is not what I want. I demand more; I expect much more from myself." This faith and this exigency, pushed to such an extent, are found in only five or six people a century. The conditions must be just right for them to be able to blossom, and the first of these conditions is to be a man. A woman does not have enough confidence in herself because no one else has enough confidence in her, and neither does she have the highest exigency, which alone can lead to the highest achievement [*réalisation*]. For lack of exigency, she does not have that long patience which Buffon said was the very essence of genius.[16] These qualities are denied to her not by a defect in her nature, but by all the conditioning to which she is subjected.

Therefore, in conclusion, I will say that many people have come up with an absolutely erroneous idea about what creation is. They imagine that it is a natural secretion, that the artist or writer produces works of art like a cow gives milk, and that women's nature is such that it precludes this fertility. In truth, creation is an extremely complex process, conditioned by society as a whole. It is understandable, then, that since circumstances are absolutely different for men and women—women's condition being unequal to that of men and their chances greatly inferior—their achievements [*réalisations*] would also be inferior. One cannot affirm that women, with equal chances, would succeed less than men, if their chances were really equal. They are not, they have never been, and they are not today in any country in the world. Perhaps a woman who is twenty years old today will amaze posterity, we can not know. What is certain is that her mother and grandmother have

167

been conditioned by traditional models. Twenty-year-old women or their granddaughters will perhaps produce works equal in number and value to those of men. We can not know since never before have the conditions of equality been realized. And I insist upon this and have chosen it as my subject for this lecture because it is a vicious circle from which I would like women to escape. People tell them over and over again that women in the past have done nothing great in order to discourage them. They are basically saying, "Be reasonable; you will never do anything great so it's not worth trying." And, given the enormous pressure of public opinion, women too often let themselves be convinced. I would like for them to understand that things are not at all like that. It is because they have not had their chances that they have not done more. If they fight for their chances, they are fighting for their accomplishments at the same time. They must not let themselves be intimidated by the past because in general, in this domain as in all others, the past can never be used to deny the future.

## NOTES

This text, the second of three lectures given by Beauvoir during a trip to Japan, was presented on September 22, 1966. The French transcription appeared in *Les écrits de Simone de Beauvoir*, ed. Claude Francis and Fernande Gontier (Paris: Gallimard, 1979), 458–74; © Éditions Gallimard, 1979. It was translated as "Women and Creativity" by Roisin Mallaghan in *French Feminist Thought*, ed. Toril Moi (Oxford: Blackwell, 1987).

1. We have translated the French noun *"réalisation"* and verb *"réaliser"* as "achievements" and "to achieve" when it designates the tangible product of an artistic creation, but have translated them as "realization" and "to realize" when the context implies a broader meaning of any sort of self-realization. The French has been inserted to indicate where Beauvoir's *"réalization"* has been translated as "achievement."

2. Virginia Woolf (1882–1941) was a British novelist, essayist, and critic, who was also a feminist, socialist, and pacifist. She is considered to be one of the foremost modernist literary figures of the twentieth century.

3. Simone de Beauvoir, *Le deuxième sexe* (Paris: Gallimard, 1949), trans. H. M. Parshley as *The Second Sex* (New York: Knopf, 1952), and a new translation by Constance Borde and Sheila Malovany-Chevallier (New York: Vintage Books, 2010); Vincent Van Gogh (1853–90) was a Dutch postimpressionist painter who was financially supported throughout his life by his brother Theo. In 1878, he moved to the impoverished coal-mining region of southern Belgium known as the Borinage as a missionary, living in extreme poverty and sharing his own resources with those he met there.

4. Stendhal (1783–1842) was the pseudonym of Marie-Henri Beyle, a French writer who played a major role in the development of the modern novel; see Beauvoir's chapter on Stendhal in *The Second Sex*.

5. The *agrégation* is the highest graduate teaching examination in France.

6. Alberto Giacometti (1901–66) was a Swiss sculptor and painter best known for his attenuated sculptures of solitary figures.

7. Germaine Richier (1904–59) was a French sculptor of provocative, biomorphic figures; Mariea Elena Vieira da Silva (1908–92) was a Portuguese-born painter of intricate, semiabstract compositions.

8. Pablo Picasso (1881–1973) was a Spanish-born painter and sculptor who was one of the founders of cubism.

9. Jean-Jacques Rousseau (1712–78) was a Swiss philosopher, writer, and political theorist.

10. Wolfgang Amadeus Mozart (1756–91) was born in Salzburg and remains one of the most popular composers of European classical music; Gustave Flaubert (1821–80) was a French novelist best known for his novel *Madame Bovary*.

11. The theory of the Oedipus complex, based on the Greek legend of King Oedipus in which the hero kills his father and marries his mother, was developed by Austrian neurologist and founder of psychoanalysis Sigmund Freud (1856–1939).

12. This important term derived from Heidegger is often translated as "forlornness" or "thrownness"; Beauvoir refers to our being "thrown" into the world later in this paragraph.

13. Murasaki Shikibu (973–1024?), sometimes known as Lady Murasaki in English, lived during Japan's Heian period and was the author of one of the earliest and most famous novels ever written, *The Tale of Genji*.

14. Marie Madeleine, countess of La Fayette (1634–93), known as Madame de La Fayette, was a French writer who is best known for the early novel *La Princesse de Clèves* (*The Princess of Cleves*).

15. Réné Descartes (1596–1650), a French mathematician, scientist, and philosopher, is considered the father of modern philosophy as well as the founder of modern mathematics.

16. Georges-Louis Leclerc, Comte de Buffon (1701–88) was a French naturalist, mathematician, biologist, cosmologist, and author. The actual quotation is "Le génie n'est qu'une plus grande aptitude à la patience" (Genius is only a greater aptitude for patience), from *Voyage à Montbar* (Voyage to Montbar), which was a biography of sorts written by Hérault de Séchelles in 1803. See *The Oxford Dictionary of Quotations* (Oxford University Press, 1979, 1985, 1999).

8

Foreword to *History: A Novel*

# INTRODUCTION

*by Margaret A. Simons*

In her 2011 introduction to Beauvoir's foreword to the 1977 American edition of Elsa Morante's *History: A Novel* reprinted in our 2011 volume of Beauvoir's literary writings, Eleanore Holveck criticizes Beauvoir for failing to appreciate Morante's achievement in "one of the finest novels to come out of World War II."[1] Holveck provides helpful background: Morante (1912–85),[2] she explains, "was born in Rome to a poor Sicilian father, a clerk, and a Jewish mother who taught school. Beauvoir and Sartre traveled to Rome every year after World War II and usually saw Morante and novelist Alberto Moravia (1907–90), her husband from 1941 to 1963.[3] Morante's first major novel, *Menzoga i Sortilegio* (*House of Liars*) (1948) received the Viareggio Prize; she wrote short stories, poems, and the well-received *L'Isola di Arturo* (*Arturo's Island*) (1958)."[4]

Holveck's criticism comes in response to Beauvoir's observation in the 1977 English version of the foreword that true history for Morante is "in the hearts and bodies of the anonymous individuals who suffer through [it]," to which Holveck remarks, "but I am neither so sure about the anonymity nor that Beauvoir gives sufficient credit to Morante's achievement." In fact, Beauvoir did not describe the individuals as "anonymous." A comparison of

173

the 1977 English version of the foreword with the original French text newly translated here, reveals that the earlier translator added the word, "anonymous," and deleted the surname of the novel's protagonist, Ida Ramundo, thus assuring her anonymity.

So Holveck's criticism in this case applies to the translation rather than to Beauvoir's interpretation. Does the original French text also contest Holveck's charge that Beauvoir fails to give "sufficient credit to Morante's achievement"? Holveck lauds as Morante's "greatest achievement" in the novel her depiction of the life of the child Useppe: "the true story is the birth and death of Useppe Ramundo. From his first movements in his mother's womb, 'the little blows he gave seemed more information than protest: I inform you that I am here and, in spite of everything, I'm coping and I'm alive. . . . What are you scared of? You're not alone.'"[5] According to Holveck, "Useppe incarnates the joy of human existence, *la joie d'exister* that Beauvoir describes so movingly in *The Ethics of Ambiguity* as the concrete flesh and blood thickness of the world that underlies all political activity and that should be its final goal.[6] Morante's ability to re-create the world from a child's viewpoint is unmatched and magnificent."[7] Holveck concludes by situating Morante's achievement in the context of Beauvoir's defense of philosophical literature. "Morante's novel," Holveck writes, "truly represents Beauvoir's position in her 1966 essay "Que peut la littérature?" (What can literature do?) based roughly on Leibniz, that the world is one totality and that each point of view on that same world expresses itself, communicating with all the others, through literature."[8]

Here, once again, the original French text shows Beauvoir—in passages deleted, paraphrased, or mistranslated in the 1977 version of the foreword—recognizing Morante's achievement in the novel. Against the Italian critics who reproached Morante for not having chosen heroes who understand events and participate in them lucidly, Beauvoir explains that for Morante, "every life, even the most humble, is a human adventure that is unique and complete." Beauvoir defends the "abundance of details" that "might seem tedious at first," as necessary "to anchor us in this foreign reality," and she praises Morante's rendering—and denouncing—the "fabulous aura" of the little boy's "awestruck love for his elders." Beauvoir concludes much as Holveck does, with an appreciation of Morante's ability to "make us feel the irreducible uniqueness of each human existence," through literature and not "abstract reasoning"—although Beauvoir quotes here not from her own work cited by Holveck, but from Sartre's famously abstract *Critique of Dialectical Reason*.

## NOTES

1. Eleanore Holveck, Introduction, in Simone de Beauvoir, *"The Useless Mouths" and Other Literary Writings*, ed. Margaret A. Simons and Marybeth Timmermann (Urbana: University of Illinois Press, 2011), 309.

2. Holveck offers the following note: "Various dates are given for Morante's birth. I am using the one from Alberto Moravia and Alain Elkann, *Life of Moravia*, trans. William Weaver (South Royalton, Vt.: Steerforth Press, 2000), 134."

3. Holveck inserts the following note: "Typically, in an interview Moravia (*Life of Moravia*, cited above, ibid., 242) mentions only Sartre and Camus, and Beauvoir mentions only Moravia in *Force of Circumstance*, trans. Richard Howard (London: Penguin, 1968), 109." Holveck notes later in her Introduction that "Alberto Moravia commented that Elsa Morante 'considered herself the greatest writer—as all writers do,' which obviously irritated him; he complained of her 'constant, obsessive affirmation of her own personality and independence' (quoting from Moravia, *Life*, 210, 213)." (Holveck, Introduction, 310).

4. Holveck, Introduction, 309.

5. Elsa Morante, *History: A Novel*, trans. William Weaver (New York: Knopf, 1977), 77–78.

6. Simone de Beauvoir, *Ethics of Ambiguity*, trans. Bernard Frechtman (New York: Citadel, 1976), 135.

7. Holveck, Introduction, 309.

8. Ibid., 310.

# FOREWORD TO *HISTORY: A NOVEL*

TRANSLATION BY MARYBETH TIMMERMANN

*History* is the title of the latest novel by Elsa Morante.[1] However, don't expect to find in these pages epic or tragic tales of the dramas that have shaken the world from antiquity to modern times. In Elsa Morante's eyes, History is not the great collective events told in newspapers, recorded in books, and scrupulously summarized by her at the beginning of each chapter. Rather, it is the obscure repercussion of these events in the hearts and bodies of the individuals who experience them, usually without even understanding them. There are a small number of specialists, such as intellectuals and politicians, who comprehend the unfolding of events and attempt to participate in them lucidly. Some Italian critics have reproached Elsa Morante for not having chosen them for her heroes. For her, every life, even the most humble, is a human adventure that is unique and complete. "All lives, really," she writes, "have the same end: and two days, in the brief passion of a kid like Useppe, are not worth less than years."[2] She shows us beings unknown to the great History, tossed about and crushed by forces that are mysterious to them.[3]

The main character in this story—which takes place from 1941 to 1947—is Ida Ramundo,[4] described by the author as a poor woman with a "dull and immature mind."[5] By her side is her bastard son, the little Useppe, growing up in the innocence of childhood. Around them revolves a miserable little world of old folks, women, young people, and children. Thanks to this diversity, we see the traces of a picture emerge: Rome occupied by the Germans, liberated by the Allies, and delivered to postwar peace. But this portrait is revealed to us only in little pieces through the anguished and confused experiences that, for Elsa Morante, represent the only truth.

She describes these experiences with such an abundance of details that it might seem tedious at first. Further on, we realize that they are necessary to anchor us in this foreign reality that little by little becomes our own. Not only do we believe in the existence of Ida, but soon her universe is imposed upon us with staggering precision.[6]

Some will say this universe is basely materialistic. Finding shelter, clothing, and food for herself and her child are Ida's only concerns. But Elsa Morante admirably shows that these so-called materialistic concerns engage in each individual the entire human condition.[7] Hunger is not only the pangs of the stomach, but an entire, complex world of sensations and fantasies. It induces dreams, and sometimes it speaks the language of poetry: there are many poems and beautiful tales in this book. And in the last part, when the grip of poverty is somewhat loosened, readers rediscover the "Lies and Spells" that made Elsa Morante's first novels so charming.[8] Yet it is a painful charm. A little boy's awestruck love for his elders gives them a fabulous aura, yet even as we are made to share in this bedazzlement, Elsa Morante denounces it. She has us touch the very modest truth of these apparitions sublimated by a child's look.[9]

A precocious child who is weakened by starvation, Useppe dies at the end of the book; most of the other characters also die throughout the story. That is why in the mind of Ida, faced with the corpse of her son and about to go crazy,[10] "the scenes of the human story (History) [ . . . ] revolved, which she perceived as the multiple coils of an interminable murder."[11] This vision is undoubtedly that of the author, for she bitterly concludes that "History continues."[12]

If one wishes to draw a philosophical conclusion from Elsa Morante's novel, one could say that for her—as for Sartre in *Critique of Dialectical Reason*—the individual is *unsurpassable*. But she does not assign us this truth through abstract reasoning.[13] With remarkable mastery—without easy effects or useless pathos—she makes us feel the irreducible uniqueness of each human existence and the horror of the mutilations he suffers at the hands of what we call History.[14]

## NOTES

Foreword by Simone de Beauvoir, to Elsa Morante, *La Storia: Romanzo* (*History: A Novel*) in *Les écrits de Simone de Beauvoir*, ed. Claude Francis and Fernande Gontier (Paris: Gallimard, 1979), 580–82; © Éditions Gallimard, 1979. This foreword was written for a first limited English edition of this book (Franklin Center, Pa.: The Franklin Library, 1977), but only a shortened version of it appeared in that edition. The shortened version also appeared in Beauvoir, *"The Useless Mouths" and Other Literary Writings* (2011). Here the foreword is translated in its entirety.

1. Elsa Morante (1918–85), a famous Italian novelist, wrote about the impact of World War II on European society, particularly the common people, which can be noted in her novel, *La Storia: Romanzo* (*History: A Novel*), published in 1974. Her first novel, *Menzogna E. Sortilegio* (*House of Liars*) (1948), won the Viareggio Prize, and her last novel, *Aracoeli* (1982), won the *Prix Médicis étranger*.

2. Elsa Morante, *History: A Novel*, trans. William Weaver (New York: Knopf, 1977), 528–29.

3. The second half of this paragraph ("There are a small number of specialists . . . mysterious to them.") is omitted in the version that was previously published in English.

4. The surname Ramundo is omitted in the previously published English translation.

5. *History*, 546.

6. From "Thanks to this diversity . . ." to " . . . with staggering precision" is paraphrased in the version that was previously published in English.

7. Beauvoir writes "Mais Elsa Morante fait admirablement sentir que les soucis dits matériels engagent en chaque individu la condition humaine tout entière." In the previously published English translation, this sentence appears as "Elsa Morante's answer is to make us deeply aware of the extent to which the human spirit is revealed through the existential necessities of physical survival."

8. *Menzogna e sortilegio* was written in 1948 and translated into English as *House of Liars* by Adrienne Foulke (New York: Harcourt Brace, 1951). Beauvoir is referring to the title as it appeared in French translation, *Mensonges et sortilèges* (Lies and spells) by Michel Arnaud (Paris: Gallimard, 1967).

9. The specific references to Morante's books are omitted in the previously published translation. The last part of this paragraph, "And in the last part . . . by a child's look," is omitted and replaced with a paraphrase of a sentence that appeared in the first paragraph of the original: "Even the humblest life is a unique human adventure."

10. Again, the references to her book are omitted in the previous translation. This paragraph begins simply with "At the end of the book . . ." with no mention of Useppe's and the other characters' deaths.

11. *History*, 546.

12. Ibid., 555.

13. The specifically philosophical references are omitted in the previous translation, thus losing Beauvoir's comment on making a philosophical claim in a literary work. The first two sentences of this paragraph are paraphrased as, "We cannot transcend the individual, according to Morante."

14. The last part of this sentence, "and the horror of the mutilations he suffers at the hands of what we call History," is omitted in the previously published translation. The foreword concludes with the following: "Simone de Beauvoir, Paris, 1977."

## 9

The MLF and the Bobigny Affair

# INTRODUCTION

*by Sylvie Chaperon*

TRANSLATION BY MARYBETH TIMMERMANN

The following texts, published initially in *Le nouvel observateur* for the most part, are able to shed some light on the partnership that unites Simone de Beauvoir with the MLF (French Women's Liberation Movement). Three generations separate Simone de Beauvoir from the movement's young activists. Activists such as Claudine Monteil, who was twenty years old and deeply moved when she met the elderly lady of Schoelcher Street, was in her mother's womb when *The Second Sex* was published in 1949.[1] Whatever could have brought together these women of the baby boom and of May 1968, these radical feminists breaking away from the left wing, with an existentialist in her sixties who had never joined any feminist group?[2] The following contributions provide some keys to the answer.

## The Birth of the MLF

The first women's demonstrations took place in the spring of 1970 at the University of Vincennes. But the act marking the public birth of the movement was the placing of a wreath of flowers beneath the Arc de Triomphe in memory of the wife of the Unknown Soldier. Paris was deserted as usual that month of August when a handful of women (nine total!) thus sought to show their solidarity with the American strikers.[3] The banners read, "One man in two is a woman";[4] "More unknown than the Unknown Soldier is his wife." The following day, the newspaper headlines spoke of the birth of the "French Woman's Liberation Movement."[5]

When summer vacation was over, the movement really took shape and expanded. As Beauvoir says in "The Rebellious Woman" interview, it thrived on the refusal of any organization and gambled on pure spontaneity. There were neither membership cards nor internal rules, nor elections. The only rallying points were the general assembly meetings held at the Beaux Arts school (sacred site of student revolts) every other week amid smoke and hubbub, with no schedule or agenda, no one presiding over the meeting, and no prearranged speakers. "Each time, the number of girls increased, as well as the confusion. A magnificent and invigorating ebullition. You could hardly understand anything, and barely see; it was absolutely impossible to get in a word," says Anne Zelensky, one of the very first activists.[6] And most of the initiatives of the movement were born of these bimonthly meetings.

In October, a special edition of *Partisans* was published, entitled *Libéra-tion des femmes, année zéro* (Women's liberation, year one), coordinated by Anne Zelensky and Jacqueline Feldman.[7] Shortly afterward, Simone de Beauvoir met with the activists who had initiated this edition. Who made the first move toward the other? This point remains unclear. In the last volume of her memoirs, Simone de Beauvoir writes, "At the end of 1970, several members of the Women's Liberation Movement contacted me."[8] Yet according to Anne Zelensky, "Our movement, called MLF, had barely gotten started when Simone asked to meet us. Noble blood cannot lie."[9]

In any case the meeting was inevitable. Anne Zelensky, Christine Delphy, and other young women wanted to launch a massive campaign to lift the restrictions on abortion. They couldn't do it without resorting to the media. *Le nouvel observateur*, started in 1964 and directed by Jean Daniel, was a weekly beacon of the New Left (with a print run climbing from 175,000 copies in 1971 to more than 400,000 three years later) and showed itself to be particularly open to the protest movements that had been flourishing since the 1960s. One of its journalists contacted them and introduced them to Jean Moreau, the director of the research department who had close ties to the Maoists and to Jean-Paul Sartre, himself a supporter of the periodical. The journal agreed to publish a manifesto on the subject as long as some celebrities were associated with it. And Simone de Beauvoir was without a doubt the most famous Frenchwoman of the time, and also the author of the most radical writing on the issue. "Well, I think it's a very good idea. As far as I'm concerned, I'll sign this manifesto," was Beauvoir's immediate response, and she then proposed a list of "personalities."[10]

The names of some well-known actresses (Catherine Deneuve, Jeanne Moreau, Delphine Seyrig) and renowned women writers (Marguerite Duras, Christiane Rochefort, Françoise Sagan) were mixed with a crowd of unknowns in the list of 343 names following the text.[11] Their presence, although condemned by a part of the movement as "celebrity hype," was indispensable for the popularization of the manifesto by the media as well as for putting a damper on possible legal prosecution. They signed their names to a short and incisive text that finished with the public statement of having broken the law: "One million women get abortions each year in France. They do it under dangerous conditions because of the secrecy to which they are condemned, although the procedure, when carried out by medical professionals, is extremely simple. These millions of women are silenced. I declare that I am one of them. I declare that I've had an abortion."[12]

To take on the responsibility of defending them an association called Choisir (To Choose) was founded by Gisèle Halimi, a lawyer known for having defended Algerian nationalists, and presided over by Simone de Beauvoir. On April 5, 1971, the manifesto was published also in *Le monde*, and it had the effect of a bombshell; the entire media was talking about it; letters of support and good wishes poured in. One success leads to another, and the activists planned a rally and public hearing to denounce crimes against women, which would take place at the Mutualité meeting hall on May 13 and 14, 1972. The idea of an interview came about during the preparation for this event. It was above all financially motivated to get the money to rent the room at the Mutualité hall. *Le nouvel observateur*'s interview with Beauvoir earned 2,000 francs and appeared on newsstands February 14, 1972.

## An Historic Interview?

Alice Schwartzer, a German radio and television journalist reporting from Paris, saw the birth of the MLF and right away got involved in the fight to legalize abortion, which incidentally, she also took back to her own country. "It was an historic interview," she asserted, "Here Simone de Beauvoir is proclaiming loud and clear, 'I am a feminist.'"[13] Indeed, the text of the interview was translated into many languages and circulated among women's groups. But the novelty of the piece did not lie in the philosopher's adherence to feminism. Simone de Beauvoir had been defining herself as a feminist for quite some time. As early as a November 1949 radio interview, soon after the publication of her book, she had this response to Claudine Chonez concerning the suffragists: "After all they were feminists and rightly so, and certainly I also am one."[14] In 1965, she declared to Francis Jeanson, "I am radically feminist."[15]

The novelty came from the fact that, from that point on, she refused socialism's leadership of women, and instead advocated autonomous women-only movements. From the last few pages of *The Second Sex* to the end of the 1960s, Simone de Beauvoir remained constant: women's equality would be gained individually through economic independence and collectively through the socialist revolution. In the autumn of 1968 she still thought that "the solution to the problem of women will be able to exist only when there is a global social solution, and the best thing that women can do is to get involved in things other than themselves. This is what I have tried to do. I mean that I have gotten involved in political issues, like the Vietnam War or the Algerian War, much more readily and with much more conviction than in women's issues strictly speaking, since I do not think they can be resolved in the current structure of society."[16]

Why did she change her mind? In the interview, Simone de Beauvoir mentions the insufficiencies of socialist countries, the inequality reigning in the organizations of the Far Left, and the women's groups that, until the MLF, "were reformist and legalistic." This last assertion is not completely true, since the French Movement for Family Planning, for example, had already chosen the path of illegality by procuring contraceptives for its members. That fight had resulted in the Neuwirth Law of 1967, which legalized contraception. But no association had taken up as its own the demand set out in the pages of *The Second Sex* for an end to the restrictions on abortion.

Her conversion to the idea of a women's movement was thus the fruit of her participation in the MLF, at least in one of its components. The movement had "different tendencies," she says. "I personally tend to want to link women's emancipation to the class struggle," she adds. But this is a truism for anything surrounding the MLF because of how much the Marxist schema and leftist ideology permeated all progressive movements in France. Revolutionary rhetoric was in full force; "petit bourgeois," and "reformist" were widespread anathemas. Several lengthy passages in the interview show that capitalist oppression of the working class remained the only accepted model, the standard to which all the other dominations were compared, or even subordinated.

Three important tendencies ran through the MLF, with no precise boundaries. Many activists were unaware of them and rallied to the actions of all three. The psychoanalysis and political group, led by Antoinette Fouque and inspired by the theories of Lacan and Luce Irigaray,[17] attempted to bring to light an unconscious and irreducible feminine nature. It refused the name *feminist* for a long time and kept itself at a distance from most of the demands and struggles of the movement, producing a rather hermetic conceptualization. The class struggle tendency leaned toward reintegrating the feminist struggle into the bosom of socialism. Finally, the revolutionary feminists, taking a Beauvoirian line, challenged any idea of feminine nature, and in addition asserted the autonomy of women's domination and resistance. This was the faction that Simone de Beauvoir joined. Two aspects of it attracted her from the beginning: the refusal of biological determinism, which was very well theorized by the revolutionary feminists, and the fight for unrestricted abortion.

Nonetheless, at that time she remained reticent about several theoretical points. Contrary to Christine Delphy, who in "L'ennemi principal" (The main enemy) asserted that women are materially oppressed by the patriarchal mode of production, Beauvoir judged these analyses to be "insufficient," refused to envision household work as a "surplus value," and spoke of women as a caste, and not a class.[18] She also found "tedious and irritating" the "mystique of the clitoris" and "all those sexual dogmas" that she attributed to homosexuals alone. Finally, she considered separatism as a necessary stage for women in overcoming their alienation, while the revolutionary feminists made it a major political claim, denying that the oppressor ever has a place in liberation struggles. On these points, her thought would be gradually radicalized over the years. In 1973, in her preface to *Avortement: une loi en procès* (Abortion: A law on trial), she speaks of the "housewife whose efforts are extorted almost gratuitously."

One could also contest Alice Schwartzer's assertion that *The Second Sex* inspired "the new women's movements." Alice Schwarzer, although born in 1942, is speaking for another generation of women, those of the "Beauvoir years":[19] "immersed in those years of the 50s and 60s, before the new Women's Movement, this book was like a secret code that we, women on the way to awakening, passed from one to another."[20] But in the second half of the 1960s, works like *The Feminine Mystique* by Betty Friedan or *La condition de la française d'aujourd 'hui* (The condition of the Frenchwoman today) by Andrée Michel and Geneviève Texier had taken the lead. Although *The Second Sex* had a prominent place in most of the young activists' libraries, it was among many other works that were more recent and more decisive. Germaine Greer, Juliet Mitchell, Shulamith Firestone, and Kate Millett, all mentioned in the interview, along with others such as Ti-Grace Atkinson, became indispensable references. Many of these theoreticians said they were indebted to Beauvoir, but they also surpassed her. The influence of the American movement, which had started two years before its French counterpart, thus showed itself to be determinant. Half of the special edition of *Partisans*, which was the first theoretical collection put forth by the brand new French movement, was made up of American translations. Faced with this renewal of feminist radicalism, even *The Second Sex* began to look seriously old-fashioned, although its fierceness had remained unequaled for a long time. And incidentally, some rather harsh words on Beauvoir can be found in *Partisans*.

Also, the collaboration of these different generations was fraught with difficulties. All the young women of the MLF were struck by Simone de Beauvoir's modesty, her attentiveness, her kindness and her availability, "a touching sign of her good education. And the way she held her purse tightly upon her knees."[21] The meetings always started late and never with the same people, everyone speaking at the same time, and decisions, frequently questioned and challenged, took a long time. "Simone de Beauvoir, frightened by this hubbub, told me that she would prefer to come to smaller meetings focused on a precise theme," related Anne Zelensky in regards to the preparation for the conference at the Mutualité meeting hall.[22] Irritated by the activists' mode of operation, Gisèle Halimi (born in 1927) slammed her door shut and withdrew from the project. She wanted the denunciation of crimes to take the shape of a trial in due form with prestigious witnesses. The young women of the MLF wanted all the speakers to be ordinary women from all walks of life.

The interview gave rise to letters and debates. Simone de Beauvoir responded in an article in *Le nouvel observateur* to the reactions of several women and one man. This allowed her to correct and expand upon her earlier remarks. Leaving behind the militant forum, she addresses more ordinary women: married women, mothers, unemployed women. It also showed all of Beauvoir's polemic talents. The man in question is Maurice Clavel, professor of philosophy, veteran of the Resistance, novelist, and essayist, who had been contributing on a regular basis to the weekly magazine since 1967, and according to its director, he knew how to "make a splash."[23] In an article entitled "Les gardiennes de l'ordre" (The female guardians of order) (*Le nouvel observateur*, February 21, 1972), he decided to "finally explain myself seriously to those women" of the MLF.[24] Basically, he reproached them for imitating men instead of feminizing the world, and had this double-entendre formula: "révolution sexuelle: piège à cons" (the sexual revolution is a stupid chick trap).[25]

## Bobigny

Gisèle Halimi and Simone de Beauvoir had known each other for a long time. Together they had fought against torture during the Algerian War and against the Vietnam War at the Russell Tribunal.[26] The "Manifeste des 343" (Manifesto of the 343) and the Choisir association brought them together again. Sixteen-year-old Marie-Claire Chevalier had had an abortion with the help of an abortionist and the support of her mother, an RATP employee who was raising her three daughters alone.[27] Marie-Claire's former boyfriend, who was responsible for the pregnancy after forcing himself on her, turned her in, and the three women were arrested. Gisèle Halimi and the Choisir association took charge of their defense. Since Marie-Claire was a minor, the trial was divided into two parts: on October 11, 1972, it went before a juvenile court (behind closed doors), while the mother and her accomplices faced the judges of the criminal court [*tribunal correctionnel*], on November 8, 1972.

At that time, abortion was still punishable by prison in France. Article 317 of the penal code of 1810 still remained in force. In addition, the law of 1920, voted on after the hemorrhaging of the Great War with the purpose of ending the neo-Malthusian movement,[28] forbade pro-contraception propaganda and the "inciting" of abortion. The repressive law wasn't working, so three years later, the law of 1923 changed the status of abortion from a felony to a misdemeanor. The legislature hoped that the judges who hear the misdemeanor cases in the *tribunal correctionnel* would show themselves to be less indulgent than the juries who decide the felony cases in the *cours d'assises*.[29] Although the number of abortions hardly decreased, the repression succeeded in breaking up the neo-Malthusian movement. Following World War II, Simone de Beauvoir stood out as one of the rare exceptions who continued the fight. The Neuwirth law of December 1967, which authorized contraception, reopened the debate. The decrees affecting the application of the law were put off indefinitely, and there was no publicity campaign informing the public of the new law, which explains the very small percentage of women using contraception cited by Beauvoir. But most proposals calling for change remained very moderate, suggesting only broader criteria for medically necessary abortions in specific cases. Only the MLF demanded that all women have the freedom to control their own bodies.

Disagreements arose during the tumultuous debates at the Choisir association's general assemblies. Gisèle Halimi, who ultimately prevailed, wanted a big political trial with Nobel Prize winners and internationally recognized scholars such as Jacques Monod, Paul Milliez, and Jean Rostand testifying. The women of the MLF, whose side Beauvoir took, wanted to let "anonymous" women speak, and not male "specialists." Above all, Gisèle Halimi insisted upon the socially unjust aspect of the law, while the activists affirmed the common oppression to which women of all socioeconomic groups were subjected. The absence of real democracy within the association also gave rise to criticism. These differences of opinion came to a head over Annie Cohen's testimony. She was a well-off MLF activist whose abortion had taken place in good conditions yet was accompanied by a feeling of distress. Her testimony was meant to illustrate the situation common to all women, rich or poor, caused by the ban on abortion. Gisèle Halimi, supported by the accused, refused to allow her to testify at the public trial. To show her disapproval, Simone de Beauvoir resigned as president of Choisir.

These tensions did not prevent Beauvoir from coming to testify at the second trial or from writing the preface to the publication of the complete record of the pleadings (a publication explicitly forbidden by law),[30] but they explain the content of her positions. In both her "Deposition" and "Preface," Simone de Beauvoir moves away noticeably from the argumentative strategy used previously in *The Second Sex*. Back then she was using any available means. The law penalized only the poorest of women since wealthy women were able to go to foreign clinics. An operation that would be benign if performed in good sanitary conditions became dangerous because of the ban. Unwanted children were increasing the numbers of those on public assistance, and too many children compromised family life. The same highly exaggerated figure (used by supporters as well as by adversaries of abortion) of one million abortions per year was still being used nearly twenty-five years later. On the other hand, new ideas—that motherhood formed the cornerstone of women's exploitation and that the abortion struggle was the means toward a much broader liberation—made sense in the context of the ideological struggles within the MLF. By emphasizing these two points, the unity of women's condition and women's liberation were assured. Through her "Deposition" and this "Preface," Simone de Beauvoir provided a platform for revolutionary feminist positions: with class struggles put aside, male dominance could be seen clearly.

Gisèle Halimi, for her part, was a socialist who supported the proposal of a bill to legalize abortion[31] and emphasized the social inequality of the law that penalized mostly the poorest classes. Should this be seen as an expression of the class struggle tendency? Probably not since, as a shrewd politician, she understood that, "this aspect was what crystallized and unified public opinion," for she wanted to reach the public as well as the judges.[32]

But beyond the tactical divergences, intensified by the importance of mobilization and by the personality of each one, the two women shared rather similar analyses. In "L'avortement des pauvres" (Abortion and the poor), which came out October 16, 1972, and therefore before the conflict and her resignation from the presidency, Beauvoir had denounced not only the risks and the high cost encountered by poor women with no "social influence," but also the "class justice" that never attacks "rich bourgeois women." Her loyalty to the MLF activists led her to change her argumentation just after that.

The controversy resurfaced a year later, when Grasset published La cause des femmes (The cause of women) in which Gisèle Halimi presented her version of the facts. Annie Cohen, "the anonymous face on duty" responded angrily to Gisèle Halimi, "the star on duty" (Le nouvel observateur, November 26, 1973). Using a moderate tone, Beauvoir brought attention to the lawyer's contradictions in a short insert. "Where are her true convictions?" she asked. But the question could just as well have been asked of her. The affair revealed the inevitable changes in opinion by intellectuals caught in the heat of action and Beauvoir's engagement with the analyses of revolutionary feminists.[33]

Marie-Claire was released and her "accomplices" received minor sentences. We can never know the magnitude that a trial organized by the MLF would have had, but the one orchestrated by Gisèle Halimi had a considerable impact. Despite the conflict in their interactions, both women were involved in the events that rocked public opinion: in 1970 only 22 percent of French people stated that they favored ending restrictions on abortion, and one year later, the number was 55 percent.[34]

## NOTES

1. Claudine Monteil, "Simone de Beauvoir et le mouvement des femmes. Un témoignage" (Simone de Beauvoir and the women's movement: A testimony) in Le cinquantenaire du "Deuxième sexe" (Fifty years after The Second Sex), edited by Christine Delphy and Sylvie Chaperon (Paris: Syllepse, 2002), 305–9. [Tr. Simone de Beauvoir lived on Schoelcher Street during the last several decades of her life.]

2. Jacques Zéphir, Le néo-féminisme de Simone de Beauvoir. Trente ans après "Le deuxième sexe": un post-scriptum (The neofeminism of Simone de Beauvoir. Thirty years after The Second Sex: A postscript) (Paris: Denoël-Gonthier, 1982). [Tr. The widespread rioting in May of 1968 involved students and workers across France who showed their discontent by erecting barricades in the streets and going on strike for several weeks.]

3. [Tr. August is traditionally vacation time for Parisians, the majority of whom close shop and leave town during this month. In the United States, on August 26, 1970, Betty Friedan led the Women's Strike for Equality in New York City on the fiftieth anniversary of women's suffrage.]

4. This famous slogan attacks the standard practice of using "man" to refer to both men and women.

5. [Tr. Although first referred to as the "Mouvement de libération de la femme" (Woman's Liberation Movement), the name was soon changed to "Mouvement de libération des femmes" (Women's Liberation Movement).]

6. Annie de Pisan and Anne Tristan, *Histoires du MLF* (Stories of the French Women's Liberation Movement) (Paris: Calmann-Lévy, 1977), 59.

7. Sylvie Chaperon, *Les années Beauvoir* (The Beauvoir years) (Paris: Fayard, 2000).

8. Simone de Beauvoir, *Tout compte fait* (*All Said and Done*) (Paris: Gallimard, 1972), 492.

9. Anne Zelensky, "Castor for ever," in *Le cinquantenaire du "Deuxième sexe,"* 310–13. [Tr. The French proverb is "Bon sang ne peut mentir," which can also be translated as "Blood will tell."]

10. Pisan and Tristan, *Histoires du MLF*, 67.

11. Bibia Pavard, "Qui sont les 343 du manifeste de 1971?" (Who are the 343 of the 1971 Manifesto?), in Christine Bard, ed., *Les féministes de la deuxième vague* (Second wave feminists) (Rennes: Presses universitaires de Rennes, 2012), 71–84.

12. *Le nouvel observateur*, March 31, 1971.

13. Alice Schwarzer, *Simone de Beauvoir aujourd'hui. Six entretiens* (Paris: Mercure de France, 1984), 16, translated as *After The Second Sex: Conversations with Simone de Beauvoir* by Marianne Howarth (New York: Pantheon, 1984), 16.

14. Retransmitted by "Les jours du siècle" (The days of the century) radio program, France Inter, February 17, 1999.

15. Francis Jeanson, *Simone de Beauvoir ou l'entreprise de vivre, suivi d'entretiens avec Simone de Beauvoir* (Simone de Beauvoir or the business of living, followed by interviews with Simone de Beauvoir) (Paris: Le Seuil, 1966), 258. [Tr. Francis Jeanson was a French author and political activist who served as one of the directors of *Les temps modernes* from 1962–67.]

16. "La femme entre le défi de la suffragette et la passivité de la femme-objet, Simone de Beauvoir trace la voie de la femme pleinement réalisée" (Woman between the defiance of the suffragist and the passivity of the woman-object, Simone de Beauvoir traces the path of the fully realized woman), an interview by Martine de Barsy in *Pénéla: Connaître et comprendre* (Know and understand), September 1968, cited by Zéphir in *Le néo-féminisme de Simone de Beauvoir. Trente ans après "Le deuxième sexe": un post-scriptum*, 36.

17. [Tr. Jacques Lacan (1901–81) was a French psychoanalyst and psychiatrist who was heavily influenced by Sigmund Freud; Luce Irigaray (1932–present) is a Belgian feminist author and interdisciplinary thinker who works among philosophy, psychoanalysis, and linguistics.]

18. Christine Delphy (Christine Dupont, pseud.), "L'ennemi principal," in *Partisans, Libération des femmes: Année zéro*, 1970, July–October. [Tr. The English translation by Lucy Ap Roberts and Diane Leonard Barker was published in 1977 by the Women's Research & Resources Centre in London.]

19. Chaperon, *Les années Beauvoir*.

20. Schwarzer, *Simone de Beauvoir aujourd'hui*, 11.

21. Ibid., 15.

22. Pisan and Tristan, *Histoires du MLF*, 89.

23. Maurice Clavel, *La suite appartient à d'autres* (What comes next belongs to others) (Paris: Stock, 1979), 8.

24. Clavel's article "Les gardiennes de l'ordre" was reprinted in his book *La suite appartient à d'autres*, 149–51.

25. [Tr. The formula was already popularized by Sartre with "élections: pièges à cons" (elections: idiot traps), but in regard to sexuality, Maurice Clavel is using the double meaning of the word "con," which is a vulgarism designating the vulva (as well as the common meaning of "idiot"). He was probably reacting to the second volume of *Le torchon brûle* (Battle brewing/ Dishcloth burning) (September 1971), the MLF's "menstrual" newspaper (in itself a play on the word "mensuel" which means "monthly"), which showed a photo supporting "the power of the 'con,'" and about which the office of the public prosecutor filed a complaint.]

26. See Simone de Beauvoir and Gisèle Halimi, *Djamila Boupacha* (Paris: Gallimard, 1962). [Tr. The Russell Tribunal was an international body organized in 1966 by British philosopher and pacifist Bertrand Russell in order to investigate and publicize war crimes committed by the United States and its allies in Vietnam.]

27. [Tr. RATP stands for *Régie Autonome des Transports Parisiens*, which is responsible for public transportation in the Parisian metropolitan area, including subway, buses, trains, etc.]

28. [Tr. This movement was based on the theories of T. R. Malthus, who believed that the increasing population would eventually deplete supplies and resources unless disease, war, or sexual restraint slowed the population rate. The neo-Malthusians advocated contraception rather than chastity to curb population growth.]

29. [Tr. In France, judges determine the sentence in the *tribunaux correctionnels*, whereas in the *cours d'assises*, the sentence is determined by the jury, which tends to be more indulgent.]

30. [Tr. *Avortement: Une loi en procès. L'affaire de Bobigny. Sténotypie intégrale des débats du tribunal de Bobigny, 8 novembre 1972*, Preface by Simone de Beauvoir (Paris: Idées/Gallimard, 1973); translated by Beryl Henderson as *Abortion: The Bobigny Affair: A Law on Trial: A Complete Record of the Pleadings at the Court of Bobigny, 8 November, 1972* (Sydney: Wild and Woolley, 1975).]

31. [Tr. This bill was passed into law on January 17, 1975, legalizing abortions in certain circumstances. It is also known as the Veil Law because Simone Veil, then Minister of Health, presented the bill to the National Assembly in November 1974.]

32. See Gisèle Halimi, *La cause des femmes* (The cause of women) (Paris: Gallimard, 1992), 96.

33. Sylvie Chaperon, "'Momone' et les 'bonnes femmes' ou Beauvoir et le MLF" (Simone and the girls, or Beauvoir and the MLF), in C. Bard, ed., *Les féministes de la deuxième vague*, 85–96.

34. Jean-Yves Le Naour and Catherine Valenti, *Histoire de l'avortement, XIXe–XXe siècle* (The history of abortion in the nineteenth and twentieth centuries) (Paris: Seuil, 2003), 228; and Catherine Valenti, *Bobigny le procès de l'avortement* (Paris: Larousse, 2010).

# THE REBELLIOUS WOMAN—
# AN INTERVIEW BY ALICE SCHWARTZER

TRANSLATION BY MARYBETH TIMMERMANN

NOTES BY MARGARET A. SIMONS

AND MARYBETH TIMMERMANN

ALICE SCHWARTZER: To this day, the analysis of the situation of women that you put forth in *The Second Sex* remains the most radical. No other author has gone as far, and it can be said that you have inspired the new women's movements. But it is only now, twenty-three years later, that you have engaged yourself personally in the concrete and collective struggle of women. So last November you participated in the international women's march in Paris. Why?

SIMONE DE BEAUVOIR: Because I find that, in the twenty years that have just passed, the situation of women in France has not really changed. They have obtained a few small things in the laws pertaining to marriage and divorce. The availability of contraception has increased, but insufficiently, since only 7 percent of French women are on the Pill. In the work world, they have not made serious gains either. There are maybe a few more women who work now than before, but not many.

In any case, they are still confined to situations of little importance. They are secretaries and not CEOs, nurses more often than doctors. The most interesting and profitable careers are practically forbidden to them, and even from within the professions, their advancement is barred. All these factors got me thinking [*réfléchir*]. I thought that women, if they wanted their situation to change, must take matters into their own hands. Besides, the women's groups that existed in France before the French Women's Liberation Movement,[1] created in 1970, were reformist and legalistic. I had no desire to join them. The new feminism is, on the contrary, radical. It reiterates the 1968 slogan: Change life this very day. Don't count on the future, but act immediately.

When the women of the MLF contacted me, I wanted to join their struggle. They asked me to work on drafting an abortion manifesto saying that we, I and others, had had abortions. I thought that it was a valid move that would attract attention to one of the most outrageous issues facing France today: the abortion problem. It was therefore very natural for me to go down into the streets and march with the MLF activists in November of 1971, adopting their slogans as my own: legal and free abortion, legal and free contraception, voluntary motherhood.

ALICE SCHWARTZER: You speak of the situation in France, but you have visited certain socialist countries. Has the situation of women fundamentally changed in those countries?

SIMONE DE BEAUVOIR: It is a bit different. For example, I have seen the situation of women in the USSR [Union of Soviet Socialist Republics] up close.[2] Almost all Soviet women work, and the women who do not work (wives of some high-ranking government workers or other very important people) are looked down upon by the others. Soviet women are very proud of working. They have rather considerable political and social responsibilities and a sense of their responsibilities. However, if you consider the number of women who are found in the central committee or in the assemblies, which have the real power, it is very small compared to the number of men. For the most part, women practice the least agreeable and least sought-after professions. In the USSR, almost all doctors are women. This is because the doctor's profession—medical treatment being free—is extremely hard, tiring, and poorly remunerated by the State.

Women are restricted to medicine and teaching while the more important careers like the sciences and professional engineering, etc., are much less accessible to them. Professionally, they are therefore not equal to men; furthermore, they and women everywhere encounter the same outrage— against which the women of the MLF are fighting: the onus of household duties and caring for children falls entirely upon women.

This is very striking, for example, in Solzhenitsyn's book *The Cancer Ward*,[3] about a woman who is a senior consultant in a hospital and a respected figure in medical science, but when she leaves her patients after an exhausting day at the hospital, she hurries home to make dinner and do the dishes for her husband and children. She is also the one who waits in line for hours in the stores. So in addition to all her extremely weighty professional tasks, she piles on her domestic duties, just as in other countries. And even maybe more so than in France, where a woman in an analogous situation would have domestic help.

Their condition is better in a sense, but more difficult, than that of women in capitalistic countries. We can draw the conclusion that in the USSR as in other countries, equality between men and women is not at all realized.

ALICE SCHWARTZER: What are the reasons for this?

SIMONE DE BEAUVOIR: Well, first of all, the socialist countries are not really socialist. A socialism that would change mankind [*l'homme*] such as Marx dreamed of, has not been realized anywhere. The relations of production have been changed, but we understand more and more that changing the relations of production is not sufficient to really change society, to change mankind.[4] And consequently, in spite of this different economic system, the traditional roles of men and women remain. It is tied to the fact that in our societies, men have profoundly internalized, through what I would call a superiority complex, the idea of their superiority. They are not ready to abandon it. They need to see women as inferior in order to valorize themselves. As for women, they are so used to believing themselves inferior that rare are the women who fight to win equality.

ALICE SCHWARTZER: There are many misunderstandings about the notion of feminism. I would like you to give me your definition.

SIMONE DE BEAUVOIR: At the end of *The Second Sex*, I said that I was not a feminist because I thought that the solution to women's problems must be found in a socialist evolution of society. By being feminist, I meant fighting for specifically women's demands independently of the class struggle. Today I maintain the same definition: I would say that feminists are women or even men who fight to change the condition of women, of course in conjunction with the class struggle, but also outside of that struggle, without totally subordinating this change to that of society. And I would say that today I am a feminist in that way, because I have come to understand that we must fight for the concrete condition of women before our dreams of socialism can come true. And, in addition, I have come to understand that, even in socialist countries, this equality has not been achieved. Women must therefore take their destiny into their own hands. That is why I have now joined the Women's Liberation Movement.

Furthermore, I have noticed—and this is also one of the reasons, in my opinion, that many women have created the movement—that even in the activities of the French Left and even in leftist movements, there has been a profound inequality between men and women. Women have always been the ones to do the most humble, tedious, and self-effacing tasks, and the men have always been the spokesmen, writing articles and doing all the most interesting things requiring the greatest responsibility.

Therefore, even at the heart of these movements which, in principle, are made to liberate everyone—young people as well as women—women have remained inferior. And it doesn't stop there. I won't say all, but many male leftists are aggressively hostile toward women's liberation. They scorn women and show it. The first time that a feminist meeting was held at Vincennes, a group of male leftists broke into the room shouting, "Power is at the end of the phallus." I think they are beginning to revise that position, but that is only because women are taking a militant action independently of them.

ALICE SCHWARTZER: In general, what are your positions toward the new feminists, those young women in the fight who are more radical than ever?

SIMONE DE BEAUVOIR: You know, there is—at least in America where the movement is the most advanced—a whole spectrum of tendencies, from Betty Friedan who is rather conservative to what is called SCUM, which is a movement for the emasculation of all men.[5] And between these two positions, there are many others. In France also, it seems to me that there are different tendencies within the movement. I personally tend to want to link women's emancipation to the class struggle. I believe that the battle women are fighting, although it is unique [*singulier*], is tied to the battle they must fight along with men. Consequently I completely reject the total repudiation of men.

ALICE SCHWARTZER: So what do you think of the women-only rule within the groups, which, at this stage, has been adopted by the majority of the women's movements?

SIMONE DE BEAUVOIR: As you just said, it is a stage. I think that, for the moment, it's a good thing, for several reasons. First, if men were admitted into these groups, they would not be able to stop themselves from the masculine reflex of wanting to take charge and impose themselves. Also, many women still have—regardless of what they say and even sometimes

195

without their being aware of it—a certain feeling of inferiority, a certain timidity. There would be many who would not dare to speak freely in front of men. And in particular, they must know that they will not feel judged by the man who shares their life, because it is in regards to him that they also must liberate themselves . . .

ALICE SCHWARTZER: . . . and analyze their specific oppression?

SIMONE DE BEAUVOIR: That's right. For the moment, neither the mentality of men nor that of women would allow for a truly honest discussion to take place in a mixed group.

ALICE SCHWARTZER: But isn't this temporary exclusion of men also a political issue?[6] Given that they represent the system and that, in addition, it is they who individually oppress women, don't feminists in this first stage see men as the "main enemy"?

SIMONE DE BEAUVOIR: Yes, but it's rather complicated because, as Marx said regarding capitalists, they are also victims. It is too abstract to say, like I used to think, that only the system should be blamed. Men should also be blamed because one can not with impunity be an accomplice and beneficiary of a system, even if one did not establish it oneself. A man living today did not found this patriarchal regime, but he profits from it, even if he is one of those who criticize it. And he has internalized it.

We must blame the system but at the same time remain, not hostile toward but at least suspicious of, men and behave prudently so as not to allow them to encroach upon our own activities, our own possibilities. We must attack the system and men at the same time. Even if a man is feminist, we must keep our distance and beware of paternalism. Women don't want equality bestowed upon them; they want to win it, which is not at all the same thing.

ALICE SCHWARTZER: And you personally, in hindsight, did you have this suspicion, this hatred toward men?

SIMONE DE BEAUVOIR: No. I always got along very well with the men who were a part of my life. Besides, many women of the MLF whom I know do not hate men either, but rather have a prudent attitude, a desire to not let themselves be devoured.

ALICE SCHWARTZER: Do you think that it is a good thing, politically, for some women to take it even further?

SIMONE DE BEAUVOIR: Perhaps. It actually might not be a bad thing that there are women who are totally radical and who completely reject men. They lead the way for those who would otherwise be willing to make certain compromises. That is very possible.

ALICE SCHWARTZER: In the majority of women's movements, there is a homosexual undercurrent—which in no way constitutes a majority, as people are often led to believe—but which gives considerable impetus to these movements. Do you think that female homosexuality—as the most radical form of excluding men—can be a political weapon in the current phase of the struggle?

SIMONE DE BEAUVOIR: I have not given it much thought [*réfléchi*]. I think that in principle, it is good that there are some very radical women. Homosexual women can play a useful role. But when they allow themselves to be obsessed with their biases, they run the risk of driving heterosexuals away from the movement. I find their mystique of the clitoris to be tedious and irritating, along with all those sexual dogmas they want to impose upon us.

ALICE SCHWARTZER: Their first argument is that, in the current circumstances, any sexual relationship with men is oppressive. They therefore refuse it. What do you think of this?

SIMONE DE BEAUVOIR: Is it really true that any sexual relationship between a man and a woman is oppressive? Couldn't one work toward, not refusing this relationship, but making it so that it isn't oppressive? The claim that all coitus is a rape shocks me. I do not believe this. When they say all coitus is a rape, they are taking up masculine myths again. That would mean that the man's sexual organ is a sword, a weapon. The issue is inventing new sexual relations that are not oppressive.

ALICE SCHWARTZER: You spoke a minute ago about your individual experience.[7] You told me, in a comment about *The Second Sex*, that the problem of femininity had not personally affected you and that you had felt you were in "a position of considerable impartiality." Did you mean that individually, a woman can escape her condition as a woman, in the professional world and in her relations with others?

SIMONE DE BEAUVOIR: Completely escape her condition as a woman? No! I have a woman's body. But really, I was very lucky. I escaped most of women's servitudes, those of motherhood and those of the housewife. And professionally, in my day fewer women pursued higher education. To graduate with an *agrégation* degree in philosophy was to be situated in a privileged way among women. As a result of my success, I was recognized by men; they were ready to give friendly recognition to a woman who succeeded as well as they did because it was rather exceptional. Now, many women pursue their studies seriously and men are afraid of losing their places. More generally, if you admit as I do that a woman is not obliged to be a wife and mother in order to have a complete and happy life, then some women can fully accomplish their lives without suffering from women's servitudes.[8]

ALICE SCHWARTZER: You have said, "The greatest success in my life is Sartre."

SIMONE DE BEAUVOIR: Yes.

ALICE SCHWARTZER: But you have always been deeply concerned with independence and fearful of being dominated. Even though an egalitarian relationship between a man and a woman is so difficult to establish, do you think that you personally achieved it?

SIMONE DE BEAUVOIR: Yes. Or, rather, the question never arose because Sartre is not at all an oppressor. If I had loved someone other than Sartre, I would never have let myself be oppressed, in any case. There are women who escape male domination—provided that they have professional autonomy. Some manage to have a balanced relationship with a man. Others have inconsequential affairs.

ALICE SCHWARTZER: You have spoken of women as an inferior class . . .

SIMONE DE BEAUVOIR: I did not speak of a class. But in *The Second Sex* I said that women were an inferior caste. The term *caste* refers to a group into which one is born and from which one can not escape. Whereas one can, in theory, escape from one class by moving into another. If you are a woman, you will never become a man. That is really being part of a caste. And the way women are treated economically, socially, and politically makes them an inferior caste.

ALICE SCHWARTZER: Some movements have gone even further. Based on domestic work, which is unpaid and without exchange value, they define women as a separate class, outside of the existing classes. That is to say that they posit patriarchal oppression as the principal, rather than secondary, contradiction. Do you agree with this analysis?

SIMONE DE BEAUVOIR: I find that the analyses on this point are insufficient. I would like to see a very serious study done on it. For example, in *Women's Estate*, Juliet Mitchell has shown how the question arises. But in this short book, she does not claim to resolve it. I remember that that was one of the first questions I posed when I met the MLF activists: According to you, how exactly are patriarchal oppression and capitalist oppression linked [*s'articule*]? For the moment I do not exactly see the answer. I would like to work on this point in the years to come. It is extremely interesting to me.

But I find that the analyses making patriarchal oppression equivalent to capitalist oppression do not ring true. The work of the housewife does not produce any surplus value: it is a different condition than that of the worker who is robbed of the surplus value of his work. I would like to know exactly what relation exists between the two. The strategy that women should follow depends entirely upon this.

It is exactly right to emphasize unpaid housework. But there are many women who earn their own living and who can not be considered as exploited in the same way as the housewife is.

ALICE SCHWARTZER: But even when a woman works outside of her home she is paid less than a man for the same job.

SIMONE DE BEAUVOIR: Yes, that's true. In general, salaries are not equal. But to return to my point, the exploitation of women as housewives differs in kind from that of workers. As I said, this is a point that has not been sufficiently studied in any of the books I have read: those by Kate Millett, Germaine Greer or [Shulamith] Firestone.

ALICE SCHWARTZER: Besides, they don't really bring up anything new as far as the analysis . . .

SIMONE DE BEAUVOIR: No. Neither Millett nor Greer. Only Firestone, who is less well-known, brought up something new in her book *Dialectic of Sex*. She associates the liberation of women with the liberation of children. This is true because women will only be liberated when they are liberated of children and at the same time children will be liberated, to a certain degree, of the adults.

ALICE SCHWARTZER: You were very much engaged in the class struggle after May of 1968. You took charge of a revolutionary newspaper[9] and demonstrated in the streets. In short you were a part of the fight. How do you see the relationship between the class struggle and the struggle between the sexes?

SIMONE DE BEAUVOIR: All that I can say, and what led me to modify the position I took in *The Second Sex*, is that the class struggle properly speaking does not emancipate women. Whether it's communists, Trotskyites, or Maoists, women are always subordinated to men. Consequently, I am convinced that women must truly be feminists, taking "the woman problem" into their own hands. Now, society must be analyzed in a completely serious way in order to try to understand the relationship between the exploitation of workers and the exploitation of women, and to what extent the elimination of capitalism would lead to more favorable conditions for women's emancipation. I don't know. That remains to be done. One thing of which I am certain is that eliminating capitalism would, at the same time, put things into a better place for women's emancipation. But it would still be far from achieved.

Eliminating capitalism does not mean the elimination of the patriarchal tradition, as long as the family remains. I think that we must not only eliminate capitalism and change the means of production, but we must also change the family structure. And that has not been done, not even in China. Of course, they have eliminated the feudal family, which brought great changes in the condition of women. But, to the extent that they accept the conjugal family, which is still basically an inheritance from the patriarchal family, I do not really think that women in China are liberated. I think the family must be eliminated. I completely agree with all the attempts by women, and also, incidentally, sometimes by men, to replace the family with either communes or other forms that have yet to be created.

ALICE SCHWARTZER: Could one say, then, that the class struggle does not inevitably resolve the condition of women, but that by bringing into question society and the existing relations between men and women, radical feminism inevitably resolves the class struggle?

SIMONE DE BEAUVOIR: No, not inevitably. If we begin by eliminating the family and family structures, it is likely that, as a result, capitalism will be weakened. But here again, I would not venture an opinion without having given the question much reflection. If women were to initiate the destruction of patriarchal society, to what extent would that achieve the elimination of every aspect of capitalism and technocracy?[10] That, I don't know.

If feminism makes totally radical demands, and if these demands prevail, then at that moment, it will truly threaten the system. But it will not be enough to reorganize the relations of production, the relations of work, and the relations between men—by that I mean human beings. There is not enough analysis on this matter because the women who were active in feminism were bourgeois women who fought politically.

They were suffragettes seeking to win the right to vote. They did not take a stand on the economy. And economically, there has been a willingness to settle for Marxist formulas such as: When socialism is here, there will automatically be equality between men and women. When I wrote *The Second Sex*, I was very surprised that it was poorly received by the Left. I remember a discussion with some Trotskyites who told me, "'The woman problem' is a false problem. There is no problem. Once the revolution takes place, women will naturally end up in their place."

There are also communists with whom I had many political disagreements at the time, and who ridiculed me a great deal. They wrote articles saying that the women working in Billancourt didn't give a damn about "the woman problem." Once the revolution had taken place, women would be men's equals. But they didn't care about what happened to women before the revolution.

I also hoped that things would improve much more in socialist countries than in capitalist countries. But in fact, nothing of the sort happened, apart from the nuances that I have already pointed out.

ALICE SCHWARTZER: After *The Second Sex* came out, you were often reproached for having stopped at analysis, without developing a strategy for women to follow in their struggle.

SIMONE DE BEAUVOIR: That's true! I recognize that this is a shortcoming in my book. I finish by expressing a vague confidence in the future, the revolution, and socialism.

ALICE SCHWARTZER: And today?

SIMONE DE BEAUVOIR: Today, I have changed. As I told you at the beginning; I have truly become a feminist.

ALICE SCHWARTZER: What concrete possibilities do you see for women's liberation, individually and collectively?

SIMONE DE BEAUVOIR: Individually, the first thing is to work, and if possible, refuse marriage. After all, I could well have gotten married to Sartre. But I believe that we were wise not to do so, because when you are married, people see you as married and at the same time it leads you to consider yourselves as married. You do not have exactly the same relationship with society if you are married or if you are not married. I believe that marriage is dangerous for women.

That said, a woman may have reasons to get married: if she wants to have children, for example. It's still very problematic to have children whose parents are not married; they will encounter all sorts of difficulties. If one really wants to be independent, what counts is having a job and working. That is the advice I give to all the women who ask me that question. It is a necessary condition that allows you, when you are married and you want to get a divorce, to leave, support your children, and assume your own existence. That said, work is not a panacea.

I know very well that work, such as it is today, has a liberating side but also an alienating side, and that consequently, women often have to choose between two sorts of alienation: that of the housewife or that of the factory worker. Work is not a panacea, but it is nevertheless the first condition of independence.

ALICE SCHWARTZER: And women who are already married and already have children?

SIMONE DE BEAUVOIR: I think that there are women who no longer have a chance. If they are already thirty-five years old, married with four children to care for and no professional qualifications, I do not really see what they can to do to liberate themselves. We can speak of liberation with a good chance of success only for the generations to come.

ALICE SCHWARTZER: Should the women who fight for their liberation limit themselves to the individual plane, or move on to collective action?

SIMONE DE BEAUVOIR: They must move on to collective action. I had not personally done so up until now because there was no organized movement with which I felt I could agree. But all the same, writing *The Second Sex* was taking an action that surpassed my own liberation. I wrote that book out of concern for the condition of women as a whole, not simply to understand what women's situation was, but also to fight, to help other women understand themselves.

Incidentally, in the last twenty years I have received an enormous number of letters from women who have told me that my book had helped them to understand their situation, to fight, to make decisions. I have always made the effort to respond to these women and have met some of them. I have always tried to help women in trouble.

ALICE SCHWARTZER: In general, how do you see the evolution of women's liberation?

SIMONE DE BEAUVOIR: I think that it should progress. But I don't know. In France, as elsewhere, most women are very conservative. They want to be "feminine." All the same, it seems to me that the new conditions of housework liberate women a little and allow them more time to reflect; so they should be led to rebel. On the professional plane, one thing is certain: women will never be given work in a capitalist country as long as there are unemployed men. That is why I think that equality for women can be won only if the system is totally overthrown.

That said, I think that the women's movement could overturn many things, just as the students' movements were limited in the beginning and then later triggered strikes all over the country. If women manage to break into the work world, then they will truly shake up the system. For now, the weakness of the French movement, and the American movement, I think, is that they have won over very few women workers.

ALICE SCHWARTZER: Isn't it a question of the stage of the struggle?

SIMONE DE BEAUVOIR: Of course. Everything is connected. When women go on strike in the factories, as they have in Troyes and Nantes, they become aware of their power and autonomy, and they will be much less likely to let themselves be walked all over at home.

ALICE SCHWARTZER: So you think that this feeling of solidarity should be developed?

SIMONE DE BEAUVOIR: Absolutely. Individual emancipation is not enough. There must be a collective effort tied to the class struggle. Women who fight for women's emancipation can not truly be feminist without being on the Left because, although socialism is not sufficient for assuring the equality of the sexes, it is necessary.

ALICE SCHWARTZER: Indeed for the first time in history, feminist movements are revolutionary movements. They no longer believe they can change women's lot in life without changing society.

SIMONE DE BEAUVOIR: That's true. There was a slogan I read in Italy that I found very apt: "No revolution without women's emancipation, no emancipation of women without revolution."

ALICE SCHWARTZER: In *The Second Sex*, you quoted a line from Rimbaud, which gives a vision of a future world in which women would be liberated.[11] Do you have a conception of this new world?

SIMONE DE BEAUVOIR: Rimbaud imagined that once liberated, women would bring something entirely different to the world. That is not what I believe. I don't think that specifically feminine values will develop once women have won their equality. I have discussed this with some Italian feminists who say that we must reject masculine values and models, that we must invent entirely different ones. I do not agree.

The fact remains that culture, civilization, and universal values have all been the feat of men because they were the ones who represented universality. Just as the proletariat, in rejecting the bourgeoisie as the dominant class, does not reject the entire bourgeois heritage, so must women, as equals with men, grab hold of the instruments created by men, without rejecting all of them. I think here again it is a question of suspicion and vigilance.

It is true that in creating these universal values—I would call mathematical science a universal value, for example—men have frequently given them a strictly masculine, male, and virile character. They have combined the two in a very subtle and underhanded way. Now it is a matter of disassociating the two and tracking down that contamination. It is possible, and it's one of the tasks that women must carry out [*faire*].[12] But we must not reject the world of men, because after all, it is also our world.

I think that liberated women will be as creative as men. But they will not bring new values. To believe the contrary is to believe that a feminine nature exists, which I have always denied. All of those concepts must be completely swept away. That women's liberation will bring about new types of relations between beings, and that men as well as women will be changed as a result, that much is certain. Women must be fully human beings [*êtres humains à part entière*], just as men are. The differences that exist between them are no more important than the individual differences there may be among women or among men.

ALICE SCHWARTZER: Are you for violence in the women's struggle?

SIMONE DE BEAUVOIR: Such as the situation is today, yes, up to a certain point, because men use violence against women, in their language as well as in their gestures. They assault women: they rape them, insult them, and certain looks are aggressions. Women must equally defend themselves with violence. Some women learn karate or other forms of combat. I am in complete agreement. This way they will be much more comfortable with their bodies and in the world than if they feel unarmed when faced with male aggressions.

ALICE SCHWARTZER: You often speak of American women. Do you have the most contact with them?

SIMONE DE BEAUVOIR: Yes. First of all, there are numerous American books, some of which I have mentioned. I have read books by Kate Millett, Germaine Greer—even though she is not American—and Firestone, whereas French women have not yet published anything. And it's true that the American movement started earlier. I also have received many letters from American women and invitations to go to America. But now I answer, "I am working with French women. I must first work here at home."

ALICE SCHWARTZER: Now that you consider yourself a militant feminist and have engaged yourself concretely in the struggle, what action do you envision taking first?

SIMONE DE BEAUVOIR: I am working with a group of women on a project to hold a public hearing denouncing the crimes committed against women. The first two meetings will focus on the problems of motherhood, contraception, and abortion. They will take place on May 13th and 14th in the main meeting room of the Mutualité hall.* There will be a sort of commission of inquiry composed of about ten women who will question wit-

---

* Organizational committee for the first public hearing denouncing crimes against women. To be held at number 15, Notre-Dame-de-Lorette on Thursday from 2 to 7:30 P.M. ; Friday from 6 to 8 P.M.; and Saturday from noon to 8 P.M.; telephone: 878-4-95 and 526-50-65.

nesses: biologists, sociologists, psychiatrists, doctors, midwives, and above all women who have suffered from the condition currently imposed upon women.

We hope to convince the public that we must secure women's right to procreate freely, that is to say help them bear the burdens of motherhood—through child-care facilities in particular—and also help them refuse unwanted pregnancies by providing contraceptive methods and abortion. We demand that it be unrestricted and decided by the woman alone.

ALICE SCHWARTZER: The women's struggle is often tied to abortion. Do you see your involvement [*engagement*] going beyond this stage?

SIMONE DE BEAUVOIR: Naturally. I think that the Women's Liberation Movement, and I along with them, must work on many other things. We are not only fighting for abortion on demand but for the massive diffusion of contraceptives, which will leave only a marginal role for abortion. On the other hand, contraception and abortion are only one starting point for women's liberation. Later we will organize other public hearings where we will denounce the exploitation of working women: housewives as well as women office workers and laborers.

## NOTES

"La femme révoltée," an interview by Alice Schwartzer, *Le nouvel observateur*, February 14, 1972, 47–54; reprinted in *Les écrits de Simone de Beauvoir*, ed. Claude Francis and Fernande Gontier (Paris: Gallimard, 1979), 482–97; © Éditions Gallimard, 1979. The interview was first translated by Helen Eustis as "The Radicalization of Simone de Beauvoir" in *Ms.* 1, 1 (July 1972); reprinted in *New French Feminisms*, ed. Elaine Marks and Isabelle de Courtivron (Amherst: University of Massachusetts Press, 1980), 142–50. The interview was later translated as "'I am a Feminist'" by Marianne Howarth in Alice Schwarzer, *Simone de Beauvoir Today; Conversations 1972–1982* (Chatto & Windus, 1984), published in the United States as *After "The Second Sex": Conversations with Simone de Beauvoir* (New York: Pantheon Books, 1984), and hereafter referred to as IAF. Note the spelling variants: "Schwartzer" in *Le nouvel observateur* and *Ms.* and "Schwarzer" in *Simone de Beauvoir Today* and *After "The Second Sex."*

The title in French, as it appears in the *Le nouvel observateur* article, is "La femme révoltée," which brings to mind the title of fellow existentialist Albert Camus' 1951 essay "L'homme révolté" (*The Rebel*). The editorial introduction in *Le nouvel observateur* is as follows: "Twenty three years after the publication of *The Second Sex*, Simone de Beauvoir has decided to join the ranks of the militants. She who in the past considered socialism to be the true remedy for the inequality of the sexes now says, 'I have become a feminist.' In this interview with Alice Schwartzer, she explains in detail her disillusions, hopes and rebellions—which she shares with the young women of the MLF [French Women's Liberation Movement]."

The editors of *Ms.* titled their 1972 translation of the interview "The Radicalization of Simone de Beauvoir," and introduced it as follows: "Twenty-three years ago, Simone de Beauvoir published *The Second Sex*, a classic study of women's condition. The book changed minds and possibly history, but the author herself remained a distant figure: a woman greatly admired, but little known even to the very women's groups her work had helped to start. She was the lone woman in the male intellectual circles of France. Here, for the first time, Simone de Beauvoir reveals a recent and very personal revolution. With Alice Schwartzer, an activist in the Frenchwoman's Liberation Movement, she discusses her conversion to feminism, her changed political philosophy, and her plans to join women at last."

Margaret Simons and Marybeth Timmermann would like to thank Terry Keefe for his permission to reprint the following review of "The Radicalization of Simone de Beauvoir" and his cooperation in modifying it for this publication. Keefe argues in his review, "Another 'Silencing of Beauvoir'? Guess What's Missing This Time" (*French Studies Bulletin*, 50, Spring 1994: 18–20), that the translation in *Ms.*, by Helen Eustis, is incomplete and at times inaccurate:

> Although accurate translations of Alice Schwartzer's interviews with Beauvoir are available, Helen Eustis's version of selected parts of the interview in February 1972 differs from the original French in a number of significant respects, of which mistranslation of particular phrases is perhaps the least worrying ("without submitting to women's limitations" for "sans souffrir des servitudes de la femme"; "Can women . . . ?" for "Les femmes . . . doivent-elles . . . ?"; "the American movement is more advanced" for "le mouvement des Américaines remonte plus haut"; "first and foremost" for "à part entière"; "getting rid of" for "dépister"; etc).
>
> Of Schwarzer's 35 interventions in the original interview—almost all explicit questions—the translation reproduces only 25, although nothing at all in *Ms. Magazine* itself suggests that the text of the interview is anything other than complete. In any case, excluding material is one thing, but modifying the material included quite another. The translation alters the order in which questions were asked late on in the interview, and the very sense of some questions is significantly modified by omission from, and distortion of, Schwarzer's words.
>
> *Thus*: "Vous parlez de la situation en France. Mais vous avez visité certains pays socialistes. La situation de la femme y a-t-elle fondamentalement changé?"
>
> *becomes*: "You spoke of the situation in Russia. What are women's lives like there?"
>
> *And*: "Certains mouvements sont allés plus loin. En partant du travail domestique, qui est gratuit et sans valeur d'échange, ils définissent les femmes comme une classe à part, hors des classes existantes. C'est-à-dire qu'elles posent l'oppression patriarcale comme contradiction principale et non secondaire. Etes-vous d'accord avec cette analyse?"
>
> *becomes*: "What do you think of the political analyses that equate patriarchal oppression of women as unpaid domestic labor with the capitalist use of workers?"
>
> It is clear from the last example that, in the process of shortening the interview, Eustis has used some of Beauvoir's omitted comments in the re-shaping of Schwarzer's questions. Hence a statement by Schwarzer in the very first sentence of the translation, of which there is no trace in her French—"you believed that

socialism was the only true remedy for the inequality of the sexes"—is presumably a formulation of what *Beauvoir* is taken to be saying in one of her replies! A consequence of all this, of course, is that in such cases Beauvoir's remarks in the translation are presented as answers to different questions from those actually posed in French.

Moreover, Beauvoir's own statements are themselves amended in a number of ways. Occasionally, utterances are put into her mouth: "socialism, as it has evolved—for example, in Russia—hasn't changed women's position, either," while somewhat contrasting ones are left out: "C'est une condition qui, dans un sens, est meilleure que celle de la femme dans les pays capitalistes." Some of Beauvoir's emphases, as marked by italics in the French text, are omitted. Paragraphing is altered. The order of her remarks is sometimes changed, and particular points are even switched from one answer to another (for example, a comment on women's strikes in Troyes and Nantes, made in answer to an omitted question about the stages of women's struggle, is tagged onto an answer to a slightly different earlier question). And an assertion about the importance of the differences between men and women is moved from the end to the beginning of an answer.

There are special problems, too, concerning the nature and range of omissions from Beauvoir's answers. These are considerable in extent, and it is not easy to decide what principles of selection were involved, or to what degree—especially in conjunction with multiple modifications of the interviewer's questions—the net effect is to produce susbtantive differences in the views expressed. Some minor omissions can be accounted for by a wish to eliminate repetitions. Others—though this is clearly a dubious procedure in itself—may seek to play down Beauvoir's uncertainty or hesitation on specific points ("C'est très possible," "je ne sais pas," etc).

But this leaves a great many cases of omissions relating to sensitive and controversial matters of feminist ideology and strategy. For instance, the exclusion of a major sequence on capitalism at the beginning of one of Beauvoir's answers undoubtedly has the effect of making her seem less anti-capitalist in the English than in the French version. Other, almost systematic, omissions result in the playing down of Beauvoir's emphasis on socialism and the class struggle ("si le socialisme n'est pas suffisant pour assurer l'égalité des sexes, il est nécessaire"), and of her insistence that she does not believe in specific feminine values. One or two strong assertions about abortion and contraception are also excised. Furthermore, the fact that the English text leaves out entirely certain striking question-and-answer sequences concerning lesbianism and women with children ("Je pense qu'il y a des femmes qui n'ont plus leur chance") is bound to alter the precise impact of the interview as a whole.

The very existence of interviews with modern writers raises some difficult matters for commentators, and translation necessarily constitutes a further complication. Nevertheless, scholars have the obvious duty to judge, wherever possible, how correctly interviews have been transcribed and translated. In this particular case, even if some of the alterations might be considered to be broadly in line with Beauvoir's thought, certain reasonable bounds have been transgressed. This is especially unfortunate when Howard Parshley has been not only severely criticized for the quality of his translation of *Le deuxième sexe*, but also—from a feminist standpoint—suspected of ideological bias. The Eustis translation—given all the more prominence by its inclusion in *New French Feminisms* (ed. Elaine Marks and Isabelle de Courtivron, Harvester Press, 1980)—seems very much like an anomaly, but this is all the more reason for ensuring that it is not taken as a full and reliable expression of Beauvoir's views.

1. Mouvement de libération des femmes (abbreviated as MLF).

2. This sentence is omitted in IAF.

3. Aleksandr Solzhenitsyn (1918–2008) was a Russian writer who won the Nobel Prize for literature in 1970.

4. According to the online Encyclopedia of Marxism, relations of production mean "The objective material relations that exist in any society independently of human consciousness, formed between all people in the process of social production, exchange, and distribution of material wealth." http://www.marxists.org/glossary/terms/r/e.htm (accessed on April 21, 2014).

5. SCUM stands for "Society for Cutting Up Men."

6. An additional question is inserted in IAF: "Is the exclusion of men at this stage simply a practical question for you, because women would be more inhibited or whatever? Or is it also a political question?" In the *Le nouvel observateur* article, the question appears as "Mais cette exclusion momentanée de l'homme n'est-elle pas aussi une question politique?"

7. This sentence is omitted in IAF.

8. The following sentence is added in IAF: "Of course they have to be born into a privileged family or possess certain intellectual abilities."

9. On September 24, 1971, Beauvoir, as the legally responsible publisher of *L'idiot international*, a radical leftist monthly, was indicted for libeling the French police, in response to two articles charging the police with "systematic" violence against demonstrators.

10. "technocratie" was translated as "democracy" in IAF.

11. Arthur Rimbaud (1854–91), was a French poet who had a great influence on the symbolists and subsequent modern poets. In *The Second Sex*, Beauvoir quotes a letter he wrote to Pierre Demeny on May 15, 1871, at the end of the chapter entitled "The Independent Woman": "The free woman is just being born; when she conquers herself, she will perhaps justify Rimbaud's prophecy: 'Poets will be! When woman's infinite servitude is broken, when she lives for herself and by herself, man—abominable until now—giving her her freedom, she, too, will be poet! Woman will find the unknown! Will her worlds of ideas differ from ours? She will find strange, unfathomable, repugnant, delicious things, we will take them, we will understand them.' Her 'worlds of ideas' are not necessarily different from men's, since she will free herself by assimilating them; to know how singular she will remain and how important these singularities will continue to be, one would have to make some foolhardy predictions. What is beyond doubt is that until now women's possibilities have been stifled and lost to humanity, and in her and everyone's interest it is high time she be left to take her own chances." See Simone de Beauvoir, *Le deuxième sexe* (Paris: Gallimard, 1949), trans. Constance Borde and Sheila Malovany-Chevallier as *The Second Sex* (New York: Knopf, 2009), 751.

12. In IAF, the following is added before the final sentence of this paragraph: "When it comes down to it, what do we mean by rejecting the male model? If a woman learns karate, it is a masculine thing."

# RESPONSE TO SOME WOMEN AND A MAN

TRANSLATION AND NOTES BY MARYBETH TIMMERMANN

Some of the women who, in their letters, claim to be fulfilled by motherhood and keeping house, display such a rude and caustic aggression that it casts doubt over the happy balance of which they boast. Others reproach me more moderately for seeing motherhood as a servitude; but without a doubt, in France today, it is one. I understand that one can choose it deliberately; I am aware of the joy that children can bring when they have been wanted. But for me, who did not wish to have any and who wanted above all to accomplish an oeuvre, I was lucky to not have any. I am not someone who wishes to impose my manner of living upon all women, since on the contrary, I am actively fighting for their freedom: freedom to choose motherhood, contraception, or abortion. The fanatics are those mothers who refuse to accept that someone might follow a path other than their own.

As far as contraception is concerned, several correspondents were astonished that only 7% of French women take the Pill. Mr. Neuwirth himself admitted that the law on contraception had been bungled.[1] Not only did they make no effort to make it known to the entire population, but counterpropaganda has turned the majority of women away from using the Pill. What's more, the pope has forbidden it to Catholics.

I have been accused of scorning unwed mothers and refusing them the right to exist. That is false. Recently I fought for young unwed mothers in Plessis-Robinson, and for those in Issy-les-Moulineaux. I think highly of a woman who chooses motherhood and does not feel obligated to bind her life to that of a man. Only it is difficult today, in France, to be an unwed mother or illegitimate child. I understand why a woman who wants children chooses the path of marriage; it appears to be safer. I say "appears to be" because a child without a father is often happier than one whose parents don't get along.

## Women and Work

Obviously, I wish that motherhood and marriage were disassociated since I am for the abolition of the family. This statement has shocked many people. They make an objection that I am used to: How can I, unmarried, with no children, speak of family? Human sciences would be impossible if one could understand nothing other than one's own particular case. Deciding how to organize the care of children is a problem, but it is a lie to claim that they could flourish nowhere else better than in the midst of the family. Parents bring their children into their sadomasochist games, projecting onto them their fantasies, obsessions, and neuroses. This is an eminently unhealthy situation. Without even counting child abuse,[*2] the world of neurotic children that our society produces is considerable. Moreover, the family is the intermediary by which this patriarchal world exploits women, extorting billions of hours of "invisible work" from them each year. In France, in 1955, forty-three billion hours were devoted to paid work, compared to forty-five billion hours devoted to unpaid work in the home.

But, they say, isn't paid work also alienating? In our society, it certainly is. At least it allows women to escape from marital dependence. How many letters I've received from women who are stuck against their wishes in the conjugal home because they can not earn a living, and they bitterly regret it! By assuring her autonomy, a job gives a woman a direct hold on the world; she can fight to change society at a factory or in an office.

There is, in that interview, a sentence spoken in haste that I retract. In speaking of women thirty-five years old or older who are married with

---

* Each year in France, 2,500 cases of child abuse go before the courts, and the number of cases that remain unreported is obviously much higher.

several children and lacking any professional qualifications, I said, "I do not really see what they can to do to liberate themselves." Several women who found themselves in that very case have written to me that it can be done; they have succeeded in finding a job and reconciling it with their children's education. Let's say then, that it is a difficult situation, but not a dead-end.

Some correspondents have asked me why I want to change the condition of women within this society. Why not have confidence in socialism? I heard this question when *The Second Sex* was published, and in my interview I once again responded to it. Socialism has brought nothing or nearly nothing to women. When they tell me that true socialism has never been realized, I respond that for the moment, authentic socialism with perfect equality is still a utopia, whereas real women of flesh and bones exist, and they do not have the time to wait for some glowing tomorrow. I will come back to this point a bit later.

## Against the Pill

Since I am writing in *Le nouvel observateur* about the condition of women, I would like to take advantage of this occasion to explain myself to Maurice Clavel.[3] I am sorry to have to rank him among the phallocrats because, on many points, I agree with him. I was dismayed when, a rather long time ago already, I read articles in which he congratulated the pope for having forbidden the Pill. "No one is forced to be Catholic," he wrote. Yet he is aware that Catholicism is imperiously imposed upon all peoples in Latin America, and that by obligating them to proliferate, the pope is condemning them to starve to death. This oversight, in a man generally sensitive to men's sufferings, is significant. The explanation lies in Clavel's enthusiasm for the fact that the pope blames sexuality. Clavel rejects "the easy and clear sexual conscience," that, in the most arbitrary manner (since it can be seen in many other civilizations), he ties to this alienated and alienating society of consumption. Without claiming that "Pleasure and Death are indissolubly linked," he proclaims his scorn for "the risk-free sperm." But for whom does sperm present a danger? Uniquely for women. To satisfy his fantasies, he finds it normal to inflict on his partner the risk of an unwanted pregnancy, or an abortion, which in current conditions is a very painful experience that can in some cases lead to death. He affirms himself as the sovereign seigneur with the utmost thoughtlessness and a clear sexual conscience, reducing women to the rank of pure instruments of pleasure.

## From the Cradle

This renders a priori rather suspect the immense respect that Clavel displays for women; in fact, this respect is only addressed to those women who bow to his desires and his mythologies. "We must be different in order to love each other," he declares. And—without considering the love that exists between homosexuals—he demands that women cultivate their difference, not caring that this difference implies an economic and social inferiority and that it would be in women's best interests to refuse it. *His* interests are that she consents, and therefore she should consent.

This leads him to ask an absurd question: Do feminist women intend to remain women? If nonfeminist women are called women, then feminist women obviously do not wish to remain women. As such, they are unfaithful to their essence, thinks Clavel, who, according to himself, believes that woman is defined by "a deep qualitative difference." Where does he situate that difference? He obviously does not adhere to the vague scientism professed by Ms. Suzanne Lilar among others. Shall we suppose that souls have a sex? In truth, the segregation of the sexes is founded on neither nature, nor essence. The genetic, endocrinal, and anatomic differences that distinguish the human female from the male are not sufficient to define either femininity or masculinity. These are cultural constructions, and all recent developments in pediatrics, pedagogy, and psychology prove it.

I want to emphasize this issue because so many of my correspondents bring it up: in order to liberate women, their education must be changed right from the cradle, as psychologists and teachers have written to me. Indeed. The fascinating experiments done at Harvard between 1966 and 1968 by Rosenthal and his collaborators showed that in any apprenticeship—whether it concerns rats, grade school children, or college students—the attitude of the teacher with regards to the apprentice plays a determining role; he gets what he expects.[4] So, parents expect something completely different from a girl than from a boy, and it shows in their behavior. Mothers "handle, caress, and carry boys differently than girls," wrote American psychoanalyst Robert J. Stoller.**[5] He resolutely abandons "the discredited idea that masculinity and femininity are, from the start, produced biologically in humans." In fact, he says that "the effects of the apprenticeship, which

---

** In an article [entitled "Création d'une illusion: l'extrême féminité chez les garçons" (Creating an illusion: Extreme femininity in boys)] published in *La nouvelle revue de psychanalyse* [The new review of psychoanalysis], no. 4, fall 1971 [pp. 55–72], where he summarizes the essentials of his theses.

starts at birth, determine the major part of sexual identity ... the choice of the name, the color and style of clothing, the manner of carrying the child, proximity and distance—all that and still many other things begin almost at birth."

The little girl's apprenticeship destines her to become the vassal of man. Clavel, in his absurdity, goes so far as to approve of a despicable television speech in which [Jean] Cau objects to Benoîte Groult, saying that although little girls are told not to imitate boys, the boys are also told they must not be like girls.***[6] But there is no symmetry here. Society does assign to women a role other than that of men; but it is the role of an inferior, and society encourages in the master the idea of his superiority.

## Strange "Superiority"

The feminist rises up against this inequality. It is not true that she intends to "take all man's privileges without losing any of her own." She does not demand "special treatment," on the contrary. She is prepared, if necessary, to face violence (by the way, does Maurice Clavel really make it a habit of throwing punches to solve differences between himself and his peers?). She simply wants to have the same possibilities as men, and to escape the exploitation and oppression that are her lot. This demand throws Maurice Clavel into a panic. If a woman speaks of equality, he supposes that she is surreptitiously aiming at superiority. As far as work is concerned, he says that she will demand a near majority quota. Didn't he see the television program about working women that revealed, among other things, that in a competitive entrance exam, a State administration accorded fifty places to women out of six hundred and fifty, the others being a priori reserved for men? We are too far from equality to accuse women of having "majoritarian" claims.

But if, through her abilities and activities, a woman shows herself to be man's equal, then she will become his superior, protests a panicked Clavel, because she, in addition, possesses the faculty of "creating life." Clavel suddenly becomes rather modest; does the man have no role in procreation? Supposing that pregnancy and giving birth constitute a "creation bonus," this advantage is largely offset by the exhaustion and pain that it entails. Not to mention the abortions from which very few women escape. In truth, what man would wish to benefit at such a price?

***

\*\*\* He even approves of Cau's remark: "In the streets, it is the men who sweep." But which men? Immigrant workers who constitute, like women, an underutilized category [in the economy].

When he denounces the hysteria of the feminist "harpies," Clavel becomes convulsive. Any argument at all seems good to him. "What will become of ugly women after the sexual revolution?" he asks. And what becomes of them before? Their chances will certainly be better in a world which no longer perpetuates the cult of the woman-object.

## An Awful Word

In his conclusion, he takes refuge in fallacious ramblings: feminists are only striving to integrate themselves into a society that must be destroyed. "You are claiming the right to success," he says. "What an awful word." So be it, but he is the one to say it. If workers revolt against oppression and exploitation, Clavel is the first to approve; he does not accuse them of wanting to "succeed." Yet women are doubly exploited and oppressed. Relegating women to the bottom rung of the social ladder on the pretext that any hierarchy is unfair is clear proof of his "machismo."

"You want reforms and everything must be redone!" Clavel also says. Here again, his bad faith bursts forth. A very large number of feminists also situate themselves in the field of the class struggle. They demand a world without classes or sexual segregation. I fail to understand why a man who claims to be leftist, like Clavel, does not show solidarity with them. He gives no valid ideological reason for his attitude. Like almost all antifeminists, his motivations—which are evident in every line he writes—are of a psychological and sexual order, and purely egotistical. It would be easy to expose them but I see no interest in that. I simply wanted to denounce the radical lack of objectivity in the columns that Clavel devotes to women.

### NOTES

"Réponse à quelques femmes et à un homme" (*Le nouvel observateur*, March 6, 1972, 40–42); reprinted in *Les écrits de Simone de Beauvoir*, ed. Claude Francis and Fernande Gontier (Paris: Gallimard, 1979), 498–504; © Éditions Gallimard, 1979. In *Le nouvel observateur* the article is preceded by the following introduction: "Simone de Beauvoir received a considerable amount of mail concerning the interview on 'La femme révoltée' [The rebellious woman] which we published in our February 13 issue. Unable to respond to each of her correspondents, she discusses here their main arguments and also uses this occasion to argue her point with our friend Maurice Clavel, who has often shown his disagreement with feminist activists, and who responds in turn in his usual column (on page 58)." A new translation of the original interview can also be found in this current volume.

1. Lucien Neuwirth (1923–2013) was a French politician best known for proposing the Neuwirth law, which legalized oral contraception in France in 1967.

2. We have preserved the footnotes that appear in the *Le nouvel observateur* article, although it is not certain whether Beauvoir authored them or whether they were inserted by the editors of *Le nouvel observateur*.

3. Maurice Clavel (1929–79) was a French philosopher, playwright, and writer who wrote for the left-wing French newspaper *Combat* as well as the weekly newsmagazine *Le nouvel observateur*. See Sylvie Chaperon's introduction to this chapter for more information regarding his article entitled "Les gardiennes de l'ordre" (The female guardians of order) (*Le nouvel observateur*, February 21, 1972).

4. See R. Rosenthal and L. Jacobson, "Pygmalion in the Classroom: Teacher Expectation and Pupils' Intellectual Development" (New York: Rinehart & Winston, 1968).

5. Robert Stoller (1924–91) was a professor of psychiatry and worked at the UCLA Gender Identity Clinic. He authored many books and articles, including *Sex and Gender: On the Development of Masculinity and Femininity* (New York: Science House, 1968).

6. Jean Cau (1925–93) was a French journalist and writer who was Jean-Paul Sartre's secretary and won the Prix Goncourt for his book *La pitié de Dieu* (God's pity) in 1961; Benoîte Groult (1920–) is a French feminist writer and journalist who was named Commander of the Légion d'honneur in 2010.

# ABORTION AND THE POOR

TRANSLATION BY MARYBETH TIMMERMANN

Each year in France, a million women have abortions with no punishment.

In practice, the law against abortion is widely repudiated by public opinion; it is so often disobeyed that the criminal courts choose to avoid it. However, on October 9, 1972, Marie-Claire C . . . went to court at Bobigny for having had an abortion—the juvenile court since she is a minor. Why this measure of exception? Was her "crime" more serious than that of the others?

Marie-Claire C . . . was fifteen and half when she let a seventeen-year-old acquaintance pull her into his room. Daniel T . . . then physically forced her to submit to him. She never saw him again. A bit later, she noticed that she was pregnant, and she confided in her mother. Not having the means to raise a child, they decided to not keep him.

Thirty-nine years old today, Ms. C . . . was abandoned by the father of her three children after living with him for five years. She worked hard to provide for their needs. As a subway employee, she earns 1500 francs a month. A perfect mother. "She is an exemplary woman," notes a police report. But she knows how much it has cost her. "I did not want my daughter to relive my Calvary," she said in court. She had trouble finding the money necessary for the procedure, which is harmless when it takes place in good conditions, when the person concerned has money and connections. For Marie-Claire, it was difficult and the young girl had to spend four days in a clinic.

Daniel T . . ., who was questioned by the police for a car theft, denounced Marie-Claire. Many denunciations bring about no consequences. The judge was free to decide to dismiss the case, which would seem to have been called for by the circumstances.

First, there is the age of the "guilty" party. In many countries, an abortion is automatically granted to minors who demand one. In France, a pregnant minor is treated as an adult since she is subject to the same law. If she breaks the law, she appears before the juvenile court. Maternity does not emancipate her. Society does not give her the means to provide for her child. The future of the child is decided by the grandparents: he will be turned over to State custody if they cannot or do not want to burden themselves with him. The labor of pregnancy and childbirth are inflicted upon the adolescent without compensation: how could she not try to escape this?

The modest resources of Ms. C . . . would not allow her to nourish one more mouth without the help of an additional family credit that would not have been granted to her.[1] It is always a great responsibility to bring a human being into this world. How can one consent to this if one is incapable of helping him find his place on Earth, if it is necessary to thrust him into the unknown and, in all probability, condemn him to unhappiness?

Shouldn't the youth of Marie-Claire C . . . and the economic condition of Ms. C. . . . have been enough to avoid charges? It would be naïve to be surprised. These were, on the contrary, the reasons for bringing charges against them.

Since those in power do not want to abolish this anachronistic, flouted, trampled upon, inoperative law on abortion, they must at least give it a semblance of existence from time to time by applying it.

But, careful! Not just anyone. In France, justice is class justice, and nowhere is this fact as flagrant as in this domain. Not only is the arrival of an unwanted child more catastrophic in a poor family than in a well-to-do family, not only is the procedure more anguishing, more painful, and more dangerous for the underprivileged than for the privileged, but it is always among the former that the forces of repression choose their victims. Rich bourgeois women, society women, wives of CEOs, industrial leaders, government officials, and judges are among the millions of French women who have had abortions in the course of these last few years. None of them has ever been charged. "Justice" only goes after women who have neither fortune nor social influence: housewives, shorthand typists, saleswomen.

From this point of view, the case of Marie-Claire C . . . is exemplary; the only reason she has been treated as a criminal is that she was thought to be defenseless. She was released, but she will not forget the ordeal of the charges and the trial. And her mother will be tried for complicity on November 8. But the risk of a trial and a conviction remains hanging over the heads of all poor and humble women who have had abortions. Arbitrariness will continue to reign as long as the laws against abortion are not abolished. Public opinion is content to ignore them; everyone gets around them as best they can, according to their own interests. This is not enough.

The proceedings brought against Marie-Claire clearly denounce the unjust manner in which they are used. We must fight for their repeal.

## NOTES

"L'avortement des pauvres" (*Le nouvel observateur* 414, October 16–22, 1972, 57); © Sylvie Le Bon de Beauvoir. The article was preceded by the following introduction: "Marie-Claire C. . . . has been acquitted. But her mother will be tried on November 8."

1. In France, each family with two or more children receives a cash benefit from the State for each child, called "allocations familiales."

# BEAUVOIR'S DEPOSITION
# AT THE BOBIGNY TRIAL

TRANSLATION BY MARYBETH TIMMERMANN

(*The witness is sworn in.*)

MS. HALIMI: Ms. de Beauvoir is a character witness. She knows Ms. Chevalier.

SIMONE DE BEAUVOIR: Ms. Chevalier is a member of the Choisir [To Choose] Association, of which I am president.

MS. H.: I would like to ask Ms. de Beauvoir why this law is above all a law that oppresses women?

S. DE B.: The law is set up to oppress women. Women's oppression is, indeed, one of the trump cards available to society. This situation is extremely advantageous for men for more than one reason: psychologically, it is always nice to have inferiors and to feel superior to someone, economically as well. One point that is not emphasized enough and that I find very important is that each year women in France provide an enormous quantity of work that can be called invisible, clandestine, unpaid. It is household work. A recent statistic said that there are 45 billion hours of household work provided by women compared to 43 billion hours of paid work.

So the volume of household work far surpasses paid work. If society had to pay for this work, its expenses would obviously be enormously multiplied. It is quite advantageous for society to have women who do this enormous work for nothing.

How to get women to do this work? They must be conditioned. As it is difficult to persuade women that they have a vocation for washing dishes, something much better has been found.

Maternity is exalted because maternity is the way to keep women at home and to make them do housework. Instead of telling a little two-, three-, or four-year-old girl, "You will be destined to wash dishes," she is told, "You will be destined to be a mommy." She is given dolls, and maternity is exalted so that when she becomes a young woman, she thinks of only one thing: to get married and have children. She has been convinced that she will not be a complete woman if she does not have children. When a woman does not have children, people say, "She is not a true woman," but when a man does not have children, people do not say, "He is not a true man."

Therefore women must be enslaved to maternity. If they at least had the freedom to be mothers when they wanted to, how they wanted to, planning the births of children, it would leave them a lot of freedom on all levels. Women could present themselves as professional rivals to men. They would not be constantly chained to the house, and that would bring up the question of why it is not the men who do the dishes.

In order to prevent this from happening, maternity must be imposed upon women, and imposed against their will. This is the reason that for as long as contraception has existed, its use has never been facilitated, to the point that currently in France there are 7% of French women using contraceptive methods; that's all. It is also for this reason that the government, at this time, is in the process of removing all subsidies from Family Planning, the only movement concerned with informing women. However, the government recognizes that it has no alternative solution. And this is a very grave matter. Not only is Family Planning being done away with and its possibilities of action are being removed, but nothing is planned to replace it. Women are thus prevented from protecting themselves against unwanted pregnancies and therefore become pregnant against their wishes.

So they end up having an abortion, and this is what a million French women do each year in spite of the law that prevents nothing at all, and therefore makes no sense. From time to time, to give the law a semblance of existence, charges are brought against a few women always chosen from among the most underprivileged because you would never see the wife of a judge, a government official, or a great industrialist sitting in the place where the accused are sitting today.

Yet one can be sure that there are as many abortions in those milieus as in the others. The law oppresses all women, even those who are privileged.

In my life, I have seen not only blue-collar women and office workers, but also middle-class women with money arriving at my house, in tears. Once I even helped the wife of a very important bank director. In spite of everything, women are isolated. Even with money, they do not always have the necessary addresses; they do not know whom to contact.

As I was saying at the beginning, such a feeling of guilt has been put into the hearts of women that abortion becomes something traumatizing for them, as would not be the case at all if it took place under legal conditions.

There was an article in the *New York Times* and in the *Herald Tribune* that quoted the director of health services of the State of New York who observed that ever since the legalization of abortion, women can have abortions without feeling any sort of distress about it. "We hope," he said, "that the example will be followed by all the other states in America."

It is not at all a question of a procedure that automatically traumatizes women. It is a procedure that is traumatizing only insofar as they have been conditioned to make maternity into a veritable calling.

I will not go into details, but the fact is that the current law is unfair because, in particular, it always falls upon women who belong to the least favored strata of society and never upon the others.

MS. H.: In your opinion, does society have the right to intervene in women's freedom to give life or to abort?

S. DE B.: In my opinion, women have bodily freedom. They can choose to have or to not have a child and no one can intervene. For me there is no doubt about it.

MS. H.: Have you had an abortion?

S. DE B.: Yes, a long time ago; but what I have also been doing frequently and for a long time, is helping women who come and ask me how to get an abortion. I give them money or I lend it to them, and I give them addresses, and sometimes I even lend them my residence so that the procedure takes place in good conditions.

THE PRESIDENT: Since you begin with the principle of everyone's bodily freedom, do you think, by applying the same principle, that the public powers should give complete freedom to people who take drugs?

S. DE B.: That is not related to the question.

THE PRESIDENT: So you admit having certain reservations about it.

S. DE B.: I would be of the opinion that people should be free to take drugs if they wanted to, while giving them sufficient information about the drugs. People must be informed and must be equally advised, and in these conditions, then, well, yes, they should be allowed that freedom.

THE PRESIDENT: The Court thanks you.

## NOTES

"Déposition de Simone de Beauvoir au procès de Bobigny," was first published by the Association Choisir (To Choose Association) in *Avortement: Une loi en procès. L'affaire de Bobigny: Sténotypie intégrale des débats du tribunal de Bobigny, 8 novembre 1972* (Paris: Gallimard, 1973), translated by Beryl Henderson as *Abortion: The Bobigny Affair: A Law on Trial: A Complete Record of the Pleadings at the Court of Bobigny, 8 November, 1972* (Sydney: Wild and Woolley, 1975), and reprinted in *Les écrits de Simone de Beauvoir*, ed. Claude Francis and Fernande Gontier (Paris: Gallimard, 1979), 510–13; © Éditions Gallimard, 1979.

# PREFACE TO *ABORTION: A LAW ON TRIAL. THE BOBIGNY AFFAIR*

TRANSLATION BY MARYBETH TIMMERMANN

On the exterior, this book resembles many others. It is, however, absolutely unusual. Never before have the proceedings of an abortion trial been brought to the public's knowledge. The Choisir [To Choose] Association has decided to publish them in their entirety because these proceedings are not like any previous proceedings. It was not Ms. Chevalier who was being judged, but the law in whose name she appeared before the court. Women and men took the witness stand one after the other in order to indict a law which makes France appear as one of the most backward countries of our time, a law which is radically divorced from the collective conscience and from the facts since it is broken each year by close to a million French women. "When the daily practice in a country gets too far away from the jurisdiction, there is a major danger to the balance and general mental health of this collectivity," Judge Casamayor has rightly written.[1] Experience proves that jurisdiction has no influence over practice; it is therefore the jurisdiction that must be changed.

I do not hesitate to call it criminal. A correctly executed abortion is an operation that is as benign as the extraction of a tooth, and less dangerous than giving birth. In England, the percentage is twenty-one deaths for every

100,000 abortions and twenty-four deaths for every 100,000 births. In the state of New York, where for two years now, any woman less than twenty-four weeks pregnant can legally have an abortion, the results have been declared an "immense success," by the director of Health Services. He would like all the states in the USA to follow New York's example. The French legislation, however, murders 5,000 women each year. Only a minute number of doctors, midwives, or nurses consent to secretly interrupt pregnancies. In the immense majority of cases, the intervention is carried out by incompetent people, in difficult conditions, so that the most elementary hygienic measures are not taken. That is why so many women who have had abortions die; that is why a large number of them find themselves sterile, sick, or no longer healthy. Most often, the anguished search for an "address," the humiliation of the steps that must be followed, insecurity, and fear make the abortion into a traumatizing ordeal. And even more so because, while breaking the law, many women fear it or even respect it. They feel guilty, and this contradiction sometimes brings about neurosis.

Of course, the risks of death, mutilation, and anguish are not equally shared by all women. It is the most underprivileged who pay the highest price. And it is always among those women that "justice" chooses its victims of repression. The spouse of a judge or a government official is never seen on the bench for the accused, but hourly employees, saleswomen, and secretaries are. Ms. Chevalier is a subway employee and a single mother.

One particularly ridiculous argument that is sometimes brandished against abortion is that by interrupting a pregnancy, you risk getting rid of a Mozart or a Mao Tse-tung. But maybe you save the world from a Hitler. All that is only nonsense. In reality, it is another crime of our code that obligates women—for the lack of an address or the necessary money—to bring forth unwanted children into this world: neglected children, abused children, children abandoned to State custody. Most delinquents and many criminals have had this sad beginning in life. They are the destitute who hang themselves in our prisons; often they finish their days in psychiatric hospitals. They would not necessarily share the same opinions as high-ranking officials with judicial authority, officials like the prosecutor of the Bobigny trial who can proudly say, "We were all fetuses once. And in general we are all happy to live."

If I examine the reasons that are officially opposed to the freedom of abortion, I do not find them more serious than the one I just mentioned. From a biological point of view, Professor Monod and Professor Jacob, whose testimonies we will read later, have shown that abortion can not be considered infanticide. To consider the fetus as a human person is a metaphysical attitude that is blatantly denied by practice. When a woman miscarries in a hospital, the administration throws the fetus in the garbage, and the Church approves. It does not consider according a religious burial to this "human person." It treats it as simple waste.

In fact, it is often said that by suppressing abortion, the regime obeys utilitarian considerations; it wants soldiers, an abundant workforce, a plethora of consumers. Questioning such birth-rate politics is not even necessary here. It suffices to repeat that each year in France there are nearly one million women who have abortions. Making abortion legal would only save them from useless suffering and not prevent the births of a million little French people each year.

So why does the idea of this freedom meet such an opposition? According to me, there is one reason, only one, but a heavy one: outlawing abortion is an essential piece in the system that society has put into place in order to oppress women.

Clearly, it is in men's interest to maintain women in a subordinate condition. It is always psychologically advantageous to belong to a caste that considers itself superior. Politically and socially, men do not intend to share with women the powers they hold. Their entire effort aims at keeping them out of public life. But it is especially on an economic level that the enslavement of women is profitable. A recent statistic indicates that in France each year, paid workers provide 43 billion hours of work. Women provide 45 billion hours of household work *that is not paid*. What the husband spends for their upkeep can not even be compared to the amount women would earn if each hour of work brought a salary, even just the salary of a maid. What an upheaval it would be if they demanded that the private production of domestic work be converted into public production, that this "invisible" work be industrialized, and therefore remunerated! The entire economy of our patriarchal society implies that women accept being overexploited. Starting in her earliest years of childhood, a girl is conditioned in order to extract this consent from her.

And for that they rely on a ruse. It is difficult to present washing dirty laundry and dishes as a sacred function to a little girl, difficult to convince her that this is her irresistible vocation. But if a woman is kept in the home by her children, she immediately becomes this housewife whose efforts are extorted almost gratuitously. So she is persuaded from early childhood on— by words, by example, by the books and games that are given to her—that she is destined for maternity. If she does not have children, she will not be a "true woman," yet a man without children is not accused of not being a "true man." In general, she follows the path that has been laid out for her: she gets married; she has children; she *keeps house*. And that does the trick.

However, she would not be a household slave if she had the means to plan her pregnancies according to her desires and her interests. She could reconcile them with her studies, a professional training, a career. She would demand and occupy positions that men consider as their right. And what men fear even more is that women would discover and reclaim their autonomy in all domains by taking their destiny into their own hands. They would refuse to be the docile vassals who wear themselves out doing unpaid tasks inside four walls. It is because they are conscious of this danger that men have joined forces to sabotage contraception, driving women to have abortions, which they forbid them to have. "Kinder, Küche, Kirche" [children, kitchen, church]:[2] the child is necessary to keep women in the kitchen. The woman who rebels against forced maternity is on the path to a more general rebellion. They will arrest her on the way, forbidding her to consider the affirmation of her will as a victory. She has chosen to have an abortion, so be it. Everything will be put into place to convince her that she should be ashamed of it. She is blamed and even punished. I have heard doctors boasting about "having given *them* a rough time of it" during curettage when they were interns. This is also one of the novelties of this trial: Marie-Claire, listed as a witness, and the accused, Ms. Chevalier and her friends, have faced it with heads held high. They have affirmed that a woman is free to control her body, that no one has the right to control it for her.

Thus, the struggle for the diffusion of contraception and for legal abortion that the Choisir Association has undertaken has more than one goal and more than one meaning. It is first of all a question of making abortion irrelevant by making more available the contraceptive methods that are officially authorized, but that only 7% of French women are using. It is a question of defending those who have had abortions and their "accomplices" against a society that, in order to breathe an appearance of existence into a dying law, arbitrarily decides to punish the most vulnerable among them. It is a question of moving public opinion, of putting pressure on the regime so that abortion is no longer suppressed. Realizing this reform will at the same time surpass it. When women—thanks to the diffusion of contraception and the freedom of abortion—have obtained control over their bodies, which will no longer be poisoned by fear or regret, they will be available for other struggles. They will understand that they must fight for changing their own status as well as the society that imposes it upon them. Women will fight. And I hope that a day will come when they will win.

## NOTES

Simone de Beauvoir, "Préface" to *Avortement: une loi en procès. L'affaire de Bobigny. Sténotypie intégrale des débats du tribunal de Bobigny, 8 novembre 1972* by the *Association Choisir* (To Choose Association) (Paris: Gallimard, 1973), translated by Beryl Henderson as *Abortion: The Bobigny Affair: A Law on Trial: A Complete Record of the Pleadings at the Court of Bobigny, 8 November, 1972* (Sydney: Wild and Woolley, 1975), and reprinted in *Les écrits de Simone de Beauvoir*, ed. Claude Francis and Fernande Gontier (Paris: Gallimard, 1979), 505–9; © Éditions Gallimard, 1979.

1. Casamayor was the pen name of Serge Fuster (1911–88), who was a French judge and writer.

2. This was a slogan used in Nazi Germany in the 1930s and promoted in France during the Nazi Occupation from June 1940 to November 1944.

## 10

Short Feminist Texts

from the Seventies and Eighties

# INTRODUCTION

*by Françoise Picq*

TRANSLATION BY MARYBETH TIMMERMANN

## Simone de Beauvoir and the MLF (1974–79)

In 1949 Simone de Beauvoir was not a feminist activist. She did not believe that feminism had ever been an autonomous movement. Noting in *The Second Sex* that equality between the sexes had been recognized in the United Nations and that many women had finally had "all the privileges of the human being restored to them" she concluded that "the quarrel about feminism" is "now almost over."[1] But the movement that burst forth in the 1970s reflected her thinking so much that she couldn't help but be touched by it.

Searching for their identity, women were seeking to define themselves, individually and collectively, in the terms that she had forged. The French Women's Liberation Movement was Simone de Beauvoir's child just as much as it was the child of May '68.[2] She recognized it as her own and followed its actions and debates with interest. She lent her support each time it was requested, putting her notoriety and her connections at the service of this movement of young rabble-rousers, without ever claiming to lead it in any certain direction. She took part in the *Manifeste des 343* [Manifesto of the 343, 1971]; she sold an interview in order to finance the renting of a room in the Mutualité meeting hall for the "public hearing denouncing the crimes against women"; and she sided with the young troublemakers when Gisèle Halimi judged the project to be irresponsible and left.[3] She was there, from the beginning to the end, fascinated by the outpouring of multiple and convergent voices.

* * *

The winter of 1973–74 marked a turning point in the history of the feminist movement. The principal battle over legalized abortion was on the verge of victory, and the movement, which had gotten considerably more developed and complex, was searching for a second wind. The opposition was stiffening and the tendencies within the movement were solidifying. Even among the "revolutionary feminists," who were closest to Simone de Beauvoir, the divisions were apparent when it came to putting their strategies into place.

For some, the time had come for a change in strategy: the incendiary actions of a minority that had allowed the movement to emerge were cutting it off from the great majority of women. The movement should now open itself up to those women through specific actions on concrete themes close to their daily lives. The image of feminists held by the general public must be corrected. Anne Zelensky, who published *Histoires du MLF* [Stories from the French Women's Liberation Movement] under the name of Anne Tristan (with Annie Sugier, whose pen name was de Pisan), was one of the women who thought this way. She had been involved in all the struggles, starting in 1968 with the creation of the FMA.[4] She was also one of the initiators of the *Manifeste des 343*, on which occasion she had contacted Simone de Beauvoir; and she had, with others, organized the public hearings at the Mutualité hall, taking charge of collective meeting places. She incarnated this new image of feminists that she wanted to promote. Anne and Annie, as Simone de Beauvoir pointed out in her preface to *Histoires*, were "thoughtful and poised women," with "nothing extravagant in their outward appearance or actions, nothing outrageous in their language." They were women like many others, who since their childhood and their adolescence had become aware of the alienation of women, which they had refused for themselves, choosing instead to be neither wives nor mothers, but to have careers that interested them and assured their independence. Simone de Beauvoir had to appreciate this itinerary that she had indicated in *The Second Sex* as being the "path to liberation." But she also appreciated the collective and subversive character of their actions. Their testimony was precious, she emphasized, because it spoke of "the problems posed by the birth and development of a revolutionary movement," since "the decolonization of women implies a radical overthrowing of society."

In *Histoires*, Anne Zelensky describes at length the context and reasons that governed the creation of the League of Women's Rights. Tired of sterile polemics, she wanted to invest her energy in a smaller group that was "more serious" and "more efficient," that would set reachable goals. Simone de Beauvoir had suggested a law against sexism, like the existing one against racism. A law would not be enough to make sexism disappear, no more than a law had made racism disappear, but at least it would be a useful strategic tool for reaction, at the disposal of concerned persons or legal entities devoted to this matter. This is the reason they decided at the same time to found an association with that as its objective: the League of Women's Rights, presided over by Simone de Beauvoir, would be a legal instrument for the movement to use.

For others, this was not at all an obvious step. To constitute an association was to break with what had been the strength and originality of the women's movement, which had been anti-institutional and extraparliamentary. Liliane Kandel, Cathy Bernheim, and Catherine Deudon were of this opinion. Anne's initiative seemed to them to be a denial, an abandonment of what constituted the richness of the MLF: a spontaneous movement with no designated leader, no membership, and no delegation of power. By putting a "recognized, responsible, representative organization of women" in place, wouldn't they be stifling and burying the women's movement and its spontaneity, its absence of structure and power? By formulating a "demand for a law" within the framework of the existing system, which was bourgeois and patriarchal, wouldn't they be collaborating with it and compromising themselves? Playing the institutional game would be to misunderstand the resulting effects of such an instrument on the movement and the women's struggle. It would be to start the irreversible process of co-optation, the taking charge of women, if not regaining control over them.[5]

The creation of the League of Women's Rights and the divergences among feminists that followed marked the end of a stage. As the first ones to take the position that social subversion was no longer called for, the founders of the League of Women's Rights decided that it was better to ensure their gains rather than lose everything. They entered into a resolutely reformist perspective, aimed at bringing the MLF out of the left wing where it had been born.

\* \* \*

Simone de Beauvoir did not take sides in this quarrel. She supported the creation, on March 8, 1974, of the League of Women's Rights, of which she was president. At the same time she offered a permanent place in *Les temps modernes* to those who preferred to fight sexism by denouncing it with perspicacity and humor, rather than demanding a legal tool. Hence the column "Everyday Sexism" was born.[6]

While the League of Women's Rights, no longer afraid of reformism, deployed an effective activism, the "Everyday Sexism" team deepened reflections that were as humorous as they were subtle. It was not a matter of constructing a radical feminist theory, as *Questions féministes* [Feminist questions] would later do, but of deciphering immediate reality within a rich and original debate to which each woman brought her own style. Simone de Beauvoir appreciated the intellectual dialogue of this small group and their freedom of tone. She very readily agreed to put herself into question ("I myself have more or less played the role of the token woman"), and to see her schemas of rational thought shaken up. This is why, besides the monthly column "Everyday Sexism," she allowed the team to produce a special issue of *Les temps modernes* called *Les femmes s'entêtent* [Women insist], which gathered together the questions and debates of the movement in that year of 1974: marriage and divorce, motherhood, homosexuality, rape, but also the difficulties of existing with these contradictions in a "Super-Ego Movement." Sociological analyses of schools and the streets appeared right next to dreams and visions. As Beauvoir points out, this issue was presented "with disruption in mind."

Other reports and special issues of *Les temps modernes* accompanied the deepening of feminist thought: *Petites filles en éducation* [Little girls in education] (May 1976) and *Est-ce ainsi que les hommes jugent?* [Is this how men judge?] (February 1979), which questioned the relationship between women and the law when feminists were criticized for appealing to justice for more effective prosecution of rape. The long history of feminism also found its place there: the history of the right to become a lawyer so difficult for women to obtain; the debates and demands for new laws by the feminist conventions at the beginning of the twentieth century; and the image of past feminism as moralistic and integrationist, which was echoed in the denigration of contemporary feminism. Indeed, the activists had discovered the history of feminism and the oblivion into which it had been thrust by official history. They endeavored to reestablish the facts, republish texts, and question men's history. Around the same time, Jean-Paul Sartre was invited to construct a series of television shows called "Sartre, Witness of His Century," and Simone de Beauvoir included the feminists in this project. Several brilliant left-wing male intellectuals involved in the project, who were competing for the attention of the philosopher, could accept that "women" have a small part in it, but certainly not that they would give their opinion on its overall construction. The "Sartre Series" would never be completed because French television in 1975 did not have enough autonomy to allow the greatest philosopher of the century to express himself freely.

The women's movement experienced a sort of renewal during the years 1977–78. Many journals and magazines came out, such as *Histoires d'elles* [Women's history] (March 1977), *La revue d'en face* [The magazine from the other side] (May 1977), *Questions féministes* (November 1977), *Parole* [Speech] (Spring 1978), *Le temps des femmes* [Women's time] (March 1978), and *Femmes travailleuses en lutte* [Working women fight back] (new edition at the end of 1978). *Des femmes en mouvement* [Women on the move] became a weekly publication.[7]

Simone de Beauvoir became the Publication Director of *Questions féministes*, a radical feminist theory magazine founded notably by Christine Delphy, Emmanuelle de Lesseps, Nicole Claude Mathieu, and later joined by Monique Wittig in 1979. After the split in the collective,[8] Beauvoir became Publication Director of the new journal, *Nouvelles questions féministes* [New feminist questions]. Not reserving her support only for "revolutionary feminists," she did an interview in *La revue d'en face* in order to help launch the new journal.

## The Urgency of an Anti-Sexist Law

The project for an anti-sexist law meant a lot to Simone de Beauvoir, as she explained in her *La revue d'en face* interview: "I do not at all believe that a law prevents struggles outside of State institutions and independent of them. . . . The fact that it would be against the law to publicly insult women . . . would not prevent women from leading struggles on their own against sexism."[9]

She called attention to its urgency on the occasion of a tragic news item, since sexism is responsible for violence against women, including murder. She emphasized in "The Urgency of an Anti-Sexist Law" that although violence originates essentially with men, it is not some "unchangeable given of nature" that makes men violent (since "one is not born, but rather becomes, a man") but a cultural and social environment that tolerates discrimination and sexism. Well before the concept of gender had been forged, Simone de Beauvoir was using it.

With the change of political power in 1981, the new government took up many feminist proposals, including the anti-sexist law. Yvette Roudy, Secretary of Women's Rights, wanted to complement her important law on professional equality with a bill "regarding the fight against sex-based discrimination," which would extend the stipulations of the law banning racism to include sexism and would give an association the legal right to fight against public ads and signs that attack the dignity of women. The uproar against this proposed law was impressive. Advertisers posed as heralds of freedom. The press, with *Libération* in the lead, stood in the way, fearing neither self-contradiction nor bad faith, and distorted the project, denouncing the Puritanism and hypocrisy of this "G-string law," in the name of the alleged mission of sexist advertisements to express fantasies. It pretended to believe that vast sections of literature were threatened. Simone de Beauvoir, in "La femme, la pub et la haine" [Women, ads and hate], attempted in vain to let the voice of reason be heard in this overheated public debate: it did not concern literature; only advertisements that, "instead of being *offered* to [individual] freedoms, are *imposed* upon all eyes that are subjected to them, willingly or not." The fact that this proposed law was abandoned but especially the terms of the debate showed the depth of sexism in French culture. Advertisements, along with the fantasies evoked by their abusive use of images of women, remained untouchable. Thirty some years later, it has hardly changed, and feminist associations such as Mix-cité [Mixed city], Encore féministes [Still feminists], and the Chiennes de garde [Female watchdogs] continue to denounce, without much success, the objectification of women's bodies.

## Marriage, Divorce, and Freedom for Mothers

Simone de Beauvoir's opposition to marriage, the patriarchal institution par excellence, is well known. For herself, she chose and made official a mode of free and egalitarian union that also allowed for secondary, contingent liaisons. This life choice may have caused outrage in her day, but for the generation of 1968 and the feminists emerging from that generation, it presented itself as an alternative model that many women (and men) would adopt. Marriage was profoundly reformed by the 1965 law on marriage settlements that notably permitted women to work and open a bank account without their husband's authorization, as well as the 1970 law instituting "parental authority" instead of "paternal power," and the 1972 law on filiation giving equality to children born inside and outside of marriage. But this "modernization" of the institution of marriage that extensively challenged the patriarchal principles of the Napoleonic code was not enough to make it an attractive option: the number of marriages decreased (25% in 10 years), and the divorce rate doubled (tripled in the big cities).

In spite of these reforms, the conjugal bond remained a form of "slavery" for many women, and those who sought to escape from it ran up against an "inhuman, bureaucratic, often absurd judicial system," as Simone de Beauvoir explains in her preface to *Divorce in France*. This is why she displayed her indignation, in "My Point of View: An Outrageous Affair," when the courts upheld "the legal fiction that the father of a child conceived during marriage is the husband" despite the "biologic and sociologic reality." This is why she wrote the preface to a book about divorce that testified to the obstacles and injustice of a system that "systematically puts women at a disadvantage," ignoring the violence done to them and refusing divorce by mutual consent. But the book is also a testimony of liberation for the woman who escapes from hell and for her child who can be "assassinated" by parents determined to live side by side in disunion. Claire Cayron's book is a plea for divorce reform. And this reform was voted into law in 1976, permitting divorce by mutual consent in order to simplify and decrease the trauma of divorce.

## Trickery and Counterrevolutions

The 1970s ended in betrayal and confusion. The Iranian revolution started an upheaval whose scope was grasped by few at the time. The Cold War had become entrenched in passive coexistence and the principal struggle would no longer be between East and West, between capitalism and Marxism. A new battleground was opening, where religion gained ground over politics, where dogma was asserted against individual freedom. The Iranian revolt was incontestably a popular movement in search of justice, with impressive determination, despite the repression, and with an anti-imperialistic character that might seem attractive to some. But how could one not be worried by the reclamation of a faith from another age, incarnated by the old Ayatollah hidden away in the Parisian suburbs. As soon as morals came into play, it was clear that women would be a central political pawn. Would women be unveiled and westernized, or would they be veiled again, like flags signaling the return to a tradition reinvented according to the needs of the moment, and diffusing throughout the world a model opposed to that of the "liberated woman"? The feminist counterrevolution had begun.

In March of 1979, women who had participated in the demonstrations against the Shah's regime and contributed to his fall, once more took to the streets of Tehran for five consecutive days. They were protesting against the obligatory veil. Attacked by counterdemonstrators, they were accused of playing into the hands of counterrevolutionaries and being manipulated by foreign agents. International feminist solidarity had to be shown, in spite of the hesitations from the Left. On March 16, a demonstration was organized in Paris with the slogans: "No Shah, no chador, no Russian tanks," "The Right veils women; the Left veils its eyes," and "Sails/veils unfurled . . . toward terror?"[10]

Simone de Beauvoir, who had been engaged in all geopolitical conflicts where freedom and human dignity were at stake, must have felt particularly concerned when it had to do with women. "We must denounce the outrages without allowing ourselves to be intimidated by the fact that we are Westerners," she declared in *La revue d'en face.* "There are interests of women and feminism that surpass all the differences between nations and regimes."[11] She therefore accepted the position of president of the International Committee for Women's Rights, whose objective, as she explained in her opening statement at a March 15, 1979, press conference, was to inform themselves and the global public of the situation of women in each country throughout the world, and to support the actions and struggles of women for their rights. On March 19, the Committee sent an "information gathering mission" to Tehran made up of female celebrities, journalists, writers, and artists: more of a publicity initiative than an effective one. In spite of the reassuring promises of the Ayatollah Taleghani, all women in Iran were soon forced to wear the veil. This attack upon the freedom of women was only the first sign of human rights violations. And the international feminist mobilization, which was a powerful symbol, was well justified.

The "feminism of the 1970s" symbolically came to a close in the year 1980 with its victory—the law on abortion was enlarged and made permanent—but also with its failure as a spontaneous movement founded on trust among women. An association named *Mouvement de libération des femmes* [MLF or French Women's Liberation Movement] was legally formed and shortly after became a commercial trademark registered with the National Institute of Industrial Property. The name MLF had legally become the property of a group that forbade any one else to use it and sued anyone who dared to publicly denounce this outrage. This time Simone de Beauvoir took a stand and in her foreword to *Chroniques d'une imposture, du mouvement de libération des femmes à une marque commerciale* [Deception chronicles: From the

Women's Liberation Movement to a commercial trademark], wrote "To reduce thousands of women to silence by claiming to speak in their stead is to exert a revolting tyranny."

## NOTES

1. Simone de Beauvoir, *Le deuxième sexe*, Folio (Paris: Gallimard, [1949], 1976), 29; trans. Constance Borde and Sheila Malovany-Chevalier, *The Second Sex* (New York: Knopf, 2010), 15, and *Le deuxième sexe*, 11; *The Second Sex*, 3.

2. [Tr. The widespread civil unrest and rioting in May of 1968 involved students and workers across France who showed their discontent by erecting barricades in the streets and refusing to work for several weeks.]

3. [Tr. The Manifesto of the 343 was a declaration signed by 343 women publicly admitting that they had had an abortion. It was published in the spring of 1971, first on March 31 in *Le nouvel observateur* and then on April 5 in *Le monde*. For more details, see Sylvie Chaperon's introduction to Chapter 9 in this volume.]

4. Féminin Masculin Avenir [Feminine masculine future].

5. "For a MLF-Renewal, or for women's sake, silence." Undated, unsigned tract (1974, League of Women's Rights file, Marguerite Durand Library).

6. Selected articles have been compiled in a book called *Le sexisme ordinaire* [Everyday sexism], with a preface by Simone de Beauvoir (Paris: Editions du Seuil, "Libre à elles," 1979).

7. See Liliane Kandel, "L'explosion de la presse féministe" [The explosion of feminist publications], *Le débat*, no. 1, 1980.

8. See Françoise Picq, *Libération des femmes, Quarante ans de mouvement* [Women's liberation: Forty years of movement] (Brest: Editions Dialogue, 2011), 376, and following.

9. "Sur quelques problèmes actuels du féminisme: entretien avec Simone de Beauvoir" [Some current issues in feminism: An interview with Simone de Beauvoir], *La revue d'en face* 9/10, 1st trimester (1981): 9.

10. [Tr. The slogans in French include plays on words referring to the obligatory veils. When spoken in French, the words for "shah," "chador," and "tanks" in the first slogan all sound similar: "Ni shah, ni tchador, ni chars russes." The second slogan, "La droite voile les femmes, la gauche se voile la face," uses the expression "se voiler la face" to mean "look the other way." The last slogan plays on the words "le voile" (veil) and "la voile" (sail): "A toutes voiles (meaning 'full speed ahead under full sail,' but also sounds like 'veils to all women') . . . vers la terreur?"]

11. *La revue d'en face* 9/10 (1981): 5.

# EVERYDAY SEXISM

TRANSLATION BY MARYBETH TIMMERMANN

An individual who calls another a "dirty nigger" in front of witnesses, or who prints insulting remarks about Jews or Arabs can be brought to trial and convicted of "racial slander." But if a man publicly shouts at a woman, calling her "a whore," or if in his written work he accuses *Woman* of treachery, foolishness, fickleness, stupidity, or hysterical behavior, he runs absolutely no risk. The notion of "sexist slander" does not exist. A certain number of women, myself included, have undertaken the creation of a League of Women's Rights. One of the many goals set forth by this association is to combat discrimination against women in public advertisements, written works, and speeches. We will demand that "sexist slander" also be considered as a crime. In the meantime, *Les temps modernes* intends to denounce the most flagrant instances each month; that is the meaning behind this new column which begins today. We ask our women readers—and men readers—to collaborate here by sending us articles or facts that tell of outrages against women. If women are responsible for them, it goes without saying that we will not hesitate to denounce them because the sexism of certain women is as virulent as the sexism of men.

## NOTES

Simone de Beauvoir wrote this preface to the column called "Everyday Sexism" in *Les temps modernes* 329, December, 1973; reprinted in *Les écrits de Simone de Beauvoir*, ed. Claude Francis and Fernande Gontier (Paris: Gallimard, 1979), 514; © Éditions Gallimard, 1979.

Selected articles from the "Everyday Sexism" column in *Les temps modernes* were collected in a book called *Le sexism ordinaire* [Everyday sexism], with a new preface by Beauvoir (Paris: Editions du Seuil, 1979) where Beauvoir comments on how the column evolved since its inception: "Male chauvinism is the most widespread thing in the world, and it is expressed shamelessly, with discouraging monotony. The editors of 'Everyday Sexism' more or less gave up on listing the quotations that tirelessly repeated the same overused clichés. They preferred to analyze articles, books, and films where sexism is disguised more subtly." She also highlights the progress that had been made during those six years: "[Sexism] is a word that did not appear in the previous editions of the *Petit Robert* dictionary. Thanks to the authors of 'Everyday Sexism,' among many others, it does appear in the 1978 edition. One might think that this is a minor victory, but one would be wrong. To name something is to disclose it, and disclosure is already an action. The discrimination based on the differences between races has been condemned for a long time under the name of racism, yet the discrimination based on the differences between the sexes has been passed over in silence, which is a way of denying it. We are amazed that so-called democratic cities such as Athens and Rome could have accepted slavery without seeing that it went against their principles. No doubt posterity will wonder how an 'egalitarian' society could take for granted the oppression of women. One might say that, even for those individuals who indignantly disapprove of oppression, there exists a sort of blind spot: they literally don't *see* the oppression that women are subjected to. In creating the column 'Everyday Sexism' in *Les temps modernes*, we have attempted to open their eyes."

# LEAGUE OF WOMEN'S RIGHTS MANIFESTO

TRANSLATION BY MARYBETH TIMMERMANN

> *When she who is crushed by the world's oldest exploitation*
> *becomes aware that it must be overthrown and not managed,*
> *then finally the world will stand a chance of changing.*

Four years ago, there was a collective resurgence of the women's movement. Why? In theory, we have rights equal to those of men, thanks to the actions of the first feminists. But what happens in practice?

We continue to assume exclusive responsibility of children and domestic work. We systematically take on the most thankless jobs and are paid on average 30% less than men. There are seven of us in the National Assembly.[1] Methods that would allow us a choice of when to become pregnant are forbidden to us. Prostitution is flourishing as never before. Parts of our bodies are displayed on the city streets for the glory of this profit-driven society.

We had to conquer a few rights in order to understand that they are but a lure of liberation in a system of exploitation that only benefits the exploiters. Fundamentally, women's servitude in male society has not changed. Are we really free and equal when we are brainwashed from childhood to be submissive and obedient to men? Are we really free and equal when our entire lives unfold in subordination and under constraints?

## "Changing ourselves"

And yet the majority of women dare not recognize their oppression. Why? Because male domination is so engrained in our minds that many women

242

believe it to be "natural" and no longer even feel it. Because for generations we have been conditioned by our education and our daily lives to feel inferior, and sometimes, we end up believing it. For these reasons our fight is not only an external one; we must also carry out this fight within ourselves. We must change ourselves if we want to change our condition.

We must become aware of our alienation without allowing ourselves to be deceived by propaganda that claims, "*It has come; you are liberated. What more do you want?*" We must do away with the notions of inferiority and passivity which have been taught to us by men, and which make us say, "It has always been this way. There is no reason for it to change."

And yet, "it" has already changed! Women have finally become aware of their solidarity. They recognize that they are part of the same "category," i.e., an oppressed majority. This very unity has succeeded, in a very short period of time, in making the outrage of backstreet abortion into a public and national debate. This is proof that when the oppressed revolt, they are heard. The moment has come for us, after centuries of silence, to speak out.

The League of Women's Rights is a new instrument of action. It allows us to get together wherever we happen to be, in order to denounce specific incidents of the discrimination of which we are victims everywhere: in the home, on the street, before the law. Each time, it is a matter of convincing more women to become aware of their situation and to engage themselves in the fight against sexism, which is at the root of our economic and social system.

The League of Women's Rights puts forth the following goals:

* *To denounce sex discrimination in all its forms.*

We must attack those who use our bodies as merchandise in their spoken or written words, on posters or billboards.

Our rights to training, work, and equal salaries and responsibilities are not respected. We are given all the economically or culturally devalued jobs: housework, teaching, or nursing care. We must do away with blatant or hypocritical discrimination in the workplace. To obtain equal qualifications and salaries, we must first obtain access to equal work.

Our rights to the free use of our bodies and sexual equality are denied. We must abolish masculine morality, which reserves the right to physical pleasure and sexual initiative to men, limiting women to the roles of virgin, and then mother or whore.

Girls are being psychologically mutilated; from childhood on, the little girl is trained to be not herself, but the man's second. All her creativity and initiative is being stifled.

243

We must attack sexism at its base, in elementary school text-books and children's books, which reinforce the image of the nice-and-pretty-little-girl-who-helps-mother-and-obeys-father.

We are everywhere treated as minors and irresponsible beings. The following type of judgment must never again be formulated: "The ORTF [Office de radio-télévision française, or French Radio and Television Office] is a difficult place, constantly agitated, lacking in-depth analysis, a place I would call feminine . . . and which indeed needs a real boss" (Mr. Malaud, October 1973).[2]

* *To defend women and inform them of their actual rights.*

Male society prevents us from applying the rights we have acquired. We will fight for the application of these rights in all domains, especially in legal matters concerning family and work.

Even worse, male society dupes us by bestowing upon us what they call women's victories, in order to reinforce their domination. We will denounce the danger of pseudo-rights, like the housewife's allocation, which prohibits women from economic independence and confines them to their house-hold burdens. With this goal in mind, the League of Women's Rights includes a legal group.

* *To undertake every action that promotes new rights for women.*

We must increase women's rights beyond the minimum of rights already won. Male society has always refused them to us because it has placed us in a fundamental situation of oppression.

We are not asking for a specific right that would contribute to reinforcing our "protected" status as minors. Much to the contrary, we want to completely transform the laws, which are nothing more than an alibi for male domination, and assert our right of access to decision-making power.

In the meantime, struggles around specific issues can encourage the general public to become aware of oppression and its profound causes. Our fight for unrestricted and free abortion must be understood in this light. Our final goal is not obtaining the right to abort, which in the current system would only be a truncated right since men continue to make the decisions about our procreation. This fight, like those to come, is a way for us to mobilize around one aspect of oppression, and to make us understand that it will not go away with a few more rights. Our goal will only be reached through a total overturning of the social relations and values that form the basis of our patriarchal civilization, which is marked by exploitation.

## NOTES

"Presidée par Simone de Beauvoir, 'La ligue du droit des femmes' veut abolir la prostitu- tion" ('The League of Women's Rights,' presided over by Simone de Beauvoir, wants to abol- ish prostitution), *Le monde*, March 8, 1974: 36; © Sylvie Le Bon de Beauvoir.

This article is preceded by the following introduction: "At the initiative of some MLF (Women's Liberation Movement) activists, a League of Women's Rights has just been cre- ated in Paris, with Ms. Simone de Beauvoir as president. Contrary to other tendencies, the 'feminist' tendency of the MLF, which is at the origin of this new creation, emphasizes the need for the Movement to periodically organize actions dealing with concrete themes con- cerning the daily lives of women, and thereby prevent feminist activists from closing them- selves off in isolation. We are publishing, as a document, the text of the League of Women's Rights manifesto, which explains the goals of this organization." The article was followed by the following address: "FMA, BP 370 75625 Paris, cedex 13."

1. The French National Assembly (*Assemblée Nationale*) is the Lower House of the French Parliament consisting of 577 elected deputies.

2. Philippe Malaud (1925–2007) was a French diplomat and politician serving in the National Assembly at the time of this article.

# PREFACE TO *DIVORCE IN FRANCE*

TRANSLATION BY MARYBETH TIMMERMANN

For most women, marriage is a trap that society sets for them starting in childhood and into which they blindly fall as soon as adolescence is over. Having no experience with life, men, or themselves, they bind their existence to that of a stranger. Certainly there are some happy unions; many are tolerable. But for many couples who have come together by chance or through misunderstandings, conjugal life is a small hell. In general, the man most easily makes the best of it because he runs away from it; he works, he is independent. Supported by him, stuck in the home, the traditional woman is imprisoned in her function as wife, even if she can no longer bear it. After several years of slavery, many women dream of liberating themselves. If they really want it, divorce is one solution that is available to them. That is what Claire Cayron has chosen. And it has not been easy for her. But she has also come to understand how fallacious are some of the arguments that condemn it. She wanted her experience to benefit all women affected by this matter.

People have objected that hers was a special case: they all are. I have met many women, either in person or through correspondence, who wished to divorce. Some of them have hesitated, and others have decided to go through with it, but on more than one point their stories confirm the one related in this book. One might also say that this is an extreme case, but that is exactly what makes it a good example.

Claire Cayron's husband was more tyrannical, more sadistic, and more neurotic than the average man, yet she waited more than three years before asking a judge for authorization to leave the conjugal home. She obtained it immediately since the abuses she had suffered were apparent in her physical appearance: she was 1.75 meters tall [5' 7"] and weighed 47 kilograms [104 lbs]. Why had she put it off for so long? That is what most women do and oftentimes for an even much longer time. They know the truth very quickly but do not want to admit it to themselves. They still have a sense of indulgence for a man whom they have loved. They refuse to admit failure and fear the criticism of their families and neighbors. They feel more or less guilty, and above all they hesitate to deprive their children of the "comforts" of home. Rather than surmounting these obstacles, many resign themselves to unhappiness.

Those who, like Claire Cayron, take the plunge, run into an inhuman, bureaucratic, often absurd judicial system that systematically puts women at a disadvantage. Both sexes suffer from the inhuman and bureaucratic absurdity of the law, since two spouses who agree to separate can not obtain a divorce by mutual consent; they must come up with evidence of grievances. Claire Cayron was stunned when she had to submit to the absurdities of the system. She complained that she had been beaten, raped, and menaced with a knife almost every day by a man whose brutality had severely traumatized their oldest daughter, yet her accusations were not upheld. She had to establish proof of adultery in order to obtain a divorce—even though she was indifferent as to whether or not her husband had cheated on her.

When it comes to adultery, the discrimination against women is flagrant. For the husband, adultery is committed only if he is caught in the act at the conjugal home. But when Claire Cayron found a job as a secretary, her lawyer advised her to never be seen with a male colleague in a car, at a restaurant, or on the street, because a photograph of her in the company of a man, taken by a private detective accompanied by a bailiff, would be sufficient to establish adultery, and the court could refuse her custody of her daughters.

Hostile toward women and disregarding practicalities, the law is hardly concerned with the best interests of the children. A doctor beyond any suspicion, professor V., had stated in an official report that little S., who had become an autistic child as a result of her father's violence, could not recover unless she were only very briefly and very rarely separated from her mother. However, even though the father had proved his indifference toward his children to the point of being given a one-month suspended prison sentence for abandonment of his family, the court accorded him "visitation rights," allowing him to take his daughters with him for half of all their vacations. (Luckily he did not take advantage of this, but one visit of a few hours was enough to throw S. into convulsions and set back her progress.)

Since she was powerless to defend herself and her children against a legal code that deliberately favors males, the young woman was forced to seek the help of professionals. The author's description of her interactions with notaries, attorneys, and especially lawyers, is appalling. She had expected their excuses that she had picked a bad time. But without well-connected friends or relatives, a woman who wants a divorce has infinitely more chances of picking the wrong time than picking a good one. In fact, the judiciary system itself encourages legal professionals to be lazy, negligent, and unscrupulous, and offers them every occasion to let themselves be corrupted.

Although the author emphasizes what she calls "the dark side" of divorce in the first part of the book, it is certainly not meant to discourage women from following this course of action. Rather, it is to persuade them to file for divorce only after seriously preparing themselves for it. They should proceed with caution, inform themselves, study the law, and if possible, contact people they can trust.

The second part of this essay is more joyful; it is the victory of a divorced mother over the disorders that living with her biological family [*foyer normal*] had caused in her oldest daughter. Well developed at one year, S., a witness and victim of her father's violence, had become an autistic child by two years old. Through much vigilance, patience, love, and with the help of intelligent educators, Claire Cayron brought S. out of her neurosis; today she is a candid and happy adolescent with a keen mind who succeeds in her studies. Those well-intentioned people who are opposed to divorce in principle claim that it is always destructive for the child, but a child can be "assassinated" by parents who insist on living side by side in disunion, and can be resuscitated thanks to their separation. Here again, the case of S. is extreme, but it has a demonstrative value. It proves the falsity of such sayings as, "better to have a bad father than no father at all."

Divorce is not a panacea. It only really liberates women if they know how to put their freedom to use in a positive way. But in order to discover their own possibilities, divorce is often a necessary condition. Claire Cayron's book will give some hesitant women the courage to face it, and will also prompt women to fight in this field against the discrimination of which they are the victims. We must obtain a modification in the law so that it no longer favors men; we must invent the means that will guarantee that we see the benefits of this change in practice. This is the only possible conclusion after having followed, along with the author, the tortuous and distressing paths imposed upon her by the current legal code.

## NOTES

Simone de Beauvoir, "Préface" to *Divorce en France* by Claire Cayron (Paris: Denoël-Gonthier, 1974), reprinted in *Les écrits de Simone de Beauvoir*, ed. Claude Francis and Fernande Gontier (Paris: Gallimard, 1979), 515–18; © Éditions Gallimard, 1979.

# INTRODUCTION TO *WOMEN INSIST*

TRANSLATION BY MARYBETH TIMMERMANN

"Disruption, my sister . . ." This issue [of *Les temps modernes*] is presented with disruption in mind. The reader expecting to find here a methodical and complete account of women's condition will be disappointed. We do not claim to denounce here all the injustices suffered by women, nor to draw up an exhaustive statement of their demands, and even less to propose a revolutionary tactic. We only hope to spark some unrest in people's minds. The prevailing principle in gathering together these texts was that of freedom. We established no preconceived plan. Some women—a few of whom have even remained anonymous to us—spontaneously chose to speak about subjects that mean a lot to them, and we welcomed their writings. A radical refusal of women's oppression was a priori a common feature among them. As a result, certain themes kept reappearing in the articles that we received, which allowed us to regroup them afterward into a small number of headings. Nevertheless there exist great differences between the articles and sometimes even contradictions. Feminist thought is far from monolithic; every woman in the struggle has her own motivations, perspectives, her singular experience, and she presents them to us in her own way.

Some readers may possibly feel disconcerted in reading some of these pages. Among the women who choose to express themselves, some believe that the language and the logic currently in use in our world are universally valid instruments, even though they have been forged by men; the issue is to steal the tool. Others, on the contrary, consider that culture itself represents one of the forms of their oppression. Because of this oppression, and by the way in which they have reacted to it, women have created a cultural universe different than that of men; they want to refer to their own values by inventing speech in which their specificity is reflected. This is a difficult invention, sometimes requiring a trial-and-error approach, but when successful, this effort enriches us with a truly new contribution.

In both cases the voices that you are going to hear want above all to *disturb* you. The oppression of women is a fact that society is so used to that even those among us who condemn it overall, in the name of abstract democratic principles, assume that many of its aspects have been amended.[1] Even to me, because I myself have more or less played the role of the token woman, it seemed for a long time that certain inconveniences inherent in women's condition ought to be simply ignored or overcome; that there was no need to attack them. What the new generation of women in rebellion made me understand is that my casual disregard entailed a certain complicity. In fact, to accept the least inequality between the two sexes is to consent to Inequality. Feminists are often seen as childish and petty for attacking vocabulary and grammar, such as the fact that in French the adjective modifying three feminine nouns and one masculine noun must be masculine. Of course it is not on these grounds that the struggle must be started. But to pass over it is to risk closing one's eyes to many things. Vigilance should be part of our slogan. And indeed the new feminists look upon the world with the ingenious, demanding look of a child. The child is weak; one listens to him and smiles. Women are and want to be stronger and stronger. They make people uncomfortable, and that is why some people try to discredit their vision of things, turn it into something ridiculous, and treat them like shrews.

Readers—women or men—who approach these texts in good faith risk feeling themselves called into question by the time they finish reading. The anti-sexist struggle is not directed, like the anticapitalist struggle, only against the structures of society taken as a whole; it attacks within each of us what is most intimate to us and what seems the most sure. It questions our very desires, the very forms of our pleasure. Do not back away from this questioning, for beyond the distress that it will perhaps provoke within us, it will destroy some of our shackles and open us to new truths.

## NOTES

Simone de Beauvoir's "Présentation" (Introduction) to *Les femmes s'entêtent* (Women insist), special issue of *Les temps modernes*, April–May 1974: 1719–20; later published as the introduction to a volume with the same title (Paris: Éditions Gallimard, 1975); reprinted in *Les écrits de Simone de Beauvoir*, ed. Claude Francis and Fernande Gontier (Paris: Gallimard, 1979), 519–21; © Éditions Gallimard, 1979.

1. The last part of this sentence reads " . . . en prennent pour amendés beaucoup d'aspects" in the *Les temps modernes* special issue, but appeared as " . . . en prennent pour avenus beaucoup d'aspects" in the *Les écrits* version.

# PREFACE TO *THROUGH WOMEN'S EYES*

TRANSLATION BY MARYBETH TIMMERMANN

When I started to write, many women writers [*auteurs féminins*] specifically refused to be classified in that category. Critics were happy to review our books in columns entitled "Works by Ladies," and that irritated us. They wanted to confine us within the narrow limits of a world reserved for our sex: house, home, children, with a few escapes to nature and the cult of Love. We rejected the notion of women's literature [*littérature féminine*] because we wanted to speak on an equal plane with men about the entire universe.

And we still want to. Only the recent evolution of feminism has made us understand that we occupy a singular situation in this universe, and that, far from denying this singularity, we must claim it.

Is this to say that in order to write we must invent a specific language for ourselves? Some among us believe so, but not I. One can not create a language artificially. This proved to be the failure of the *précieuses*[1]—whose feminism was very close to our own—but whose speech was only understood within their group and quickly faded away. The same is true today; *l'écriture au féminin* [writing in the feminine] reaches only a small circle of initiates. It seems elitist to me, destined to satisfy the narcissism of the author rather than establish a communication with others.

I know that everyday language is full of traps. Claiming universality, it in fact carries the mark of the males who developed it; it reflects their values, their pretensions, and their prejudices. So it must be used only with caution. Nevertheless, it is the instrument chosen by the three novelists in this book—Claire Etcherelli, Christiane Rochefort, and myself[2]—because it seemed to us to be the best suited for making heard what we had to say.

What all three of us wanted to express, through our very different works, was certainly not the women's universe [*l'univers féminin*] in which tradition tried to confine us in times past, but the whole of society today, such as it is revealed to us, based on our condition as women. In the novels that Anne Ophir has chosen to study, Christiane Rochefort denounces, through her heroine, consumer society. Claire Etcherelli describes, through the eyes of Élise, the horrors of working on an assembly line and the ravages of racism. As for me, I attempted, in *La femme rompue* [*The Woman Destroyed*], to depict the critical moments of three female existences: the encounter with old age, the exasperation of solitude, and the brutal end of a love affair.[3] What interested me essentially in these stories was the bad faith to which my heroines clung more or less stubbornly throughout their struggles. I was pleasantly surprised, in reading Anne Ophir's essay, to see that my narratives could be viewed in a completely different way. Critics rarely teach me something about my books. Most of them are content with a superficial summary. Some want to appear too intelligent and read too much into my intentions. Anne Ophir, on the contrary, led me to make some discoveries. It may seem strange that an author doesn't know exactly what he has written. But the fact is that he follows a certain line and is more or less blind to the background upon which this line is traced. Anne Ophir showed that the consumer society, of which I speak implicitly in *Les belles images*, is the implicit context in which my three narratives unfold. Murielle in "Monologue" [The Monologue] is the victim of it; the woman in "L'âge de discrétion" [The Age of Discretion] rejects it violently; Monique in "La femme rompue" tries to escape from it, but in all three cases it is present without my really being aware of it. I told the stories of women, and, just as a fan who is passionate about one of the protagonists in a tennis or boxing match ends up not seeing the other during the match, I hardly sought to elucidate the role of the men. Anne Ophir asks me some very pertinent questions about them: why did André, for three years, let his wife write a book that he thought was bad? What are Maurice's faults and the limits of his good intentions? What events, injustices, and misfortunes made Murielle sink down into paranoid spitefulness?

On the other hand, there are themes that I consciously treated without understanding their importance, which are highlighted by Anne Ophir. The rejection of time, for example. Murielle has stopped time: she lives in a perpetually renewed present of hatred and anger; the woman in "L'âge de discrétion" refuses to admit that she is getting older; "La femme rompue" doesn't want to understand that feelings change. Above all, the problem that haunts these three narratives is that of communication: impossible in "Monologue," almost impossible in "La femme rompue," and difficult in "L'âge de discrétion."

I think that the greatest praise one can give a critical study is that it brings an unexpected light to the work of the writer. As far as I'm concerned, that is why I hope Anne Ophir's book will have a great many readers.

## NOTES

Simone de Beauvoir, "Préface" to *Regards féminins* ("Through Women's Eyes," my translation) by Anne Ophir, Collection Femmes (Paris: Denoël-Gonthier, 1976); reprinted in *Les écrits de Simone de Beauvoir*, ed. Claude Francis and Fernande Gontier (Paris: Gallimard, 1979), 577–79; © Éditions Gallimard, 1979.

1. *Précieuses* are women of seventeenth-century France who flaunted an excessive refinement and affectation of language and manners known as *preciosity*. Beginning among the aristocracy in Paris, the movement peaked to a fad that swept all France after midcentury and then died in ridicule in the 1660s. Dismissed as a silly pretentiousness of conceited, pedantic women, it has also been identified as a feminist search for identity and self-expression (*Women's Studies Encyclopedia*, ed. Helen Tierney, Greenwood Press, 2002).

2. Claire Etcherelli (1934–) is a French novelist who won the *Prix Femina* for her novel *Elise, ou la vraie vie* (*Elise, or The Real Life*) (1967); Christiane Rochefort (1917–98) was a French feminist writer who won the *Prix Médicis* in 1988. Her bestselling novel *Le repos du guerrier* (*Warrior's Rest*) was made into a film starring Brigitte Bardot in 1962.

3. *La femme rompue* (Paris: Gallimard, 1968) is a collection of three short stories, "La femme rompue," "Monologue," and "L'âge de discrétion." It was translated as *The Woman Destroyed* by Patrick O'Brian (New York: Putnam, 1969).

# WHEN ALL THE WOMEN
# OF THE WORLD . . .

TRANSLATION AND NOTES BY MARYBETH TIMMERMANN

From March 4 through March 8, 1976, the International Tribunal on Crimes Against Women will be held in Brussels. It is not by accident that this Tribunal opens just after the close of the laughable "Year of the Woman," organized by male society for the mystification of women. The feminists gathered in Brussels mean to take their destiny into their own hands. Contrary to what happened in Mexico,[1] they are mandated by neither political parties, nor by nations, nor by any political or economic group. They will express themselves as women. Indeed, whatever the regimes, laws, morality, and social environment happen to be, all women are subjected to a specific oppression. They are meeting in Brussels to denounce it. They rightly declare it to be criminal. Indeed, in institutionalized forms or not, it results in true violations against the human person.

A woman's freedom is violated when unwanted pregnancies are imposed upon her; her body is hideously mutilated when she is sterilized without her consent, when certain medical or psychiatric treatments are inflicted upon her, when she is made to undergo that cruel operation that a great number of Islamic people practice: excision. Economically speaking, women are the victims of a discrimination as unacceptable as the racial discrimination which is condemned by society in the name of human rights. Unpaid domestic work is extorted from women, they are doomed to perform the least appreciated tasks, and their salaries are less than that of their male counterparts.

In spite of the inferior status to which males have reduced them, women are the favored object of their aggressiveness. Nearly everywhere—including in the United States and in France—the number of rapes is increasing; physical cruelty is considered normal, even the psychological or frankly brutal attacks that women are faced with, for example, when walking alone in the street.

This widespread violence is unanimously ignored and passed over in silence. Even against blatant violence—rapes, grievous bodily harm—there is no legal recourse in the immense majority of cases. It seems that the lot of women is to suffer and remain silent.

The women who are going to gather together in Brussels boldly refuse this lot. In order to lead this struggle, they have been forming groups in many countries for a long time already. But separated by distance and by difficulties in communication, these groups are more or less unaware of each other. For the first time, they are going to come together, and women coming from all over the world will realize the common core of oppression that underlies the diversity of their problems. They will develop defense tactics, the first being precisely what they are preparing to put into practice: to speak to each other, to speak out, to shed light on the scandalous truths that half of humanity tries so hard to cover up. In itself, the Tribunal of Brussels is one act. By the international solidarity that it is going to create among women, it heralds many others. Given the impact that this Tribunal will have on the process of women's decolonization, I think it must be considered as a great historic event.

## NOTES

"Quand toutes les femmes du monde. . . ." (*Le nouvel observateur*, March 1, 1976, 52) is an expanded version of a letter published in *The Proceedings of the International Tribunal on Crimes Against Women*, ed. Diana E. H. Russell and Nicole Van de Ven (Millbrae, Calif.: Les Femmes, 1976); reprinted in *Les écrits de Simone de Beauvoir*, ed. Claude Francis and Fernande Gontier (Paris: Gallimard, 1979), 566–67; © Éditions Gallimard, 1979.

1. The first World Conference on Women was held in Mexico City, Mexico, from June 19 to July 2, 1975. Over 100 nations were represented and 22 governments adopted the "World Plan of Action" that was later adopted as a UN resolution. The Conference kicked off the UN's "Decade for Women" (1976–85) and was followed by three more UN World Conferences on Women (in Copenhagen, 1980; in Nairobi, 1985; and in Beijing, 1995).

# MY POINT OF VIEW: AN OUTRAGEOUS AFFAIR

TRANSLATION BY DEBBIE MANN AND MARYBETH TIMMERMANN

To the Presiding Judge of the 26th Chamber:

Having been informed by Marie Bataille of the situation which, after two years of proceedings, will take her before the criminal court, I wish to convey to you my point of view about this affair.

For a long time I have been an activist for voluntary motherhood. I believe that a woman has the right to choose to have or to not have a child, and in the first case, to choose the father of her child. Therefore I welcomed the recent law on abortion and before that, the 1972 law on filiation, which requires that the child be recognized in its biologic and sociologic reality.

In Marie Bataille's case, that reality is easily verifiable. Her liaison with A . . . is confirmed by many witnesses. She has publicly declared that he is the father of the child, and she has gone to live with him and the baby.

It was possible to conduct blood tests that would have proven this filiation. However, regardless of the law of 1972, the appellate court refused to examine the facts and hid behind the legal fiction that the father of a child conceived during marriage is the husband. Based on this fiction, the judicial system has denied the mother her right to speak; it did not listen to her.

It is outrageous that, contrary to legislation that calls for the establishment of the truth, a mother finds herself reduced to silence in an affair that essentially concerns her. Why this arbitrary decision from the court? Obviously because Marie Bataille shamelessly claims to be an adulterous woman: a woman who has chosen the man from whom she wanted a child and has chosen to raise this child with him.

An unjust jurisprudence has attacked her freedom as a mother. And for having wanted and affirmed this freedom, she risks paying a very high price . . .

One of the commonplaces of our society is the glorification of motherhood. Yet in Marie Bataille's case, the act of assuming this role freely and faithfully is considered by the courts as an offense. The patriarchal moral code triumphs. The woman is subjugated, even in her motherhood, to the capricious will of her husband. He is the one who is granted the privilege to impose *his* truth, even if in doing so, *the* truth is defied.

So this affair goes far beyond the singular case of Marie Bataille; it shows all women that the conjugal bond remains for them a chain of slavery, in spite of the efforts of the 1972 legislation.

I wish that a more enlightened justice would break this chain and acknowledge the rights of Marie Bataille and the truth.

## NOTES

The article "Mon point de vue, par Simone de Beauvoir: une affaire scandaleuse," (*Marie Claire* 286, June, 1976, 6; © Sylvie Le Bon de Beauvoir) was preceded by the following: "A woman is convicted for wanting and affirming her freedom as a mother."

# PREFACE TO *STORIES FROM THE FRENCH WOMEN'S LIBERATION MOVEMENT*

TRANSLATION BY MARYBETH TIMMERMANN

In August, 1970, barely six years ago, a few women demonstrated at the Arc de Triomphe in honor of "the wife of the unknown soldier." And so for the first time the newspapers mentioned the MLF [Mouvement de libération des femmes or French Women's Liberation Movement]. This name, similar to the American "Women's Lib," was given to the movement by the press, and the militants took it on for themselves. Ever since, the MLF has become very well known, or rather very poorly known, because the image propagated about them is one of hysterical shrews and lesbians. The primary merit of this book is to completely refute this cliché.

The book does not tell the history of the MLF. Such a history is currently impossible to write. The MLF is not a political party, nor even a unified coalition [*rassemblement*]. In spite of a common element, which is the revolt against the oppression of women, diverse groups coexist within the MLF, often in opposition or clashing with each other. Hence the book is entitled *Histoires du MLF* [Stories from the French Women's Liberation Movement]. Two militants of the early days relate their experiences in this book. Their stories follow each other chronologically, Anne having participated in the creation of the Movement into which Annie did not enter until a bit later.

Through their stories and their descriptions of one another, they appear as thoughtful and poised women, and, knowing them well, I can testify to the truth of this description. There is nothing extravagant in their outward appearance or actions, nothing outrageous in their language. Two women similar to many others, different only in that they have felt women's bondage with an exceptional force and have tried with exceptional perseverance to liberate their sisters.

They soberly tell us the reasons for this revolt and for this stubbornness. Their childhood and adolescence took place in very different circumstances, but both suffered from the condition inflicted upon women and vehemently refused it. Anne's formative experience was the most painful because of her father's brutality. Annie was strongly motivated by the contempt for women and the injustices they suffer in the professional sphere.

Both are of foreign origin, and that partly explains how they could stand back to assess our society. This distance allowed them to escape the role "normally" imposed upon women. Well before the MLF existed, they deliberately chose to be neither wives nor mothers. They gave themselves to careers that interested them and assured their independence.

Annie reveals very few things about her personal life. Anne, on the contrary, has chosen to share it with us. She believes that feminism is not only a public undertaking, but that it should also be lived out in one's private life. Having first assumed the role of "bitch"[1]—in opposition to the gentle submission of maternity—her path eventually led her to decide to renounce men. By telling us about her transition to homosexuality, she attempts to show that it signifies the search for an authentic human relationship. Two beings who share the same condition and the same lived experiences, she thinks, have a better chance of understanding each other and loving each other than two individuals separated by the diversity of their experience.

Before carrying out this intimate revolution, Anne was engaged in a collective action. The beginning was difficult. When, after having been activists in the Mouvement démocratique féminin [Women's Democratic Movement or MDF] for want of anything better, Anne and her friend Jacqueline [Feldman] created Féminin Masculin Avenir [Feminine Masculine Future or FMA]; the group included only about fifteen members, men and women. Its numbers rose suddenly in 1968 after a debate about the condition of women organized by Anne at the Sorbonne, but it dissolved quickly. In 1970, only six members remained, two of whom were men. But Anne's attempt came within a favorable historical context. Other groups, pursuing analogous goals, had been formed and made contact with the FMA. One day, thirty women were assembled, which seemed miraculous to Anne. Serious differences of opinion appeared right away. The other groups reproached the FMA for accepting both men and women. Anne and her friends were in agreement; it was up to women and women alone to lead the fight for the liberation of women. This principle was never questioned again. But there was no possible conciliation on another point; certain militants wanted to subordinate the struggle of women to the class struggle. The FMA declared itself radically feminist; the struggle of women seemed to them to be fundamental and not secondary. This is also my position. In countries all over the world I have heard it said—from men but also from women—that one must first worry about the revolution, the triumph of socialism, and national security; later one could take an interest in the problems of women. But from my experience this later means never. Of course, both struggles must be linked. But the example of the countries known as socialist proves that an economic change in no way leads to the decolonization of women.

Sometimes Anne and Annie have been criticized for their apolitical attitude, in other words their disinterest in the politics of men. But it is precisely because they were not confined to any party, and because no ideology was blinding them that they were able to rightly appreciate the subversive value of a feminist engagement.

In spite of these disagreements, all the groups fused into the vast movement that was thereafter called the MLF. General meetings were held at the Beaux-Arts school twice a month. Right away a problem arose which was never resolved: that of organization. In opposition to hierarchies and male bureaucracy, the women refused all organization. This resulted in tumultuous meetings that Anne qualifies as "invigorating," but that disconcerted the newcomers. Annie, who joined the MLF after having read the special issue of *Partisans* called *Liberation of Women: Year Zero*, published by Maspero in 1970,[2] admits that she felt very uneasy in the general meetings, which gave her a difficult start as a militant. To tell the truth, despite the rejection of organization, there was no true democracy within the MLF. The women who had the loudest voices or were most gifted with speech dominated the meetings. Ultimately, the most motivated and most committed ones assumed a maximum of responsibility, and as a result found themselves having the power of a leader. This is how it was for Anne. It flattered her for a while, but soon this role as leader overwhelmed her, especially as it aroused a certain hostility or at least defiance in her comrades. It was necessary not only to fight against the hostile male world but against the many factions that, while pursuing the same goal, differed radically on the means of attaining it.

The miracle is that despite these disputes and inconsistencies, actions were being carried out: the Manifesto of the 343 on abortion and the public hearings at the Mutualité meeting hall were brilliant successes.[3] So Anne and Annie experienced moments of triumphant joy that repaid their efforts. But reconciling their activism with their jobs led to excessive fatigue that sometimes made them want to give it all up. In order to mobilize the mass of women, an exhausting effort of imagination and invention was necessary. After the Women's Fair and the creation of a Women's Center in Trévise, 1974 seemed to Annie to be "the blackest year of the movement."

Yet they stood their ground. They created the League of Women's Rights, which plans to lead an anti-sexist campaign on many fronts. Annie describes in detail its diverse activities and the obstacles that were encountered. At the very heart of the MLF a division emerged between the League and other groups which refused any recourse to the legal system. They accused the League of reformism. As for me, I believe that extracting reforms from the government can be a step on the way to revolution—as long as one is not satisfied with that, of course, and instead turns it into a point of departure toward new demands. While developing projects for anti-sexist laws, the League also devoted itself to specific and important actions. It initiated a campaign to condemn rape. It created S.O.S. Alternatives to offer help to battered women. It resorted to legal means—seeking the intervention of Françoise Giroud[4]—and illegal means—such as occupying the Plessis-Robinson City Hall—in order to assure a shelter for them.

This struggle against the rapes and violence suffered by women was harshly criticized by journalists—both male and female. To prosecute a man in Strasbourg who beat his wife to death with his fists, or to demand that rape be considered a felony, we were told, is to accept bourgeois justice. Annie responds very well to this objection. If a migrant worker is mistreated or killed, journalists have no problem with the prosecution of his aggressor or murderer. And rightly so. But why should women give up and accept anything? Today any revolutionary attitude entails a certain amount of compromise with the current state of things. To refuse us the means of revolting is to refuse our revolt.

One sees that this book is far from anecdotal. From the outset, it plunges you into the heart of the problems posed by the birth and development of a revolutionary movement, because for me it is beyond doubt that the decolonization of women implies a radical overthrowing of society. How can democracy and efficacy be reconciled within the movement? How can the traps of power and disorder be avoided? What compromises can one accept or should one not accept with the world as it is?

Such are the questions that appeal to the reader, in a way that is far from abstract since we participate in the lived experience of two women who have dedicated their existence to resolving them. In discussing these questions for us, they [Anne and Annie] shed a vivid and cruel light on the condition of women. In telling the stories of their struggle, they make us understand the reasons for this struggle.

And I hope that all—men and women alike—who claim to be unaware of these reasons finish this book with a sense of unease.

## NOTES

"Préface," *Histoires du MLF* by Annie de Pisan and Anne Tristan (Paris: Calmann-Lévy, 1977), 7–12; © Sylvie Le Bon de Beauvoir.

1. In French, this is *garce*, which originally meant "girl" as it is the feminine form of *garçon*, meaning "boy." In modern language, it can mean "prostitute" or slut and is commonly used as a crude insult to any annoying or mean woman.

2. The publishing house created by François Maspero in 1959 was known for publishing leftist books during the 1970s and later became Éditions de la Découverte. Maspero also created the leftist review *Partisans*, whose May 1970 special issue was entitled *Libération des Femmes, année zéro*.

3. See Françoise Picq's introduction to this chapter as well as Sylvie Chaperon's introduction to Chapter 9 in this volume for more information on these events.

4. Françoise Giroud (1916–2003) was a French journalist and writer who served as Secretary of State for Women (*Secrétaire d'État à la Condition féminine*) from 1974–76, and French Minister of Culture from 1976–77.

# THE URGENCY OF AN ANTI-SEXIST LAW

TRANSLATION AND NOTES BY MARYBETH TIMMERMANN

The Yvelines criminal court has recently acquitted Mr. Leber (see *Le monde*, January 24),[1] who had fatally beaten his wife and who had left her to slowly die on the kitchen floor all night long.

What we are calling into question are the sexist motivations that have led to this acquittal. For having broken a few windows, young people are sentenced to years of imprisonment. For having killed his wife, Mr. Leber will receive no penalty on the pretext that this offense falls under the domain of "love" or the conjugal relationship. It is worth questioning a judicial system where circumstances that are usually aggravating become, in this case, attenuating circumstances.

\* \* \*

The defense's argument, which won the support of the jury, is the following: grievous bodily harm does not necessarily imply the intention to kill. In truth, especially when it is repeated, violence is always a way, more or less disguised, of wanting to kill the other. The thousands of calls from beaten women to *S.O.S. Femmes-Alternative* [S.O.S. Women-Alternative] and the women taken in at the Flora-Tristan shelter* have confirmed to us that a violent man beats regularly. Subsequent offenses are, in all other cases, aggravating circumstances; why do they make an exception when it is a matter of conjugal violence?

Likewise, alcoholism is considered aggravating when it is a matter of driving a car, yet it becomes attenuating in cases of conjugal violence. In a general manner, crimes of passion are attenuating circumstances. Does loving, then, implicitly authorize killing?

\* \* \*

The Yvelines verdict seems to us extremely revealing of the sexist mentality. Contrary to what people claim, we, feminists, do not wish to take our revenge on men. But the fact is that we do not have the choice; in order to protect women, certain men must be put away. We do not consider that sufficient; we would like to eliminate violence, and for that it is necessary to attack its very roots.

Violence is mainly perpetrated by men (95% of it, according to the Peyrefitte report).[2] But that is not an unchangeable given of nature. One is not born, but rather becomes, a man [*mâle*]. The Minister of Justice makes a false analysis of violence when he limits it to its exterior appearance. Violence takes root in the intimacy of the individual. The manifestation of violence outside of oneself is generally what logically follows violence "within oneself."

We would like to act upon these masculine mentalities turned into aggression against women by the entire cultural environment: advertisements, pornography, literature. An anti-sexist law would allow us to publicly denounce each case of sexist discrimination. In the long term, we would create an anti-sexist reflex that would have kept Mrs. Leber from dying. She would not have allowed herself to be beaten, he would not have dared to systematically beat her up, the neighbors would have intervened, the social services would have responded . . .

In order for women, in the short term, to be able to preserve their lives and their dignity, and in order for the violence of men, in the long term, to be nothing more than a bad memory, it suffices to add one small word to the law banning racism: the word *sex*. It has already been five years since we started, in this same column (*Le monde*, March 8, 1974), a campaign for an anti-sexist law. It seems to me high time that it comes to pass.

---

\* Flora-Tristan, 7, rue du Landy, 92 Clichy. [This address for the Flora-Tristan shelter was footnoted in the original article.]

266

## NOTES

"De l'urgence d'une loi antisexiste," *Le monde*, March 18–19, 1979, 1; © Sylvie Le Bon de Beauvoir.

1. Yvelines is a French department in the region of Île-de-France.
2. In 1977, a commission chaired by Alain Peyrefitte, who was then the French Minister of Justice, published a report entitled "Réponses à la violence" (Responses to violence). This Peyrefitte Report was a study of violence in France at the time, notably the first occurrences of violent unrest in the *banlieues* (suburbs) and contained recommendations for policies that the government could implement in reaction to this violence.

# PRESS CONFERENCE OF THE INTERNATIONAL COMMITTEE FOR WOMEN'S RIGHTS

TRANSLATION BY MARYBETH TIMMERMANN

Well! We have created the *Comité international du droit des femmes* [CIDF or International Committee for Women's Rights] in response to calls from a large number of Iranian women, whose situation and revolt have greatly moved us. We have decided to create this committee with several tasks in mind. The first task: information. It is a matter of becoming informed about the situation of women across the world, a situation which, to a very, very large extent is extremely difficult, painful, and I will even say odious. Therefore, we wish to inform ourselves, in very precise cases, of this situation.

We then wish to inform others of it; that is to say to communicate through articles the knowledge that we have gained. And finally, we wish to support the struggle of the women who fight against the situation affecting them. That is the general idea of the CIDF (ICWR).

And the first task assigned to us concerns a very, very burning case today. It is the task of informing, communicating our knowledge, and supporting the struggle of Iranian women. Because we have received a call [*appel*] from a very large number of them, and we have also seen, without even having a direct call, how they were struggling, how they were fighting, what they were doing. We have appreciated the depth of the utter humiliation with which they are threatened, and we have therefore resolved to fight for them.

And so the first practical act that is going to concretize our call to action is a precise action: we are sending a delegation of women to Tehran, in order to inform themselves, essentially in order to inform themselves. We have sent a telegram to Mr. Bazargan,[1] asking him if he will see us. I say we, although I personally, for health reasons, I am not going there. But I have many women friends who are going to go there on Monday. So we have asked that he receive us. If he does not answer, well! In that case we are going there anyway. But in that case, it will no longer be a dialogue with a head of state, but solely an information gathering effort. Unless they turn us away immediately, which is still very possible. It is very possible that the mission will fail, inasmuch as they might turn it away the moment it arrives. Nevertheless the die will have been cast, and it is important to show the demonstration of solidarity of a very large number of Western women, French women, Italian women, or others, with the struggle of Iranian women.

But I repeat that this matter is essentially an effort of gathering information, an information gathering mission in order to put ourselves in contact with Iranian women, in order to know their demands and the ways in which they plan to struggle.

## NOTES

"Discours d'introduction," given at a press conference of the International Committee for Women's Rights, March 15, 1979; © Sylvie Le Bon de Beauvoir.

1. Mehdi Bazargan (1907–95) was an Islamic scholar and prodemocracy activist who served briefly as Prime Minister of Iran after the Iranian Revolution in 1979.

# FOREWORD TO *DECEPTION CHRONICLES: FROM THE WOMEN'S LIBERATION MOVEMENT TO A COMMERCIAL TRADEMARK*

TRANSLATION BY MARYBETH TIMMERMANN

In 1971, when I first made contact with the MLF [Mouvement de Libération des Femmes, or French Women's Liberation Movement] about the manifesto that 343 women signed saying that they had had abortions, I only met a few isolated representatives. Later I learned that they belonged to different groups with diverse tendencies that all coexisted without trying to get organized. The movement questioned any centralized, bureaucratic, or hierarchical militant movements, and therefore had no leader. In order to belong, it was enough to be a woman, aware of the oppression endured by women and eager to combat it. This resulted in a certain disorder, sometimes annoying, but overall enriching. Unity was realized through actions accomplished in common.

I had heard of one group that was more cohesive than the others, whose leader was a woman named Antoinette [Fouque]. This group was characterized by "a strange mixture of leftism revised by a feminism that didn't declare itself, all of which was expressed in erudite language that was absolutely incomprehensible for anyone who had not read Marx or spent time with Lacan."*[1] It was called "Psych et Po"** and, at the time, hardly ever appeared publicly. In 1972, when it saw that, after months of meetings, the public hearings at the Mutualité hall denouncing crimes against women were going well, it finally decided to get involved, but without providing us with any financial support, which would have been very useful and which "Psych et Po" could have done since the group had enormous resources due to the presence of an inherited wealth. The same thing happened with the "Women's Fair" (Vincennes, 1973) and with the March for abortion (Paris, October 6, 1979): when it seemed clear that the undertakings were going to succeed, "Psych et Po" ended up following along, but without contributing in any way to their success.

This cenacle was very closed in upon itself and soon devoted itself almost exclusively to a publishing house called "Éditions des Femmes" [Women's press]. Cultivating paradox, or more accurately, lies, this group was part of the MLF, yet called itself antifeminist; had considerable funds at its disposal, yet claimed to be anticapitalist; and even went so far as to say that, as a group, it was not participating in the Book Fair in Nice, even though it had a booth there.

When three women who had been published by them went public with accounts of the difficulties they had experienced when dealing with them, the leaders of the "Éditions des Femmes" turned the tables on the plaintiffs and sued them for defamation. Yet they were the ones defaming all the other feminists by constructing a ridiculous and obnoxious image of feminists and then using their fortune to mount an advertising campaign that flooded the press with this image.

Over the years, feminists from the other groups tried to fight back, but timidly. They thought that it was better to "wash their dirty linen in private" and avoid providing their adversaries—both male and female—with the spectacle of their dissensions.

This policy of silence did not pay off. On the contrary, it encouraged "Psych et Po" to unleash their ambitions. For a long time, this little sect asserted itself overseas as the only valid incarnation of the MLF. It went much further than that in October 1979 by registering itself as a nonprofit association legally known as "Mouvement de Libération des Femmes—MLF." The initials MLF had thus become its property.

---

* Anne Tristan, Annie de Pisan, *Histoires du MLF* [Stories from the French Women's Liberation Movement] (Paris: Calmann-Lévy, 1977).
** "Psychoanalysis and Politics."

All the other feminist groups in France signed protest manifestos. And in 1980, at the large meeting of women held in Copenhagen,[2] eleven feminist publishing houses drafted a tract denouncing the appropriation of the initials MLF by the "Éditions des Femmes." Ten of them were foreign; only Éditions Tierce is French, and the "Éditions des Femmes" limited liability company (created by "Psych et Po") filed a commercial lawsuit against them for "unfair competition." Tierce, whose means are very modest, and who was only trying to distribute feminist ideas without necessarily gaining a profit, is now threatened with destruction by a sect of antifeminist feminists, anticapitalist capitalists, and mercenary ideologists. In response to this threat, several authentic and disinterested feminists have decided to bring this affair to the public's attention. I hope the public does not think that this is simply a matter of a frivolous local dispute. To reduce thousands of women to silence by claiming to speak in their stead is to exert a revolting tyranny; and in whatever form it takes, the refusal of this tyranny concerns us all. This abuse is all the more outrageous considering that Antoinette and her followers claim to be lovers of social justice and in rebellion against the world of the affluent. Yet their affluence is what has allowed them to accomplish this seizure of power which has been their sole goal for a long time. We must read this document,[3] and against the triumph of money that once again has carried the day, and against the slander and lies that it has perpetuated, we must help women regain their voices and express themselves through their difficulties and even their contradictions within their multifaceted truth.

## NOTES

"Foreword," *Chroniques d'une imposture: du mouvement de libération des femmes à une marque commerciale* (Paris: l'Association Mouvement pour les Luttes Féministes, 1981); © Sylvie Le Bon de Beauvoir.

1. Jacques Lacan (1901–81) was a leading French psychiatrist and psychoanalyst.

2. This was the second World Conference on Women, held five years after the first one in Mexico City, both organized by the UN as part of their Decade for Women initiative.

3. According to the editors' preface to *Chroniques d'une imposture*, "The collection presented here is composed of published and unpublished texts treating different aspects of the 'Psychépo' phenomenon such as they appeared at various times during the Women's Liberation Movement."

# WOMEN, ADS, AND HATE

TRANSLATION AND NOTES BY MARYBETH TIMMERMANN

If it weren't so disturbing, the flood of misogyny set in motion by Ms. Yvette Roudy's anti-sexist law would warrant peals of laughter.[1] These gentlemen—and ladies—who reproach feminists for lacking a sense of humor are showing that they regrettably lack one themselves. With much pomp they call on their sense of responsibility and professional conscience in order to claim the right to cover the walls with images that—in their minds—will best fill their pockets! They are quick to invoke the highest cultural values: according to them, advertisements shower us with beauty, and it would take a complete lack of aesthetic sensibility to not compare these creations with the most famous paintings of the Louvre and their "messages" with the greatest works in French literature.

Such weighty pretensions are astounding! But, above all, they claim to be inspired by the respect for sacrosanct freedom—what freedom? The law that allows women to freely choose their maternities is supposedly "an interference in personal life" and therefore an attack on freedom. (It is true that one hundred years ago when the first high school for girls opened up in Rouen, there were men who declared that it was an attack on freedom.)

273

Freedom! What idiocies are uttered in your name! Freedom is used as an excuse, for example, to compare Yvette Roudy to an ayatollah, yet I am not aware that she has demanded her compatriots to cover themselves in veils, nor called for the stoning of adulteresses. And what connection is there between Queen Victoria and the woman who spearheaded the legalization of free abortion? I see nothing humorous or cleverly witty in these clumsy and hateful sarcasms.

Some prefer arguments that seem to them to be more serious. *La croix,*[2] whose continued efforts in favor of sexual liberation are well known, accuses Yvette Roudy of wanting to forbid love and pleasure. Ms. Giroud, among others, reproaches her for curtailing "the right to fantasies."[3] Does this mean that people are only able to invent their dreams from the flat images of advertisements? It is not necessary to be a great psychologist to know that fantasies have altogether different origins.

However, "knowing winks" and complicit "nudges" are not sufficient to respond to these attacks because this small minority of profiteers, who have gone mad like dogs threatened with losing their bone, might cause harm due to their solidly orchestrated campaign. They are supported by many journalists since the printed press—except *Le canard enchaîné*, which has not really taken sides in this campaign[4]—lives in large part off advertisements. We must therefore denounce more precisely the bad faith of the arguments they muster.

First of all, they overlook important distinctions. The law does not affect books, films, paintings, or any artistic creation; it does not go after reviews or magazines. Only advertisements are targeted because only they, instead of being *offered* to [individual] freedoms, are *imposed* upon all eyes that are subjected to them, willingly or not. No one is indignant about limiting the freedom of exhibitionists, and certain advertising exhibitions are no less shocking. It seems logical to me to protect the passersby. Besides, this protection is very discreet. They brandish the word *censure*, but it is not at all a matter of censorship. The law simply accords women who feel attacked the power to *dispute* an ad, i.e., the right of opposition [*contre-pouvoir*] in a democracy. In the end, there will be judges to decide whether or not their protests are well-founded.

Why women? Because they are the ones in question: they are the ones depicted in the degrading images displayed by advertisements in order to sell products, never a man. Except, in the past, Blacks. But the antiracist law made Banania's "*ya bon*" ads of my childhood obsolete.[5] They tell us that laws can do nothing and that racism has remained just as alive since the antiracist law. There are a thousand reasons why it has not been eradicated, but at least it can no longer be expressed without any punishment at all. Certain public displays have been removed from our walls. After some lawsuits, cafés no longer dare to refuse to serve "*bicots*"[6] or "niggers." A law does not change mentalities overnight, true. But it plays a part in forming them. One fool asked in *Le nouvel observateur*,[7] "Will burning images be enough to liberate women?" Of course not, that would be too simple. But it is not useless to act on images. Children also have eyes, and the images make an impression on them. Preventing these images from inspiring in them a scorn for women would already be a victory.

It seems inconceivable to these gentlemen that a woman's body could be used as "advertising material" without inflicting a degrading attitude upon her. To refuse this degradation would be to forbid any image of a woman, and by extrapolation, any image at all. A world without images? That would be the tyrannous austerity of the Eastern Bloc countries! The gulag is not far behind! These absurd insinuations find a receptive audience among the enemies of the regime because we must not forget that this campaign is also—and perhaps essentially—political.[8]

However, this aspect is more or less hidden. Loudly denounced are the excesses that feminists will carry out if the Roudy law gets passed. Advertisers repeatedly insist that we must have confidence in women. So? So then feminists are not women. The most far-fetched arguments are used against them. They are "tormented and sexually maladjusted," declared Mr. J.-F. Fabry, the eminent inventor of the ads featuring a bound woman wearing Buffalo jeans. "They are intellectuals who have no contact with reality," diagnoses another. I know feminists who are doctors, lawyers, engineers, and full-time mothers. It does not seem to me that the director of an advertisement agency has, a priori, a better connection with reality, unless "reality" signifies for him money with which he certainly has a more enriching experience. In any case, and I repeat, associations will not settle anything, but judges will. All that we hope for is that the prospect of a lawsuit will have— as with racism—a deterring effect.

What is disturbing in this whole affair is the real reason behind this general outcry.

Under duress, men are giving up openly boasting about their superiority in the economic sphere and are leading a more underhanded fight against equal pay and against ending job discrimination based on sex. But they remain deeply convinced that woman is an object to manipulate and that they are the masters of this manipulation. They will not be changed so easily.

275

But every step that hinders their claims to domination should be welcomed with gratitude, not only by feminists, but by all women, at least by all those who refuse to let themselves be ruled by an iron fist, even if that fist is full of diamonds.

## NOTES

"La femme, la pub et la haine," *Le monde*, Wednesday, May 4, 1983, 1, 10; © Sylvie Le Bon de Beauvoir.

This article was preceded by the following editorial introduction entitled "The 'Anti-sexist' Bill": "At a press conference on May 2, Ms. Yvette Roudy, Deputy Minister of women's rights, stated that she would 'pursue to the end' this 'anti-sexist' bill presented—by herself—on March 9 to the cabinet of ministers. Here, Ms. Simone de Beauvoir presents the reasons that, in her opinion, should convince women to support this bill and respond to the uproar it has incited, particularly from journalists and advertisers."

1. Yvette Roudy (1929–) is a French socialist politician and feminist who was the Minister of Women's Rights at the time of this article. Roudy was also a delegate to the European Parliament from 1979 to 1981 and a delegate to the French General Assembly and mayor of Liseux from 1989 to 2001.

2. *La croix* is a French daily newspaper associated with the Roman Catholic Church that covers topics of general interest.

3. Françoise Giroud (1916–2003) was a French journalist and writer who served as Secretary of State for Women (*Secrétaire d'État à la Condition féminine*) from 1974–76 and French Minister of Culture from 1976–77.

4. *Le canard enchaîné* is a satirical weekly French newspaper known for its investigative reporting and featuring bogus interviews, political cartoons, and inside information about French politics and politicians.

5. Banania is a popular French chocolate breakfast drink whose packaging and advertisements featured a smiling Senegalese man saying "y'a bon," which was supposedly the way the Senegalese soldiers said "It's good" in pidgin French.

6. This is an extremely offensive racial slur used against Arabs or French people of Arab descent.

7. *Le nouvel observateur* is a prominent French weekly newsmagazine for general information.

8. François Mitterrand, President of the French Republic from 1981–95, was the leader of the Socialist Party, and the first socialist president of the Fifth Republic.

## 11

Preface to *Mihloud*

# INTRODUCTION

*by Lillian S. Robinson and Julien Murphy*

It begins with "love" and ends with "AIDS," but, in between, Simone de Beauvoir's last piece of writing, her preface to *Mihloud*, is only a brief summary of the book. By agreeing to place her name on the cover of this memoir, whose author's name is conspicuously absent, Beauvoir called attention to two related issues that were still considered virtually unmentionable in 1980s France: same-sex relations between men and the disease that was decimating the gay community. (For example, the cause of Michel Foucault's death in 1984 was initially listed as septicemia and only later revealed as AIDS.) If Beauvoir did not interpret "Alan's" text or even situate it in its history, she nonetheless helped make it available to a general audience.

In her three-page preface, Beauvoir recapitulates the story the memoir tells, of the love affair, at once tragic and banal, that brought together a prosperous American businessman, living as an expatriate in Paris, and a devastatingly attractive Moroccan immigrant worker some thirty years younger. Alan, the narrator, is committed to telling his story as he experienced and remembers it, with his own feelings at the center. Larger questions about sexuality and power, about masculinity and patriarchy, about the social meanings of class, cultural, and age differences between lovers are outside his scope. And Beauvoir keeps them outside hers, as well.

The books for which Beauvoir wrote prefaces during the last three decades of her life told stories that were difficult and often dangerous to make public: the Holocaust, the rape and torture of an Algerian woman militant by her French captors, the struggles of the emerging feminist movement, the radical alienation of a gifted lesbian. Her endorsement of *Mihloud* placed a homosexual love story touched by AIDS in this militant context. Alan's narrative resonates with concerns in Beauvoir's own writings—both fiction and nonfiction—and in her personal history. The critique of traditional family structures, the presence of death, the experience of love across national and generational boundaries mattered in both her work and her life. That the preface does not directly address these issues may be attributed to her sense of loss after Sartre's death in 1980 and the waning of her intellectual and literary powers.

Yet this is the way all Beauvoir's prefaces make their principal contribution. In her prime, as in her decline, she exercised her role as a public intellectual by calling attention to important works and, within them, to the key issues they raise, advocating for a cause by her advocacy on behalf of a book and its author. This is as true of her prefaces to *Djamila Boupacha* and *La grand'peur d'aimer* (The great fear of loving) or her testimony in *Avortement: une loi en procès. L'affaire de Bobigny* (Abortion: A law on trial. The Bobigny affair), in all of which she was personally and passionately involved as an activist for the human rights of women (against torture, for contraception and abortion), as it is of her preface to a work like *Treblinka*, where her involvement was less immediate.[1] Only her penultimate preface, introducing the published version of Claude Lanzmann's script for *Shoah* (1985),[2] is colored by her longtime relationship with the author and his project, and even here her passion is directed to telling us that we knew nothing of the Holocaust hitherto and that we must look at this account now. Right now.

Even in her 1964 preface for Violette Leduc's *La bâtarde* (The bastard), where there is no "cause" beyond sponsorship of a gifted writer whose career she had been championing for some twenty years, Beauvoir limits herself to pointing out the author's powerful style and the themes it conveys.[3] Many of these themes echo those she identifies in *Mihloud*: the same-sex relationships and the erotic frankness employed to describe them, the pain of family ties, the pervasiveness of money in a story about love and sex. Ironically, although she opens the preface to *La bâtarde* by telling us there are no longer any unrecognized writers, her preface supporting Leduc's sixth book gained it a much wider following. And, in a similar way, her sponsorship of "Alan's" memoir won him the only recognition as a writer that he was ever to have.

According to the publisher's note, Alan's next of kin, espousing precisely those puritanical values that Alan moved to Paris to escape, tried very hard to keep his memoir from seeing the light of day and insisted that the book remain anonymous. From this perspective, Beauvoir's preface allows her to strike one last blow against all the repressive, narrow-minded families she had encountered in her lifetime. And it was to be the last, for *Mihloud*, in some sense validated by her preface, was published in April 1986, within days of her death.

## NOTES

1. Beauvoir, "Preface to *Djamilia Boupacha*" and "Preface to *Treblinka*" in *Political Writings* (Urbana: University of Illinois Press, 2012), 272–82 and 305–10, respectively. For translations of Beauvoir's prefaces to *La grand'peur d'aimer* and *L'avortement: une loi en procès—l'affaire de Bobigny*, see chapters 4 and 9, respectively, in this current volume of her feminist writings.

2. Beauvoir, "Preface to *Shoah*" in *Political Writings*, 324–28.

3. Beauvoir, "Preface to *La Bâtarde*" in *"The Useless Mouths" and Other Literary Writings* (Urbana: University of Illinois Press, 2011), 174–87.

# PREFACE TO *MIHLOUD*

TRANSLATION BY LILLIAN S. ROBINSON

Love—can it be strong enough to overcome clashes between civilizations and cultures? This is the question poignantly raised by this fine book written by an anonymous author.

An abyss separates the two lovers. Alan, the narrator, is a very well off and very cultured American, around fifty years old; he owns an art jewelry shop in Paris and a lovely apartment across the street. Mihloud is a young Moroccan, ignorant and poor, who shares a room in Belleville with his brother and works as a laborer. However, they have some things in common. Not only is Mihloud living far away from his own country, but his father, in repudiating his first wife, also disowned him, so he bears his mother's name. This two-fold exile is very painful to him. In the United States, Alan, who had come from Poland with his parents, also felt like an exile, and his homosexuality exacerbated his solitude. He sorrowfully calls to mind "the uprooting that homosexuality causes, the desolation that is born when you realize you are different." He tried to become part of the "gay" world,[1] but this kind of "ghetto" rapidly became unbearable for him. He moved to Paris. There, he had several affairs with young Arabs. But for them, these were only meaningless erotic games, whereas he tended to get attached to them; once, after a breakup, he attempted suicide. When he fell for Mihloud, his friends told him, "Watch out! It's going to start all over again!" He replied, "Mihloud is different."

And indeed he was. One of the author's great achievements is to show us Mihloud's personality in a compelling way. We first see him buried up to the waist in one of those trenches that rip through Paris, wearing on his beautiful head a funny little hat that makes him look amused and cynical at the same time. He is highly intelligent, passionately interested in the world, curious about all experience. He readily agrees to exchange sexual pleasure with Alan. But there is no equality between them. It is Mihloud who "has" Alan, and he vehemently refuses the reciprocity that would undermine his masculinity. Alan, most importantly, commits himself entirely to this relationship; he derives "infinite sexual and emotional satisfaction" from it. The two are so intimately attached to one another that the (often very crude) descriptions of their lovemaking are never obscene. Mihloud's body—as a whole and in each of its parts—is itself transfigured by Alan's love.

For his part, Mihloud is deeply attached. The joy that he feels on the nights he spends at Alan's place certainly stems in part from the comfort of the apartment, but is also connected to the pleasure of their embraces and, more importantly, to a tenderness from which he had always been cut off. Proud, touchy, he is sensitive to the respect and confidence his friend shows him. On the evening when Alan, upon returning from a trip to India, gives him the keys to the apartment, Mihloud is so moved that he performs a marriage rite, removing all his body hair, before joining Alan in bed. Outside of bed, as well, they enjoy intense moments of harmony: nighttime walks in Paris, a brief trip to Etretat.

However, for Alan, this idyll is not always serene, first and foremost because of Mihloud's capricious temperament: he is very cheerful; he hates waking up at five in the morning; he has pains all over his body from hours of lifting stones that are too heavy for him. Alan repeatedly offers to support him, which, of course, he resents. What remains most mysterious is his refusal of all the less exhausting jobs he could qualify for that Alan has managed in vain to find for him.

And then there are the phone calls. While they are out together at a restaurant, a café, a movie, Mihloud slips away; he has to make a call. Coming home from the shop, Alan often catches him on the telephone and Mihloud hangs up right away. "It's my family," he says. "They want to talk to me every day!" Despite his sense of solitude, he does in fact have a family living in the outskirts of Paris, a crowd of half-brothers and -sisters, the children of his father's second marriage, plus uncles, aunts, and cousins of both sexes. When Alan—who, incidentally doesn't care about any heterosexual relationships that Mihloud might have—hears a woman's voice on the phone, it is always one of his cousins. While they are out on a walk, Mihloud even points out one of them, a blonde who works in a beauty parlor. Alan also glimpses a brunette driving a car. Alan is disoriented by the lies—or half-truths—Mihloud tells to protect himself from Alan's hold over him; one day, he confides, "They want to marry me off to my cousin Rheta. But I want to live with you."

Alan wants to share everything with his friend; he takes him to the theater and to fashionable parties. Mihloud readily goes along with this; he is always eager for new experiences, but he is also ill at ease, feeling out of place. Nor does he like it much when Alan tries to follow him back in to his own life, but he can't prevent Alan from going to Belleville with him, which means the reader is provided with a compelling description of the neighborhood. Alan meets some of Mihloud's friends. And he insists on attending the engagement (or wedding, he doesn't know which) celebration of a male cousin. During this ceremony, he feels himself vaguely threatened—by the presence of the whole assembled clan, by the music, the dances, a radically alien world. He is even more upset that evening, when Mihloud murmurs nostalgically, "They're going to have a l'il baby."

To tear Mihloud away from the clan's strong influence, Alan suggests taking him to America. Mihloud is enthusiastic about this plan. He throws himself into learning English. Alan sells his shop and his apartment and buys a little house in California. They are going to live happily ever after. But all of a sudden, Mihloud disappears. One of the most moving passages in the book describes Alan's desperate search through the cafés and lower depths of Belleville in an attempt to find him. He succeeds. Mihloud is lying in a hovel where a friend has sheltered him: sick, feverish, starving, with a suppurating wound in his side. He greets Alan with such joy that, in the ardor of their embrace, he lets himself be penetrated for the first time. Alan takes him away, nurses him, and heals him. In tears, Mihloud confides that he ran away on the day set for his marriage to Rheta—which is confirmed by hateful telephone calls from his family. He hates her. He hates them all. He just wants to leave for America with Alan and share his whole life with him. From now on they spend their days and nights in a paroxysm of passion and total loving reciprocity, while waiting for their departure for America, which they're dreaming of together.

All the arrangements have been completed, the tickets purchased, the departure near, when, one morning, Mihloud receives a telegram and then a phone call from Morocco; his father has lost a foot in a work-related accident. Unable henceforth to support his family, he turns all his responsibilities over to Mihloud, his firstborn, who will bear his name from now on. Dumbfounded, Mihloud immediately goes to see his family. And when he comes back one morning appearing truculent, hostile, almost hateful, he announces, "I married Rheta." Alan's pleas for their love are in vain: "I am now the head of the family; I want a son." When Alan reminds him of everything he has given up for him, he replies, "You've given up nothing. You have no family." He is certainly upset, but he goes ahead anyway; he packs his bags and closes the door behind him forever.

The book stops here. Alan adds nothing. In the whole story, he speaks very little about himself. We see his personality, complex and troubled, only in silhouette. He sharply criticizes America, but he is not at home in Europe. He is a man from nowhere. Rich in multiple interests, capable of warm friendship, such as he feels for Stella, he nonetheless has a pathetic need for a definitive and absolute passion to anchor him in the world. The failure of his relationship with Mihloud is more than a failure in love; it is the collapse of his entire being.

Note: Handsome, intelligent, disillusioned but full of humor, the author, shortly after writing this book that he would have so much wanted to see published, died of a disease then little known in France: AIDS.

## NOTES

Simone de Beauvoir wrote this "Préface" to *Mihloud* for the French publication of *Mihloud* (Aix-en-Provence: Alinea, 1986). *Mihloud* was written by an anonymous author and translated, as the publisher explains, "From the American" by Bruno Monthureux and Ghislaine Byramjee, but was never published in the original.

1. The word "gay" appears in English in the original.

# Contributors

**NANCY BAUER** is dean of Academic Affairs for Arts and Sciences and professor of Philosophy at Tufts University. She is the author of numerous papers on Simone de Beauvoir and of *Simone de Beauvoir, Philosophy, and Feminism* (Columbia University Press, 2001). She is the coeditor, with Laura Hengehold, of the forthcoming *Blackwell Companion to Simone de Beauvoir*, as well as the forthcoming *Routledge Guidebook to Beauvoir and "The Second Sex."*

**DEBRA BERGOFFEN** is professor emerita of philosophy at George Mason University and the Bishop Hamilton Lecturer of Philosophy at American University. Her writings include *The Philosophy of Simone de Beauvoir: Gendered Phenomenologies, Erotic Generosities, Contesting the Politics of Genocidal Rape: Affirming the Dignity of the Vulnerable Body*, and the coedited anthology *Confronting Global Gender Justice: Human Rights, Women's Lives.*

**SYLVIE LE BON DE BEAUVOIR**, the adopted daughter of Simone de Beauvoir, is editor of several volumes by Simone de Beauvoir, including *Lettres à Sartre* (1990); *Journal de guerre* (1990); *Lettres à Nelson Algren: Un amour* *transatlantique* (1997); *Correspondance croisée*, with Jacques-Laurent Bost (2004); and *Cahiers de jeunesse* (2008).

**SYLVIE CHAPERON** is professor of history at the University of Toulouse le Mirail in France. She has a PhD from the European University Institute (Florence, Italy) where she spent three years. She organized, with Christine Delphy, the January 1999 international conference in Paris for the fiftieth anniversary of Beauvoir's *The Second Sex* and coedited with Delphy and Kate and Edward Fullbrook, *Cinquantenaire du Deuxième Sexe* (2002). She is the author of *Les années Beauvoir: 1945–1970* (2000) and several articles and book chapters, including "Kinsey en France: les sexualités féminine et masculine en débat" in *Le Mouvement Social* 2002/1 (no 198), 91–110; and "Beauvoir et le féminisme français" in *Beauvoir*, ed. Eliane Lecarme-Tabone and Jean-Louis Jeannelle (2012), 277–83.

**ELIZABETH FALLAIZE** (1950–2009) was pro–vice chancellor of the University of Oxford. In 1989 she was the first woman ever appointed an Official Fellow of St. John's College, Oxford, and, in 2002, she was awarded a professorship in French literature. She was coeditor of *French Studies* (1996–2004) and a series editor for the Oxford University Press. Her books include *The Novels of Simone de Beauvoir* (1988); *French Women's Writing: Recent Fiction* (1993); *Simone de Beauvoir: A Critical Reader* (1998); *French Fiction in the Mitterrand Years*, cowritten with Colin Davis (2000); and *The Oxford Book of French Short Stories* (2002). She was appointed by the French Government an Officier dans l'ordre des palmes académiques in 2002 and promoted to Commandeur in 2009.

**J. DEBBIE MANN** holds the rank of professor in the department of foreign languages and literature at Southern Illinois University Edwardsville where she teaches French language and French and francophone literature and culture. Recent publications include articles on works by Andrée Chedid, Jacques Poulin, and Louis Hémon.

**FREDERICK M. MORRISON** (1943–2007) was associate professor of Spanish in the Department of Foreign Languages and Literature at Southern Illinois University Edwardsville. The translator and annotator, Véronique Zaytzeff, began collaborating with him in 1991. Their work includes *Mussorgsky Remembered*, sections of *Shostakovich Reconsidered*, Beauvoir's "Literature and Metaphysics" in *Philosophical Writings* (2004), and "Merleau-Ponty and Pseudo-Sartreanism" in *Political Writings* (2012).

**JULIEN S. MURPHY** is professor and chair of Philosophy and coordinator of Liberal Studies at the University of Southern Maine. She is the author of *The Constructed Body: AIDS, Reproductive Technology and Ethics* (1995), editor of *Feminist Interpretations of Jean-Paul Sartre* (1999), and coeditor of *Gender Struggles: Recent Writings in Feminist Philosophy* (2002). She is currently conducting funded research on cybersecurity.

**SHANNON M. MUSSETT** is associate professor of philosophy and chair of the Department of Philosophy and Humanities at Utah Valley University. She has served as the secretary-treasurer of the Society for Phenomenology and Existential Philosophy. She is coeditor (with William Wilkerson) of *Beauvoir and the History of Philosophy from Plato to Butler* (2012) and (with Sally J. Scholz) *The Contradictions of Freedom: Philosophical Essays on Simone de Beauvoir's "The Mandarins"* (2005). Recent publications on Beauvoir's philosophy include "Nature and Anti-Nature in Simone de Beauvoir's Philosophy," *Philosophy Today* 53, Supplement, 2009, 130–37; "Conditions of Servitude: The Peculiar Role of the Master-Slave Dialectic in Simone de Beauvoir's *The Second Sex*," *The Philosophy of Simone de Beauvoir: Critical Essays*, ed. Margaret A. Simons (2006); "Ageing and Existentialism: Simone de Beauvoir and the Limits of Freedom," *Death and Anti-Death*, Volume 4, ed. Charles Tandy (2006); and an introduction to "An Existentialist Looks at Americans," in Beauvoir's *Philosophical Writings* (2005).

**FRANÇOISE PICQ**, PhD in political science, is assistant professor (Maître de Conférences) at the University of Paris IX-Dauphine. She was involved in the French Women's Liberation Movement (MLF) and participated in developing feminist studies in France. She is a founder and past president of National Feminist Studies Association (ANEF), and was the National contact of the European Network for Women's Studies (ENWS). She has been editor of several feminist journals and special journal issues on feminism. Her publications include *Féministe, encore et toujours* (2012), *Libération des femmes: quarante ans de mouvement* (2011), *Libération des femmes: les années mouvement* (1993), and *Crises de la société, féminisme et changement* (1991).

**LILLIAN S. ROBINSON** (1941–2006), a Marxist feminist writer and activist, was principal of the Simone de Beauvoir Institute and professor of Women's Studies at Concordia University. Among her books were the essay anthology, *Sex, Class and Culture* (1978), *Night Market: Sexual Cultures and the Thai Economic Miracle* (1998) (cowritten with Ryan Bishop), and *Wonder Women: Feminisms and Superheroes* (2004).

**MARGARET A. SIMONS**, Distinguished Research Professor Emerita, Southern Illinois University Edwardsville, is author of *Beauvoir and The Second Sex* (1999); editor of *Feminist Interpretations of Simone de Beauvoir* (1995) and *The Philosophy of Simone de Beauvoir: Critical Essays* (2006); and coeditor of Beauvoir's *Philosophical Writings* (2004), *Diary of a Philosophy Student: 1926–27* (2006), *Wartime Diary* (2009), *"The Useless Mouths" and Other Literary Writings* (2011), and *Political Writings* (2012).

**URSULA TIDD** is senior lecturer in twentieth-century French studies at the University of Manchester, U.K. She is the author of *Simone de Beauvoir, Gender and Testimony* (1999), *Simone de Beauvoir* (2004), and *Simone de Beauvoir* (2009), and (with Jean-Pierre Boulé) the editor of *Existentialism and Contemporary Cinema: A Beauvoirian Perspective* (2012). Her most recent monograph, *Jorge Semprún: Writing the European Other*, was published by Legenda/Maney in 2014.

**MARYBETH TIMMERMANN** is a certified French to English translator of the American Translators Association, and has taught an online translation course for the University of Illinois at Urbana-Champaign. She was a contributing translator to Beauvoir's *Philosophical Writings* (2004), *"The Useless Mouths" and Other Literary Writings* (2011), and *Political Writings* (2012); assistant editor of *Philosophical Writings* and *Diary of a Philosophy Student: 1926–1927* (2006); and coeditor with Margaret A. Simons of *"The Useless Mouths" and Other Literary Writings* and *Political Writings*.

**KAREN VINTGES** teaches social and political philosophy in the Department of Philosophy at the University of Amsterdam. She, among others, published *Philosophy as Passion. The Thinking of Simone de Beauvoir* (1996 [orig. in Dutch 1992]) and *Feminism and the Final Foucault*, ed. D. Taylor and K. Vintges (2004). Her current research project is entitled "Rewriting *The Second Sex* from a Global Perspective" in the forthcoming *A New Dawn for "The Second Sex"* (2015). She initiated and coordinated a research program funded by the Netherlands Organisation for Scientific Research: "Women and Islam: New Perspectives" (2008–13).

**VÉRONIQUE ZAYTZEFF** (1937–2010) was associate professor emerita in the Department of Foreign Languages and Literature at Southern Illinois University Edwardsville. She translated from French and Russian. Her translations include *Mussorgsky Remembered*, several articles in *Shostakovich Reconsidered*, and Beauvoir's "Literature and Metaphysics" and "Merleau-Ponty and Pseudo-Sartreanism." She collaborated on translations with Frederick M. Morrison until his untimely death in 2007.

# Index

Féminin Masculin Avenir (Feminine masculine future, FMA), 232, 261–62

feminism: avoidance of association with, 6; Beauvoir's comments on, 11–12, 145, 183–84, 194–95, 231; cross-national issues, 238–39; debates about, 26, 234–35; differences in, 232–33, 250–51; equality not superiority sought in, 213–14; film criticism based in, 113n5, 121–23; "identity," 70; inspirational texts noted, 185–86; language issues, 253–55; literary theory based in, 150–51; lived experience of, 261; as necessary cause, 145, 199–200; second wave, 69, 70; as threat to capitalism, 200; turning point in movement, 232–33; values and models for, 203–4. *See also* second feminist wave

Feminist questions (*Questions féministes,* periodical), 234, 235

"La femme, la pub, et la haine" ("Women, Ads, and Hate," Beauvoir), 236, 273–76

*La femme et l'amour* (special issue of *La NEF*), 72. *See also* "The Condition of Women"

*La femme et le travail* (special issue of *La NEF*), 72

"*femme fatale*" types, 116

*La femme rompue* (*The Woman Destroyed,* Beauvoir), 10, 254, 255

"Femmes de lettres." *See* "Women of Letters"

*Des femmes en mouvement* (Women on the move, periodical), 235

*Femmes travailleuses en lutte* (Working women fight back, periodical), 235

feudalism, 89, 93, 200

*Le Figaro,* 5

*Le Figaro littéraire,* 15n20

film and television: Beauvoir's enthusiasm for, 109; constructed images in, 111, 123–24; fetishization in, 112; love vs. eroticism in, 115–16, 120–25; Sartre's television series, 234–35; spectator's gaze in, 113n5, 121–23; Stalinist show trials in, 74. *See also* "Brigitte Bardot and the Lolita Syndrome"; *specific films*

Firestone, Shulamith, 185–86, 199

*Flair,* 70. *See also* "It's About Time Women Put a New Face on Love"

Flaubert, Gustave, 162, 169n10

Flora-Tristan shelter, 266

FMA (Féminin Masculin Avenir; Feminine masculine future), 232, 261–62

*The Force of Circumstance* (Beauvoir), 52, 110, 153, 175n3

forewords by Beauvoir. *See Deception Chronicles; History: A Novel*

forlornness (*délaissement*), 162–63, 169n12

Foucault, Michel, 12, 279

Foulke, Adrienne, 181n8

Fouque, Antoinette, 185, 270, 272

"La Française et la démocratie" (French-women and democracy, Michel), 72, 88

France: "allocations familiales" in, 217, 218n1; Brigitte Bardot unpopular in, 110, 114–15, 119–20, 124–25; conditions for women's creativity in, 155; female attorneys in, 137; hoped-for social, economic, and structural changes in, 90–95; love of cows in, 123; Nabokov's *Lolita* banned in, 110; number of deaths due to abortions in, 224; objectification of women's bodies in, 236; percentage of women in workforce, 142; political power shift in (1981), 236; *précieuses* in, 253, 255n1; protests of 1960–70s in, 181–83, 189n2, 231, 239n2, 260–61; social, economic, and political context of women in, 129–31, 132–34, 135–37, 139–43; values (*Liberté-Egalité-Fraternité*) in, 5; Women's Center in Trévise, 263; women writers in, 166–67. *See also* French laws; French Resistance; Nazi Occupation; Paris

*France-Amérique* (periodical): context of Beauvoir's two-part article for, 2, 14n3. *See also* "Problems for women's literature"; "Women of Letters"

Francis, Claude. *See Les écrits de Simone de Beauvoir*

Franco, Francisco, 29n3

*Francs Tireurs et Partisans* (FTP), 103, 105n2

Frazer, James George, 62, 66n8

freedom: to choose motherhood or not, 209, 220, 258–59, 273; communal relationships

earning combined with, 90–93. *See also* children; household duties; marriage
Mouvement de libération des femmes. *See* Women's Liberation Movement
Mouvement démocratique féminin (Women's Democratic Movement, MDF), 261
Mozart, Wolfgang Amadeus, 162, 169n10, 224
*Ms.*, "The Radicalization of Simone de Beauvoir," 206–8n. *See also* "The Rebellious Woman"
Murasaki Shikibu (Lady Murasaki): Beauvoir's appreciation for, 9, 16n36, 151; biographical information, 169n13; father's encouragement for, 10, 163–64; high but marginalized position of, 164–65; Woolf's appreciation for, 151; work: *The Tale of the Genji*, 9, 151, 165
murder, 265–66
Murngin people, 59, 65n2
Murphy, Julien: introduction to Beauvoir's preface to *Milhoud*, 13, 279–81
Mussett, Shannon M.: introduction to Beauvoir's review of Lévi-Strauss's text, 4, 51–57
Mutualité hall, public hearings at, 183, 186, 204–5, 232, 263, 271
"My Experience as a Writer" (Beauvoir), 149–50
"My Point of View: An Outrageous Affair" (Beauvoir), 237, 258–59
mythologies: "Reign of women" as, 61; roles assigned to women in, 44, 46. *See also* men: superiority complex of

Nabokov, Vladimir, 7, 110, 116. *See also* "Brigitte Bardot and the Lolita Syndrome"
Napoleonic civil code, 38, 237
National Institute of Industrial Property, 238
nature: man's overall conquering of, 72, 81, 86; man's view of woman as, 41, 43; women writers' treatment of, 21, 30, 31–32
Nazi Occupation: Beauvoir's work denounced in, 5–6; exodus of French before, 26, 29n3; impact on Beauvoir's philosophical development, 57n11; Lise London's escape from, 103. *See also* French Resistance

*La NEF* (*La nouvelle équipe française*): d'Ormesson's letters in, 96n10; special issues of, 72–73, 95n, 95n1. *See also* "The Condition of Women"
Neuwirth, Lucien, 209–10, 215n1
Neuwirth Law (1967), 184, 187, 209–10, 215n1
New Left ideology: gender inequalities in, 194–95; second feminist wave linked to, 69–70. See also *Le nouvel observateur*
new novel concept, 121–22, 125n6. *See also* journalistic novel
New York (state): abortion legalized in, 221, 224
*New York Herald Tribune*, 221
*New York Times*, 221
Nietzsche, Friedrich, 78
Noailles, Anne de, 21–22, 31, 34n5
Nourissier, François, 109
*Nouvelles questions féministes* (New feminist questions), 235
*Le nouvel observateur*: anti-sexist law critiqued in, 275; Beauvoir's "Abortion and the Poor," 189, 216–18; Beauvoir's "Love and Politics" in, 10, 74–75, 103–5; Beauvoir's "When All the Women of the World . . ." in, 256–57; campaign to legalize abortion and contraception, 182–83, 189, 239n3; Clavel's critique of MLF in, 186–87, 191n25, 211–14. *See also* "The Rebellious Woman"; "Response to Some Women and a Man"

Office de radio-télévision française (French Radio and Television Office, ORTF), 244
Office of National Education (Vichy government), 5
old age study, 51, 56n3
"One man in two is a woman" slogan, 182, 190n4
*On joue perdant* (Playing a losing game, Audry), 26, 33n3
Ophir, Anne, 253–55
d'Ormesson, Jean, 72, 94, 96n10
ORTF (Office de radio-télévision française; French Radio and Television Office), 244
other/Other: falling in love with, 101; recognition of self in, xii; sexuality impacted by

## BOOKS IN THE BEAUVOIR SERIES

Series edited by Margaret A. Simons and
Sylvie Le Bon de Beauvoir

*Philosophical Writings*
Edited by Margaret A. Simons
with Marybeth Timmermann
and Mary Beth Mader
Foreword by
Sylvie Le Bon de Beauvoir

*Diary of a Philosophy Student:*
*Volume 1, 1926–27*
Edited by Barbara Klaw,
Sylvie Le Bon de Beauvoir,
and Margaret A. Simons,
with Marybeth Timmermann
Translation and Notes
by Barbara Klaw
Foreword by
Sylvie Le Bon de Beauvoir

*Wartime Diary*
Edited by Margaret A. Simons
and Sylvie Le Bon de Beauvoir
Translation and Notes
by Anne Deing Cordero
Foreword by
Sylvie Le Bon de Beauvoir

*"The Useless Mouths" and Other*
*Literary Writings*
Edited by Margaret A. Simons
and Marybeth Timmermann
and Foreword by
Sylvie Le Bon de Beauvoir

*Political Writings*
Edited by Margaret A. Simons
and Marybeth Timmermann
and Foreword by
Sylvie Le Bon de Beauvoir

*Feminist Writings*
Edited by Margaret A. Simons
and Marybeth Timmermann
Foreword by
Sylvie Le Bon de Beauvoir

*Diary of a Philosophy Student:*
*Volume 2, 1928–29*
Edited by Barbara Klaw,
Sylvie Le Bon de Beauvoir,
Margaret A. Simons,
and Marybeth Timmermann
Translation and Notes by
Barbara Klaw
Foreword by
Sylvie Le Bon de Beauvoir

The University of Illinois Press
is a founding member of the
Association of University Presses.

_____

**UNIVERSITY OF ILLINOIS PRESS**
1325 South Oak Street    Champaign, IL 61820-6903
www.press.uillinois.edu